Smiling Places

*Two Bumbling Idiots
Hit the Road*

by

*Melodee Tomsu
and
Doug Tomsu*

Capriccio Publishing   Titusville, Florida

Smiling Places (Two Bumbling Idiots Hit the Road)
Copyright © 2005 by Melodee Tomsu and Doug Tomsu

All rights reserved. Printed in the United States of America and published August 2005 in Titusville, Florida. No part of this book may be reproduced or transmitted in any form or by any means, electronic or mechanical, including photocopying, recording, or by any information storage and retrieval system, without written permission from the publisher; except for brief quotations embodied in critical articles and reviews. For information address:

    Capriccio Publishing
    182 Windsong Way
    Titusville, Florida 32780-2331

Disclaimer: This book describes the author's experiences while traveling around the U.S.A. and reflect their opinions relating to those experiences. Some names and identifying details of individuals have been changed to protect their privacy.

Library of Congress Control Number: 2005904732

Publisher Cataloging In Publication Data
Tomsu, Melodee and Doug.
Smiling Places (Two Bumbling Idiots Hit the Road)/Melodee and Doug Tomsu. — 1st ed.
  ISBN: 0-9770076-3-4
  1. Travel—Humor. 2. Marriage—Humor I. Title.
  II. Title: Two Bumbling Idiots Hit the Road.
818'.5402—dc20

Cover Design by Jeanne Tomsu and Doug Tomsu
Chapter Illustrations by Jeanne Tomsu
Proof-reading/text editing by Adele Ilijanich and Doug Tomsu

Dedications

For Inspiring the Writing of this Book,
Erma Bombeck
Dave Barry
Jerry Seinfield
Stephen King

For Making the Writing of this Book Possible,
Joel D. Greenberg
Leonard Van Eaton
Thomas A. Barnard

For Family and Friends, Past and Present,
Whose Love and Care Shaped Our
Lives Forever

Table of Contents

1	No Air to Spare	1
2	Thar She Blows Matey!	3
3	The Canned Tourists	7
4	Manikin Love	9
5	Selling Under the Influence	12
6	Survival of the Fittest	15
7	Honey, I Think You Need a Shrink	19
8	Honey, I Think I Need a Shrink	23
9	You Gotta Start Somewhere	27
10	Frumpy Old Alumnus	33
11	Queen of the Trailer	39
12	A Big Muddy Runs Through It	43
13	TV, Corn and Chocolate Mints	51
14	Extreme Eating	57
15	A Visit from Murphy	65
16	Murphy Takes a Hiatus	71
17	Murphy Overstays His Welcome	81
18	This is the Oldest I've Ever Been	91
19	Tickphobia	101
20	Driving Mrs. Flatlander	113

21	Bumbling Through	139
22	Doubts and Certainty	157
23	It's Better than Nothing, Isn't It?	159
24	Keeping a Safe Distance, Mind You	165
25	As Luck Would Have It	171
26	The Great Escape	174
27	The Out Of Towners Revisited	176
28	Laughing with Buffalo	181
29	Off Track Out Back	185
30	You Bet	189
31	The Pillsbury Dough Girl	195
32	Parting the Headwaters	197
33	Shore was Great	199
34	Running from the Cold	202
35	My Bridge of Revenge	205
36	Pictures In the Eye of the Beholder	209
37	Life Comes Full Circle	212

Postscript 214

1 - No Air to Spare

Just over a year before my husband Doug and I hitched a trailer to our truck and traveled aimlessly about, our spirits soared at the thought of sleeping in a tent and cooking over an open fire. To fulfill this inner desire, we would take a few days off from work, pile our camping gear in our car, and drive from our hometown, Dayton, Ohio, to a favorite campground.

One such place, Ludington State Park, mysteriously beaconed us 450 miles north. Hugging the eastern shore of Lake Michigan, large white-capped waves crash against the beaches of the park. Blowing sand from tall dunes quickly cover access roads, while hardwood forests stand vigil at the stroke of genius of Mother Nature. Arriving at this gem always brought a smile to my face, but not today. The flat tire incident one hundred miles back must have had something to do with it. After 24 years of marriage, I still believed men promised to love, honor, and inflate.

"I have a suggestion," I said after examining our car's flat tire and my husband's middle aged spread. "Why don't you call roadside assistance?"

Doug gave me a surprised look. He puffed out his chest like a rooster and sucked in his stomach so his pant size dropped from a size 36 to 29, in a matter of seconds. He looked like Mr. Universe on steroids.

"Mel, you know I don't need any help changing a tire, I just have to get the spare out of the trunk," he said as veins bulged in his forehead.

"Good luck," I thought as Doug strutted to the back of our car. The tightly packed trunk flew open like a jack-in-the-box. Camping gear, food, and clothing fell to the side of the road. A woman pulled over and jumped out of her van. She offered me $2.00 for our parka lying on the ground. I grabbed the coat and told her we weren't selling.

Doug had a puzzled look on his face from the minute he surveyed the remaining contents of the trunk. He picked up a black evening dress, which had been secured by a case of toilet paper. The plastic wrap covering my best dress crackled softly in the breeze.

Smiling Places

"What is this for?" Doug asked.

"That's in case you take me out to a nice dinner," I answered. "I just love it when you surprise me."

He looked at me in amazement. "Are you serious? We will be camping in a tent for two days and cooking over an open fire. I guess if you want to dress up for burnt marshmallows and canned beans, be my guest."

Luckily, the man stuck the dress and his head back in the trunk before I could reply. I heard more items being shuffled about in Doug's quest to reach the spare tire. I wondered which genius had designed the spare tire feature in the floor of the trunk.

"OK, this is a classic," Doug said. He beamed proudly as he held up his latest find. "Why did you pack a crock-pot?"

"How about to soak your dirty clothes in, instead of beating them against a rock," I smirked.

Frankly, Doug's little jabs were getting on my nerves. But then I saw it, the little *whatchamacallit* that unscrews the cover of the spare tire compartment. I peered over the side of the trunk as Doug ceremoniously began unscrewing the top. Twenty minutes later, Doug was still unscrewing the top. And then, all of a sudden, the top pulled loose and...

"Oh, oh," I said. "Your spare tire is as flat as a pancake. Now you have two flat tires."

Let's face it, a man with no air to spare cannot be reasoned with. My husband began speaking in disturbing tongues that, thankfully, I could not understand. He stormed around to the side of the car and began kicking our number one flat tire. A few hundred kicks and a very sore foot later, he calmed down. Anyway, a nice mechanic with flashing yellow lights came to fix our tires, and we were on our way.

2 - Thar She Blows Matey!

A few hours later, we arrived at Ludington, Michigan and passed its beautiful city park. Many an evening we had sat at this park with friendly townspeople and watched spectacular sunsets. Our summer days had been filled with swimming, biking, and blueberries—sweet, succulent, the size of quarters. But this year the blueberries had already been harvested and the waters had turned much colder. Even the salmon had taken their last run in early fall. We hoped for one more camping trip to Ludington State Park before the snows blew. Perhaps we were too optimistic.

Little funnels of colored leaves danced around us as we pulled into our campsite. The crowds had long since departed for the year. A few hearty souls remained in recreational vehicles, and we would brave the elements in our height-challenged nylon dome tent.

We threaded the plastic tent poles through the seams of our collapsed tent and inserted three metal flexible poles that raised the tent to a full-blown dome position. Doug returned to the car to retrieve the tent stakes to secure the tent. I watched a red-bellied woodpecker pecking a hardwood tree trunk nearby. A distinctive gust of wind rushed through the campground, picking up our tent and tossing it end-over-end, down the gravel road, connecting all the campsites.

"Thar she blows, Matey!" I yelled, obviously caught up in the moment.

Doug dropped the tent stakes by the car and scampered after the tent, which had quite a measurable lead. It bounded off in all its glory, happy to be free of the confines of human owners. Every so often the tent would stop, until the wind caught its breath, and then go running off again, just out of the grasp of my exhausted husband. It might have blown all the way across the state of Michigan to Lake Huron—had it not been for Jim.

Jim's parked motor home caught the brunt of the impact with the tent, but no damage was inflicted to either object. His slide-out exten-

Smiling Places

sion wedged the tent firmly in place until my husband caught up with it. Jim helped Doug carry the still intact tent back to our campsite, battling winds every step of the way. He invited us to his motor home for a cup of coffee after we settled in. I, for one, didn't hesitate to accept Jim's kind gesture as the weather was taking a turn for the worse.

By dusk, Jim's motor home was brightly illuminated. and an easy walk from our tent site to the other side of the campground. The mechanic who fixed our flat tires had been right about the weather. I could smell snow in the crispy daggers of wind as we left our heated car, the shelter of choice for the moment. We hurried past our cold tent seeking the confines of yet another warm structure. Once inside Jim's motor home, we sunk into overstuffed recliners with steaming mugs of coffee and barely noticed the outside elements. The inside conversation is what held our attention.

"So, when we retired three years ago, we took off and started traveling," Jim's wife Ann explained. "We sold most everything and bought this rig to live in."

"Do you have a permanent home somewhere?" I asked.

"We did in Nashville, but sold that, too, after a year on the road. It just didn't make sense to keep it since we were never there."

"So you live in this motor home?" Doug concluded.

"Hard to believe, isn't it?" Jim piped in. "Living in 300 square feet with this woman can be a challenge."

"Oh, is that so?" Ann laughed. "Speaking of challenges, why don't you tell them about the sprinkler system?"

"You just had to mention that one, didn't you?" Jim said with a wink. "Well, when we first started out, I backed over a sprinkler system at a campground in Florida. Darn campsite looked like Old Faithful had erupted before they capped it off. Had to pay for it, too. They should mark those things better," Jim sighed.

Then Ann added, "Another time, we were driving down the road, and our awning just flew off the side of our motor home. It landed in a ditch at the side of the road. All I can say is thank goodness for duct tape."

"You mean you put that heavy thing back up with duct tape?" Doug asked.

"And rode that way for 300 miles, until we could get it fixed," Jim smiled.

"Well that's really something, Jim," Doug said. "You know, I just

Thar She Blows Matey!

used duct tape to put my mailbox back together. It was whacked with a baseball bat. A prank most likely."

Ann and I were speechless. Our eyes met and we knew we had just witnessed one of those male bonding moments...with duct tape no less. I decided to quickly change the subject.

"Speaking of mail boxes," I said, "how do you get your mail on the road?"

"Our daughter collects it from a PO Box in Nashville and forwards it to campgrounds we are staying at," Ann answered quickly, as if on cue.

"Do all campgrounds accept your mail like that?" I asked.

"Well, you need to check with them first. If the campground won't, usually you can do a general delivery at the local post office," Ann said.

"Living on the road is easier than most people imagine," Jim said. "Take for example your medical. We still use our doctors and dentist in Nashville for examinations if possible. Of course, we carry a copy of our medical records with us in case of emergencies."

"One time, we had a medical problem in Montana and found a walk-in clinic that accepted our medical insurance," Ann added.

"What about emails?" Doug asked.

"Most campgrounds or local libraries now have email capabilities. I've been told that a few years back, email hook-ups were hard to find. Cell phone signals are what concern me today. They just aren't that strong in remote areas. We are OK in most places we visit. We just made sure we got a nationwide plan that didn't make us pay for roaming charges," Jim said.

What a splendid evening we spent with this fascinating couple. They were living their retirement dream, a yearning not only to see our magnificent country, but taste its cultures and feel its history. They spoke of an insatiable appetite that only travel would cure. When the open road called, they roamed again and put down their temporary roots often in unfamiliar places. And they had pictures, hundreds of them, of their experiences that they shared with us. I know what you are thinking right now. "Oh please, not the dreaded vacation pictures!"

In most cases I would tend to agree with you; when Jim and Ann brought the pictures out, I was thinking that lying in a cryogenic state in our sub-artic tent had to be better than this. But, their precious memories were different. Grizzly bear traffic jams at Yellowstone. Hot air balloon rides in Albuquerque, New Mexico. The changing of the leaves in the Great Smoky Mountains. Civil War reenactments at Gettysburg. Don-

Smiling Places

key rides in the Grand Canyon. Rafting the whitewaters of West Virginia. We had just touched the surface. In three years, Jim and Ann had traveled 60,000 miles in 39 states. They had documented their travels with these amazing pictures and planned to add hundreds more to their collection.

I have to admit, by the end of the evening, I felt a longing to join these modern pioneers of our times.

"Oh, please take me with you," I silently begged them.

And for the first time that I could remember, I wanted to be anywhere but Dayton, Ohio, my hometown of forty-six years. I didn't want to return to the piles of paperwork on my desk. I didn't want to nest at my home anymore. I craved the freedom that came with the open road... a hike in the mountains, a bike ride by the ocean.

As we said our good-byes to Jim and Ann, they told us they would be heading south for warmer weather the next morning. As soon as we stepped out of their toasty home on wheels, I too, wanted to head south for warmer weather. The cold was shocking, the wind still untamed. Tiny specks of snow stung our cheeks as our shoes shuffled through a glistening blanket of white covering the fallen red and yellow leaves. Our dome tent had morphed into an igloo, and our air mattress had sprung a leak. Yes, another flat.

Doug and I looked at each other, shook our heads, and drove south that evening...to a motel in Ludington. The next day it was still bitterly cold with snow flurries, so we packed up our campsite and left for home. We never saw Jim and Ann again. They were gone by the time we returned from the motel the next morning. But inside our tent, lying on our sleeping bag, was a postcard with a picture of a motor home parked by a wooded lake—the caption read:

>"Home Is Where You Park It.
>Happy Trails,
>Jim and Ann"

3 - The Canned Tourists

Model T's or Tin Lizzies were built, and thousands of tourists flocked to Florida in the early 1900's. They came from New York, Des Moines, St. Louis, and Toronto. Construction workers, accountants, farm workers, and doctors were drawn to the tropical breezes and sandy beaches of the Sunshine State. Their love of the automobile bound these tourists in lifelong friendships. Many lived for weeks, months, or some year-round in their vehicles or tents." In 1919, one such group formally organized in Tampa, Florida as the "Tin Can Tourists". These members sported tin cans they had soldered to their radiator caps. Canned food dominated their diets.

Around this time, a man named Wally Byam began building travel trailers. His visionary direction was no doubt shaped by his youth. He traveled with his grandfather on a mule train in Oregon, and lived as a shepherd in a donkey cart. He designed the inside of his trailers so people could stand straight up. He incorporated construction methods to decrease wind resistance. In 1934, Wally introduced the name "Airstream" calling his trailers "a stream of air" because of the way they navigated the roads. These trailers became nationally known, and out of 300 trailer manufacturers operating in the mid 1930's, only Airstream survived.

Since that time, more and more people have taken to the road. RV manufacturers have responded by improving vehicle designs and adding dynamic features. An RV club's recent estimate has put the number of people who live full-time on the road today at well over a million. Seasonal travelers or vacationers make up many more millions.

Jim and Ann gave us good insight into this unique full-time lifestyle, but after returning from Ludington, I often wondered if Doug and I could live it. My impetuous self gave one big resounding yes and came up with a simple, yet concise, plan on how to hit the road. I could hardly contain my enthusiasm when I explained this plan to my husband:

Smiling Places

Step 1: Buy a motor home.
Step 2: Start the engine.
Step 3: Drive away.

I concluded that our age-related incredible shrinking genes had not yet kicked in, and that was the icing on the cake: We could still see over the motor home steering wheel *and* reach the floor pedals.

At that point my husband added a step 4 to my plan: Eliminate steps 1 through 3. He also concluded that my brain had incredibly shrunk. Imagine that!

My other side, my cautious self, surfaced usually at night, as I was falling asleep.

"Melodee!" it whispered and started my heart racing. "Have either one of you ever driven a motor home before?"

"No," I'd answer.

"What about towing an RV?"

"You know we haven't!"

"And may I remind you about the wrecked travel trailer on the highway last year? You know, the one that looked like a peeled banana!"

"Oh, will you please shut up; I am trying to go to sleep!"

Then I would lie in bed staring at the ceiling while hives broke out on my arms.

Family, money, friends, jobs, and everything else ping-ponged in my brain for weeks. How could I say good-bye to family and life-long friends? Would my mom do OK without me? Did I want to leave my comfortable home for the unknown? Would we have enough money to live on the road? I felt like I was in a constant tug-of-war with neither side being pulled over the line. My husband finally came to my rescue. Doug didn't say much, but you could sit and watch his hair catch fire as his brain kicked into warped analytical mode. He simply concluded we still had to work and couldn't pick up on the spur of the moment and leave unless some type of early out retirement package was offered to him at work...OR we won the lottery. Now why hadn't I thought of that?

So, with Doug's plan in mind, me, myself, and I laid down our tug-of-war rope and called it a draw. Unfortunately, my husband and I returned to our workaholic obsessions. We became so immersed in our jobs that the tin lizzies and streams of air would have to wait, at least for now.

4 - Manikin Love

Our job-driven lives could be described in two words: hamster wheel. Round and round and round we'd go, how to stop, we didn't know.

For many years I had worked in finance, but my latest endeavor was in real estate. I had been a practicing agent in the Dayton area for seven years. Believe me when I tell you, people are still trying to forget me.

"There's a man taking a shower in the master bathroom," my buyer said as I was showing her a home for sale.

I didn't stop to ask her how she knew it was a man, but hurried her down the stairway and out of the house.

Another time, a lady called, and informed me her daughter had picked up fleas from the last house I had showed them that day.

"I know. I gave fleas to my indoor cat today," I said while I flicked another flea off my cat's ear.

And please, don't even remind me about the two Boa Constrictors in the basement. I rivaled Carl Lewis doing the long jump before I found out they were contained in a glass cage.

Everyday across America, more than 700,000 real estate agents become a danger to society. Everyone knows an agent or has been one at some point in their life. I applied for my real estate license along with my social security number when I was three months old. My husband waited to get his license until he was six months of age.

Doug assisted me with real estate and also worked for the Department of Defense as a Civil Engineer. He had worked in the same organization for 25 years. Manpower studies were being performed in the spirit of "downsizing" at Doug's place of employment. Eventually they called it "rightsizing" because of the negative connotation of the word "down." What they forgot was how "down" many of the workers felt. Vacant job positions were not filled and the extra work was doled out to remaining employees. Financial shortfalls made it difficult to perform daily duties let alone long-term projects. Not enough copy paper? Come

Smiling Places

on, we are talking the Government, the enclave of all things paper and in triplicate. And my husband felt the stress of all this.

"Work is no fun anymore," he told me on several occasions.

We also bought small homes that needed fixing up and resold them. Many nights Doug burned the midnight oil changing out faucets, tiling bathrooms, installing ceiling fans, fixing doors and windows, and replacing drapery rods. In between real estate commitments, I cleaned the house, mowed the grass, decorated, and painted. I can't tell you the number of times I showed homes for sale to perspective buyers with my hair frosted in satin latex paint.

I couldn't escape from my real estate job. My home phone and cell phone rang eight or more hours a day. Each call brought more problems or new clients to work with. One Sunday afternoon, I climbed into a large drainage pipe with a piece of turkey in my hand. Why? To capture my client's cat who had escaped during an open house. While showing another home, I watched as a buyer pushed up a ceiling tile and the whole ceiling suspension system fell on her head. Don't worry. I lured the cat back inside. The buyer had a small bruise but bought the house anyway.

Doug and I were living to work, not working to live. Somewhere along the way, we had lost sight of the things in life that really mattered. Several years before, we had faced a very difficult time in our marriage: we couldn't have children. Somehow, we managed to get through that huge disappointment. We volunteered in church youth activities and became very close to our nieces. My elderly mother lived close-by, and I was her caregiver.

Now, we had forgotten those important things and excused ourselves from family get-togethers. What wonderful family memories we missed. My mother needed a quart of milk, but I had appointments. Our friends received belated birthday cards instead of dinners. We no longer served food to the needy, and our spiritual souls suffered. Our daily hugs were forgotten.

When planning for vacations, we would search for hotels with modems and fax machines, not four-star ratings. Our refrigerator looked like a wasteland for paper wrappers and Styrofoam containers. We had ridden our exercise bike for twenty-two miles—in three years. And our home was packed with two decades of clutter. We had no idea what was lurking in the 288,000 square inches of space we lived in.

One day in early spring, I opened our family room closet door to

Manikin Love

search for tax papers. Our plastic manikin, a left-over from my Dad's business, came bounding out of the closet and hit me on the head. Maybe it was a wake-up call. I like to think it was. I sat in the middle of the family room floor and cried for a long time. Not because I was hurt, but the stress of our lives was overpowering. I looked around and saw an out-of-control mess, and realized we had no one to blame but ourselves.

That same day, Doug finished installing a new closet organizer in our family room to help me with my new goal: simplify our lives and slow down that hamster wheel. A small step perhaps, but an important one. Now we needed to find more storage space for all the stuff that would not fit back into our organized closet. We worked until midnight.

I fell into bed exhausted that evening. There he was, my wonderful husband, with arms extended, dreamy eyes, ready to embrace, and a mouth that was as hard as a rock with no teeth.

"What in the world?" I gasped as his arm broke off and hit me between the eyes.

"It's our manikin from the closet I organized," Doug said from somewhere in the bed. "I couldn't find anyplace to put it."

5 - Selling Under the Influence

For the next several months, I should have sold real estate. Instead, I sold clutter. Even the palm sander didn't deter me. I thought I had turned the switch to "off" when I laid it on my front porch floor. Garage sale shoppers scattered when it became alive and vibrated across the cement toward them. Too bad the outdoor extension cord I had used on the sander was fifty feet long. It followed one screaming woman to her car. I never saw the woman or the palm sander again.

But other than that small incident, the sale of our clutter was flawless. Well, almost. I forgot to tell you about the dead cow from our garage sale.

"Mr. Brown's cow died last night," Doug said early one morning while reading the newspaper.

"How do you know that?" I asked.

"Because she is flat on her back in the field back there," he pointed.

I ran to the window for a look. The cow's legs—straight up in the air.

Doug continued. "Mr. Brown told me he can get some equipment and move her by noon."

"By noon," I yelled. "My garage sale starts in a couple of hours. I can't have a dead cow out in that field. Everyone will see her. Think of what that will do to sales."

Doug went back to reading the paper. Didn't anything ever bother that man? I thought a long hard minute and came up with a plan.

"We have to hide her," I said.

Doug looked over the top of his newspaper. "The shovel is in the garage," he said.

"Go park your Ford Ranger on the knoll in front of her. That will block the view from our front porch," I said.

After begging and promising him the world, Doug drove our Ranger to the field. My plan worked great until Mr. Brown showed up with his front-end loader and scooped the cow up. From our front porch vantage

Selling Under the Influence

point, it looked like a cow with extended legs was floating mysteriously over our truck. Poor Martha dropped the stack of towels she was going to buy.

"Do you see that floating cow?" she asked me.

"What cow?" I answered, trying to divert her attention.

"The cow with stiff legs," she said.

"Now Martha, I am surprised at you—and this early in the day. What would Harry say?"

Martha burned rubber as the cow disappeared over the hill. I heard she poured herself a stiff one when she arrived home.

The more pounds of stuff I shed, the happier I became. I had not had this much fun since the five-cent lemonade stands of my youth. And slowing down my real estate activities only added to my exuberance. So much so, that one day I woke up and told Doug I thought we should get out of real estate all together. He thought it was a good idea but wanted us to sell our own home first.

"And move to an apartment?" I thought.

At first the idea did not sound appealing. But after thinking of the weekly chores we did to maintain our home on seven acres, I was ready. I could fit into a two-bedroom apartment with the sale of a few more items. We didn't know how long Doug would be working but craved the freedom. Soon, I found myself turning in the paperwork to sell our own home. And like other normal people who sell their personal residences, I turned into a raving maniac.

"Why are you selling?" a co-worker asked.

"Because our house has outgrown us, just like your dress!" I snapped before I could control myself.

My co-worker squared her shoulders and smiled just like the photograph on her real estate sign.

"And wipe that silly smile off your face," I said. "I am sick and tired of seeing smiling faces on real estate signs stuck in yards around this town. How about a mug shot with a look of "Do You Feel Lucky Today?" instead of "Mrs. Congeniality?"

Later, another co-worker asked me what price I was selling my house for.

"Well, c'mon down," I shouted. "The price is right!"

It never fails. As soon as you put your house up for sale you find a spot on the wall that needs to be repainted. One day, I opened up our seven-year-old paint can to touch up some wall blemishes. I peered in-

Smiling Places

side and discovered the paint looked like the dry cracked earth of the *Grapes of Wrath*. For hours, I worked on creating liquid paint again. After adding some water and vegetable oil, and chopping the dry paint up into little pieces, I discovered I could cover the blemishes. Well, my walls caught a case of the shiny chicken pox. I bought new paint and repainted the whole room.

I also called out a local roofing company to look at our twenty-two year old roof. I walked outside with the roofer.

"Ma'am, your roof has middle-age bulge and its shingles are sagging," he said politely.

Feeling embarrassed, I looked down at my feet. I asked him if I should enroll our roof in an aerobics class. Later that week, the sound of air hammers filled our neighborhood as new shingles were being nailed to our roof.

I always advised my clients to put a real estate sign on their front lawn. Those signs produced results. The fine print reads, "Over one billion sold." House sales are keeping pace with McDonald's hamburgers. Teenagers love signs and move them, run over them, and use them for sleds. One night my country property was the target of their mischief. They took my real estate sign from my front yard.

At six a.m., the phone rang. An irate lady woke me up.

"How dare you try to sell my house!" she screamed in my sleepy ear.

I assured her I didn't know what she was talking about.

"Well, your sign is standing in my front yard."

I asked her if she had offered it a cup of coffee.

In my opinion, the best way to sell your home is through an open house. Every Sunday, thousands of dogs are locked up in cages and bark for two hours. People take on new identities while searching for their dream home.

"I am Richard Smith III from West Palm Beach, Florida and I will be paying cash," says Pete Johnson who lives two streets over and has multiple mortgages on his house. Pete filed for bankruptcy last week.

In our case, we sold our home at our second open house. We had just shut the door on the last family when the phone rang.

"I know it is a little late," the voice said on the phone, "but we won't take long."

Five minutes later they arrived, and fifteen minutes later we agreed on a price. We signed the purchase contract the next evening and left our home two months later.

6 - Survival of the Fittest

Here was a novel idea—apartment living. We now occupied a space below Kathy and beside Tom. Kathy worked an early shift. We heard her footsteps at three a.m. Tom did his laundry on Saturdays. His washing machine shook my mirror. Every Tuesday the mower crew cut our grass. And every Friday night, the complex had a party. When our faucet leaked, the handyman found his wrench. When our siding needed sprucing, the painters found their ladders. And when we stopped to smell the roses, the landscapers pruned them.

Our lives had transformed from a hamster wheel to a Princess Cruise. We had sold our real estate properties and ended our real estate careers. Our twenty-plus years of accumulated stuff had found new homes—except for my old, rusty, black metal desk with the wood grained top. That came with us. We had to remove the office door in our apartment to fit it through the door frame. Shush...don't tell maintenance. Doug still had his hammer and screwdrivers.

So, the only familiar constant from our old life was Doug's engineering job. And Bill Murray thought he had it bad. We had experienced our *Groundhog Day* five days a week, for twenty-four years: it is Monday morning, and the alarm rings at 5:45 a.m. My husband disappears, and I don't see his shadow for ten hours. He reappears at 3:45 p.m. to be fed, watered, and quartered for the evening. The next morning the alarm rings at 5:45 a.m. and the same thing starts all over again...for twenty-four years.

We didn't fully realize it at the time, but Doug and I had mentally left Dayton when we met Jim and Ann. Since Ludington, we had been reading books, articles, and the Internet about people who lived and traveled in recreational vehicles on a full-time basis. We visualized ourselves as the Dayton Dillbillies, who loaded up our RV and drove around the back-roads of America. We felt that was our calling. Our family and

Smiling Places

friends agreed and insisted we "seize the moment" if it should arise. So everything was in place, and we waited—waited to hear about Doug's job.

The days turned into weeks, and the weeks into months. Still, we heard nothing. Doug became discouraged when December came and went. Usually, all early-outs for the year were announced in December, but I never lost hope. In fact, the day before Doug's big news arrived, I spread the essential items we had saved for our journey on the living room floor. I unzipped our hefty backpack and found what I was looking for – our survival guide – a book that was almost as old as our marriage.

Doug and I began hiking in the Great Smoky Mountains exactly 53 days after we were married. Fifty-four days after we were married, we came close to getting hopelessly lost when a mountain trail disappeared and the towering Tennessee trees closed in on us. Luckily, Doug's internal compass rescued us. As a precautionary measure, and based on sound advice from a park ranger, we bought one of those handy survival guides that can bring you through any emergency. We never read it but always kept it in our backpack figuring that we could burn it if we ever got caught out in the cold. Most of the time though, the backpack stayed at our campground since it was stuffed full of survival gear and too heavy for us to carry on day hikes. Would we ever learn?

I truly wanted to. I figured this would be an excellent time for us to brush up on our survival skills since we were planning to go to who-knows-where and venture into who-knows-what. A quick read of our guidebook indicated the most important point of survival was to not get lost in the first place. OK, that made sense. And it suggested you should always orient yourself at the starting point of your hike with a map and compass before a panic situation took place. Good advice, but generally when you lived in the same town for forty-six years like I had, it was hard to lose yourself. I thought for a moment and came up with what I considered a brilliant idea. When Doug came home after work, I dragged him out of the door and up the street to our newly built, neighborhood Fairfield Mall. What a better place to practice our survival skills than in that intertwined concrete and steel structural nightmare.

Now for those of you who have never visited the Fairfield Mall, the think-tank who designed it were marketing geniuses. They built the mall to lure you in, with top name anchor stores and hidden treasures inside, which they advertised widely. Who could resist the temptation of this Shopping Mecca? And once these geniuses got you inside, they deliber-

Survival of the Fittest

ately laid out the floor plan so you couldn't find your way out—until they had you so discombobulated that you paid any amount for just about anything—even $3.00 for a single cookie. Personally, I would have much rather been in the mountains bushwhacking my way through the forests than trying to find my way around that mall. Being pursued by some of those salespeople was worse than running from a black bear after opening a six-pack of Hershey's chocolate candy bars.

So, Doug and I walked into one of the entrances of the mall after carefully noting landmarks outside. At each entrance, those thoughtful designers had placed a map with a little red arrow that said "You Are Here." (We may be here, Buddy, but which way is our car?) Using the map, I pointed our compass in the general direction of the Yankee Candle Shop. It was 270 degrees. With obstacles all around us, we both started to panic. There were not one, two, or three JC Penny entrances, but four!!! How could we use those as landmarks? (There may have been more—has anyone ever successfully counted them?) Just then a woman came toward us and distracted us from our orienteering lesson.

"I am so lost," she muttered. She looked like she has been wandering around the mall for days on end—she was bug-eyed, her clothes were rumpled, and her hair looked like Ozzie Osborne's. I felt so sorry for her that I shared our survival guide's pertinent wisdom with her.

"Buy a whistle," I told her. "That way people can hear you and find you if you are lost."

"Oh, thank you so much," she said. "I definitely must have one of those." And she hurried off to search for her life-saving equipment.

We walked and walked through hordes of people. Buckets of sweat dripped from our brows. Distractions were everywhere—I couldn't resist a Bath and Body Works shop and bought a bottle of Sweet Pea Body Lotion. Doug veered off at a Sears store to check out the Craftsmen tools. But all the while, we didn't lose sight of our primary mission, the Yankee Candle Shop. When we could not take one more step, we both collapsed on an empty bench. Exhausted, but steadfast, we watched people swarming all around us, some with built in directional radar in their brains and others who didn't have a clue as to where they were. Oh, to be caught in the bowels of the food court and not able to get out!

We eventually found the Yankee Candle Shop but stashed the compass and followed our noses. We left the mall at closing time, nine p.m. As we climbed into our car, people started coming toward us with a glazed look in their eyes. "Help me, please help me find my car," they

Smiling Places

pleaded. There were dozens of them, and they just kept coming and coming. It was like being caught in the *Night of the Living Dead*. We floored it out of the mall parking lot as fast as we could. As we did, we heard a whistle desperately blowing in the distance.

Unfortunately, we never did learn how to use that orienteering compass. We didn't have enough time. The next morning I was on the Internet reading about—what else—living on the road, and my computer said, "You've got mail." A message from Doug floated across my screen.

"Get off the computer. I need to talk to you."

I quickly closed AOL, and the phone rang two seconds later.

"Hello," I said cautiously.

"Hi there! Have I got some news for you," my husband said.

"Good or bad?" I said.

"Great news! My early out was approved."

"In February?" I asked.

"Yep, they had one slot left. I can leave work within a month."

"In a month?" I asked.

"Yes, in one month. Do you still want me to take it?"

Doug paused.

"Hello, Mel, are you still there?"

I was still there, but I could feel my heart pounding in my chest. I felt scared and elated, strong and weak, all at the same time. We had talked about this for months, but now it was real. My husband sounded so relieved. I stood by my convictions.

"Yes, I want you to take it," I said. "I am so happy for the both of us."

"I am, too. My parole finally came through," he laughed.

Three weeks later, Doug said good-bye to his fellow workers at his retirement luncheon. Our groundhog days had come to an end. I wasn't sure what the future held for us. I wasn't even sure if we had made the right decision. All I know is we were happy—exuberant may be a better term. For the first time in years, Doug wore a smile on his stress-weary face. And, I made sure I added two whistles to our survival backpack.

You just never know, do you?

7 - Honey, I Think You Need a Shrink

Doug's mother always said, "Retirement is just a change in management." Now I know what she meant. Doug's reign of terror started the day after he retired and lasted exactly sixty days, which coincidentally was the number of days we had until our departure. That sixty-day deadline turned my mild mannered husband into a dictator from a Third World Banana Republic.

His assessment of our "readiness posture" to hit the road was "You gotta be kidding me!" He went to work at once to organize our metamorphosis from apartment living to our new life on wheels. I called his work at once to organize a recall of my husband, until he was at least ninety-nine years old.

The Big Banana's first-proclaimed task was to find the "right rig" for us to travel in.

"Selecting the right rig for our lifestyle is crucial for our full-timing enjoyment," Doug barked. "I will research every option available to us."

"Yeah, right. Who are you kidding anyways? You've been tethered to a desk for twenty-five years. I see a teenager trapped in a Tyrannosaurus's scaly body. As a sane workingman, you drove VWs, Vegas, and Ford Rangers. Now you want to kick that testosterone level up a notch, don't you? I've seen you hide those monster truck magazines in your underwear drawer. If you think for one second that I'm driving all over America with a truck tall enough to run over pedestrians crossing the street and still leave them standing with grease slicks in their hair, then think again, Mister. And your little research excursions you take without me! I know you've been driving some pretty powerful vehicles. I see that sinister look in your eyes—like *Carrie* having a bad prom night."

So, I knew from the get-go that we were going to buy the *Superman* of trucks. I just hoped there was a little Clark Kent in the truck for me.

Then one day it just happened. My husband simply fell in love. We spied her through our car's windshield as we were driving down the

Smiling Places

highway. Showcased high on a platform, dressed in rich burgundy, was the mother of all trucks: four x four, extended cab, 4.7 liter I-Force V-8, double overhead cam 32-valve engine, variable assist power rack and pinion steering, 245 horses, 315 lb-ft @ 3400 rpm, 7,100 pounds towing capacity with a class IV hitch, and best of all, a dual cup holder with 32 oz. capacity.

"Do you see that gorgeous truck up there?" Doug asked me as we swung on two wheels into a Toyota dealer's parking lot. He jumped out of our car and hurried up the hill like some child who had just found his best friend.

"And the Tundra is the Truck of the Year," the salesman spouted. "This beauty was just delivered yesterday and has four miles on it. They build them in Indiana, you know. Real nice plant up there."

The salesman studied my husband's poker face that was lit up like a Christmas tree. I knew what the salesman was thinking. "What an easy sale *this* is going to be."

"Would you like to take it out for a test drive?" the salesman innocently asked.

I have to admit, as soon as the odometer turned over to 4.1 miles, I was impressed. She rode like a dream, her seats were luxurious, she kicked into four-wheel drive smoothly, and her extended cab was "purrfect" for our cat Sushi, who would be traveling with us. We walked away that afternoon, much to the chagrin of the salesman. I insisted we think about it.

The next morning Doug carried in a dealer invoice obtained off the Internet and negotiated an excellent price. The first part of our puzzle was solved: we had purchased our tow vehicle. Given Doug's child-like attitude, I nicknamed the truck—Toy. Boys just have to have their toys, you know.

Doug's attention now turned toward our apartment—and the search for our home on wheels—a travel trailer was put on hold.

The dictator took it upon himself to visit several storage units. He solely decided a ten-foot by ten-foot storage unit would be large enough to store belongings we would not take with us on the road.

"Everything we keep has to fit in this space," Doug said as he roped off a ten by ten foot floor space in our apartment. "This floor space may look small, but the ceilings in the storage unit are ten-foot high. I am going to stage our items here in the apartment to make sure they will fit. I will rent the unit a week before we leave so we can move our items into

Honey, I Think You Need a Shrink

storage then."

One afternoon, shortly after that conversation, I walked into our bedroom and all the furniture was gone except the bed. A large stack of clothes was piled on the floor. From the other room a voice announced, "I moved the bedroom furniture into our roped apartment storage area. I didn't think you'd mind."

I walked out to where the voice was coming from and found my whole bedroom suite, which was five pieces of furniture, stacked on top of each other, seven feet high in the air. I was speechless. I just looked at this structure with my mouth hanging open. Did my husband really believe that he was exhibiting normal behavior?

Unfortunately, our staged storage area kept growing. My husband even had his ladder at hand, and would walk up and down those rungs with boxes, books, or whatever he could find to pack that space all the way to the top of our eight-foot ceiling. Other pieces of furniture had also been crammed into this area including my Lazy Boy.

"Where am I supposed to sit?" I asked.

"At the kitchen table," he answered.

"It's in staged storage," I snapped.

"The love seat?" he asked like this was Twenty Questions.

"In staged storage," I snapped again.

He was behaving like Richard Dryfuss in the movie *Close Encounters*. Doug was building it so they would come. I wondered what alien forces my husband was in contact with.

Word traveled quickly throughout the apartment complex, and neighbors would show up at our front door just to see this marvel Doug was creating.

"Oh look," one neighbor commented. "He took her Lazy Boy."

"That takes a lot of guts," another neighbor answered. "Where is she going to sit?"

He then looked around the apartment to find something else to torture me with. He obliterated my office. Doug gave away my thirty-year old desk and sold my lateral file. He put the contents of my desk and lateral file into two large boxes that he pushed against the office wall. The little dictator was sitting next to the boxes when I walked in one day.

"You don't understand the concept of a travel trailer. We don't have space, and we must travel light," Doug said to me as he threw away another stack of papers.

"I really think you have gone off the deep end," I said. "When is

Smiling Places

Scotty going to beam you up?"

"Listen, didn't I clean out your files in 1988?" he asked.

"Yes, and I am still writing to places asking for copies of important documents," I said.

Doug picked up another file and ripped it in half.

"Oh, oh," I said. "Trouble—those were this year's tax documents."

"Didn't we already file?"

"No, I better get the scotch tape."

Then one day, the marvel had to come down. The Big Banana had packed everything into the staged storage area. I didn't have any items left to take with me on the road, much less sit on.

"Whoops," he said. He only said, "Whoops."

Then the ladder was unfolded again and up and down those rungs he went carrying boxes and furniture down from the heights of the ceiling. Thank goodness Doug lost interest in his marvel after dismantling it.

The turning point of whatever sanity Doug had displayed up to this point was the day he opened our mail forwarding service account we needed for the road. The service rep told him he would have to pay postage and handling on junk mail that was forwarded while on the road.

He armed himself with form letters and phone to stop all the junk mail we received. He was successful, too, except for one company. No matter what he did, they would not quit sending their sweepstakes contest letter.

"Rub off your lucky number and then bring it down to our car dealership showroom to see if it matches our winning number," the sweepstakes letter said.

After receiving the one-too-many-sweepstakes letter, Doug muttered, "This is the last straw." He sat down and created a letter specifically for the bothersome car dealership and mailed it the same day. The letter was entitled "My Death Certificate." Under cause of death he wrote, "mysterious infection due to rubbing off sweepstakes number received from car dealership." Under the remarks section he wrote, "estate filing suit to sue car dealership." The sweepstake letters stopped immediately.

The man was driving me crazy. I had to get out of the apartment, if only for an afternoon. Why not look for a travel trailer myself? After all, I knew absolutely nothing about them. I do believe, at the end of my foray into this uncharted RV territory, that it was I who needed the shrink—not the Big Banana.

8 - Honey, I Think I Need a Shrink

In the spirit of my celebration of escaping from the Big Banana, I invited my girlfriend Emma (not her real name, but I've always loved Emma) to lunch. Emma was all excited when she hopped into my car. She asked me where we were going, and I told her it was a big surprise. Forty-five minutes later, Emma told me she was starving. I told her we were almost there. One hour later, Emma was tearing apart my glove compartment to devour an old breath mint: date stamped—1982.

We finally arrived at my destination. Emma had a puzzled look on her face as we drove into "the largest RV dealership in the world."

"Didn't we just see that sign at another RV dealer five miles back?" Emma asked.

"Probably. All the RV dealers seem to be the largest something in the world."

Emma and I entered the showroom building and could smell the roasted hot dogs and fresh brewed coffee.

"Wow, free hot dogs and coffee," I said while reading the sign in the concession area. "I'll even buy you a bag of chips. My treat."

I told Emma to sit down and eat as much as she wanted.

"Have a great lunch," I said. "I'll be back in an hour."

I know. I wasn't very nice to Emma and tricked her into lunch. But she didn't mind, really. She loved hot dogs! And I needed to learn about travel trailers since Doug had already chosen Toy.

As I waded into a sea of travel trailers, the sharks were circling and ready to attack when one jumped out from behind a travel trailer and handed me his business card.

"Hi, I am Joe. And you are?"

"Looking for a defibrillator to shock my heart back into rhythm," I answered.

"No, seriously, what is your name?"

"I am serious," I replied.

"Well, Ms. Serious, are you in the market for a travel trailer today?"

23

Smiling Places

the pesky little salesman asked.

"Today?" I said, "No, I don't think so. I would like to check under the hood of one though."

"Check under the hood," he stammered, "Ma'am, travel trailers don't have engines. This is a towed vehicle."

"A toad vehicle? Like those beer commercials?"

"What?" he asked obviously confused.

"BUD," I said with images of campfires and beers.

"Oh, I get it. You are quite the comedian," he smiled.

"No, I am serious," I said.

"I remember. See, right here. I wrote your name down in my book."

Not amused, I walked to the front of the travel trailer.

"What is under this plastic cover?"

"Those are the gas tanks," he said.

I was dumbfounded. "Gas tanks? I thought you said these don't have engines. And if this doesn't have an engine, how come it has gas tanks?" I babbled.

Joe took a deep breath.

"Gas, or more correctly, propane gas, is used for most of the appliances in the trailer like the refrigerator, stove, furnace, and water heater. The air conditioning can only use electric, but the refrigerator and hot water heater can use gas or electric. And then you have the batteries to consider, and of course you could purchase a generator."

"Wait a minute," I pleaded, obviously in a state of confusion. "You mentioned electric?"

"Yes, Ms. Serious. Your trailer has an electric cord."

"It does? And where does it get plugged?" I asked.

"Into an electric outlet," he said while rolling his eyeballs.

"Listen, Joe. I don't want to camp by my house, I want to go places."

"No, no, you plug it in at campgrounds."

"Which campgrounds?" I asked.

"Any campgrounds that have electric. Some have water, too."

"Water? Where does that go?"

"In this trailer, under the bed," he said.

"Under the bed?" I gasped.

"Yes, into a holding tank."

"A holding tank? I thought that was on the back of a toilet."

"Well, normally, it is," he said.

"What do you mean by *normally*?" I asked.

Honey, I Think I Need a Shrink

"Well, the toilet in a trailer doesn't have a tank. You flush it and fill it with pedals on the floor."

"Oh, so that is where the accelerator and brake is."

"No, this doesn't have an engine," he answered somewhat exasperated.

"Wait a minute. Now let me get this straight. You are telling me that I sleep on a holding tank and I flush with my feet."

"Well that is basically true," he said. "By the way, do you own a truck to pull a trailer with?" he asked while wiping the sweat off his brow.

"Yes, my husband already picked out our truck," I said.

"What is your gross weight?" he asked.

"My gross weight? How dare you! That is a personal question."

"No, ma'am, not *your* weight but the gross weight your truck can pull.

"Oh. I don't know. Why, do I need to be concerned?"

"Yes, most definitely. The weight of your truck plus the weight of your trailer should not exceed the GCWR."

"Did you say gee see double you are?" I asked, thinking he needed his glasses and brain adjusted.

"Yes. The gross combined weight rating."

"O.K., if you say so."

I glanced at my watch. "Poor Emma," I thought.

"Hey Joe, I really need to get going."

He wiped his brow again and reluctantly asked me if I still had his business card.

"Of course I do," I smiled sweetly.

"The largest RV sales force in the world" was printed across the bottom of the card. I told Joe I would definitely be calling him. For a split second, I thought I saw a look of terror in that man's eyes. I don't understand why.

I went back to the lobby to find Emma. She was signing some paperwork. She had bought a pop up camper. I was astounded. Emma had never camped a day in her life. I wonder if she knew that a Volkswagen could not pull a pop up camper.

When I got home that evening, I relayed to Doug what I had learned from Joe. "First, you grab a Bud beer. Then, make sure you are not plugged in, or you won't get any gas. Then you sit on the toilet. That is where the accelerator and brake is.

25

Smiling Places

Doug cut me off and wondered if I had been hitting the cooking sherry again.

"Honey, I think this has been too much on you. Why don't we take you into the bedroom so you can lie down," he said gently.

"But I still don't understand why I have to sleep on a holding tank and flush the toilet with my feet." I said while he led me away.

Five days later, we ordered the perfect travel trailer for us. The height and length appeared to be a good fit to our truck. The width measured eight feet, and the weight of our trailer including options, personal belongings, and full tanks, did not exceed eighty percent of the maximum "*gee see double you are*". The interior floor plan provided a walk around bed, a comfortable toilet, air conditioning, a couch and dinette, excellent cabinetry, and bright walls with many windows. We also ordered a heavy-duty suspension system anticipating some camping in remote places. With the travel trailer on order, the next piece of the puzzle was set—we now had this "Thing" that would be ever present in our rearview mirror as we traveled down the highways and byways. Actually, Thing is more than "present" in the rearview mirror. It "eclipses" the rearview mirror—so we bought extenders to use for Toy's side view mirrors in order to see traffic behind Thing.

On day sixty, we drove to Indianapolis, Indiana to pick up Thing, our new home on wheels. The sun was radiant and the sky deep blue with no clouds in sight. For forty-six years of my life, I had stood at doorways in Dayton waving goodbye to visitors from far and near. Now I was the one leaving. I didn't know if we would ever live here again. Life seemed different now. As we pulled out of our apartment complex, I remembered our wonderful relatives and friends and felt like the loneliest person in the world.

9 - You Gotta Start Somewhere

I read a newspaper article before we left, where a husband and wife were driving down the interstate in their RV, and the wife was waving a gun at her husband. The state highway patrol pulled the RV over, hurried the husband to safety, and drove the wife to a psychiatric hospital.

I have to tell you that I know why that woman had reached her breaking point. It wasn't because her husband had an affair, nor did he gamble or drink too much. He made the mistake of buying their first RV so they could travel, and that was the very first day the woman had traveled in one.

In many ways, I can relate to that traumatized woman. We arrived in Indianapolis, Indiana sometime after 9 a.m. to pick up our very first RV.

The double doors to the warehouse slammed behind us as workmen were putting the finishing touches on our new home on wheels. From across the warehouse, the trailer sparkled in the sunlight that drifted through large window openings. I noticed a salesman had parked Toy in front of Thing so it could be hitched up with the towing assembly.

The closer we got to our new rig, the more I watched Thing *grow* in size, while Toy kept *shrinking*. By the time we reached the front door, I had convinced myself that this was Goliath, the giant of trailers, which at any time would consume our little burgundy matchbox truck.

I started to panic when I visualized this behemoth following our truck on roads all over America. All I wanted to do was climb back into our tent, zip it up, and hide.

"Good morning," the customer service representative said to Doug and I. "My name is Bob, and I am the trailer wizard. Let's go inside, and I will show you around."

"Please Mr. Wizard, make it disappear," I silently begged him.

As we stepped inside the middle of the trailer and all crammed into the living room, I wondered why this trailer had appeared so large on the outside.

"We will begin our tour in the kitchen," Bob said as he took one step

Smiling Places

from the living room towards the front of the trailer into the kitchen.

"Oh, isn't that stove cute?" I thought. "Now if I just had my pots and pans from My Little Magic Stove that I played with when I was eight years old, I would be all ready to cook 'Our Little Magic Meal.' "

The doubts were mounting in my mind. What had I gotten myself into? I wondered how much this trailer had depreciated in five minutes. Maybe we wouldn't lose too much money if the dealership bought it back right now.

I snapped out of my thoughts as Bob told us to crowd inside the bathroom. As if on cue, we all took one step from the living room, towards the back of the trailer, through the tiny door opening, and into the bathroom. Were we trying to set a new world record of cramming three people into a trailer bathroom? I stepped into the shower to watch the tour while Doug and Bob huddled together to explore what I considered the most important room in any trailer.

And then I noticed it. There it sat, in all its crowning glory: the trailer toilet.

"Hey feet, learn the toilet shuffle," I thought as I visualized how people might flush with their feet. Did they stand up or sit down? Did they use both the left and right foot? Did one flush take care of all? These are the intricate details Bob didn't go over. I didn't ask him either.

"And lastly, your queen-sized walk-around bed," Bob said. Then, he held his breath and squeezed into the space between the wall and the bed. He didn't dare breathe, or he would have popped the wall paneling as his stomach and chest expanded to take in more air.

I glanced at the bed. If that bed was queen sized, it was sized for a very short queen who didn't mind her feet dangling off the edges at night; yet there was something else wrong in the bedroom that I couldn't put my finger on.

"Oh, the colors!" I said out loud. Doug turned towards me and Bob still held his breath and didn't move.

"The colors in this bedroom clash with the other part of the trailer," I said.

Sure enough, it looked like someone had taken the fabric pattern from the living room couch, turned it inside out, and applied leftover dyes from the 1950's to the bedspread and bedroom drape valances.

"It's renovation time, it's renovation time," I sang secretly in my head to the tune of "It's Howdy Doody Time."

At the same time, I turned towards Bob, whose veins were popping

You Gotta Start Somewhere

out of his forehead from holding his breath, and sweetly said,

"Bob, please don't worry about it. We can take care of it."

My husband looked at me suspiciously. Did Doug sense my decorating hormones kicking in? Bob ran for the living room and took his first breath of air in two minutes. I bet he didn't like that part of the tour at all.

Outside the trailer, I began videotaping the hitching of our truck to assist my husband in his future hitching endeavors. Thirty seconds later, the camera ran out of battery power, which wouldn't assist my husband in his future hitching endeavors. "I can remember this," I thought as the discussion turned to the equalizer bars and the sway bar we had purchased.

Doug commented to Bob that he wanted to be "hitched to the hilt." Bob agreed buying those bars was a good idea.

Bob explain the hitching process as I watched through the camera viewfinder so Doug would not suspect the camera was not taping. I became very confused and thought, "Now where do you put that fifth link of the chain? Did he say helper bar? There are too many bars to remember. And how did they get that big round steel ball into that inverted steel teacup? And when do you tighten that other bar? What about that little lever? Did Bob just flip it forward?" "Hmm, hope Doug is getting this all down the first time."

Soon, we were ready to leave, and my heart was beating in time to Ricky Martin's fast paced Latin hit "Livin' La Vida Loca". Doug had never driven a truck/trailer combination (a rig) before. He appeared calm and was looking forward to our maiden voyage, a campground about ten miles away from our RV dealership. We decided to stage the trailer there to ensure everything was operational.

I clutched the dashboard as Doug made his first right turn out of the parking lot and missed the utility pole that *stepped out* in front of our trailer. We were finally on our way.

I wish I could say that we arrived at our campground twenty minutes later without incident, but let's increase the time it took us to drive the ten miles to one hour and forty-five minutes. The first five miles went smoothly. We were rolling down the two lane state highway and Doug was handling our rig like he had been driving it for years. I had even managed to relax a bit and started to enjoy the ride. Until the detour from Hades.

The detour from Hades took us through the side streets in a small

Smiling Places

town with vehicles parked on both sides of these side streets. I had to get out of our truck a few times to let Doug know that he had one-inch clearance on each side of the trailer to maneuver through the streets. And we only had an eight-foot wide trailer.

After we left that detour behind and turned south on a narrow country road, we started to relax again. The blood had flowed back into Doug's knuckles, and my cheeks were rosy again. Until a semi-truck came roaring past us at a high rate of speed, and the wind from the semi pulled Toy and Thing to the middle of the road.

"What in the world was that?" I gasped as my face became pale again. It felt like I had taken the helix turn on the Mantis roller coaster at Cedar Point.

"That was a bow wave. It's air pressure created by a large vehicle, such as a semi-truck," Doug said as his knuckles turned white again.

"How sweet. Our *first bow wave* together," I thought. I was a little shaken up, to say the least. No wonder, as we accidentally drove past our campground entrance, that I could only manage to point my finger and say, "Uh-oh. Boo-boo."

"We will just turn around somewhere," Doug said while scanning the farm fields all around him.

"Driveway?" I asked still pointing with my finger.

"No, I am not backing up on these country roads. They are too narrow and have ditches on both sides of them. We need to find a parking lot."

"Out here?" I managed to say.

"Either that or go around the block."

Going around the block in Indiana farmland is a lot different than scurrying around a city block. Twenty-four miles later we arrived at our campground. This time we didn't miss the driveway.

"This is my first night, so could I have a pull-through space, please?" Doug asked the campground manager.

"Sure, but you will have to go up that hill," the manager said while pointing in the direction of the hill.

I didn't know they had mountains in Indiana. That hill must have been a ten percent grade with ruts and mud and loose gravel. We finally reached the top after spinning our wheels, and then kicking Toy into four-wheel drive to finish our ascent.

When we reached the top, I saw the little number on the metal post and told Doug this was our space. We pulled in at a strange angle and

You Gotta Start Somewhere

jumped out.

"We made it," I said as I noticed Toy and Thing were facing the opposite direction of everybody else parked in our row.

"Here are the utility hook-ups," Doug said. "They are on the opposite side of where our hook ups are on the trailer. I hope the electric plug reaches."

He told me to go stand on the other side of the trailer, and he would throw the electric cord to me from underneath.

"OK," I said, while peering under the trailer. "I am over here."

We made eye contact, Doug peering from his side, and me from mine. He threw the electric cord, and I was able to reach it.

"Nice throw," I said as a man approached with a smile on his face.

"You should probably turn yourself around," the man said. "You pulled into your space backward. Is this your first time out?"

Was it the temporary license plates on our trailer that gave us away? Or was it throwing the electric cord underneath the trailer? It certainly wasn't our parking. Doug had done a fine job, even if he did pull in backwards.

Back down that hill, and up again we went. This time the utilities were on the correct side, and we didn't have to play lasso the electric plug.

There was only one small problem remaining. Doug wouldn't unhook Toy from Thing. All of a sudden, my truck had mated with a giant sardine can.

"I want to watch the video you made this morning of the hitching process before I unhitch," he said.

"Oh, no," I thought. "I hope he wasn't having one of those senior moments while he was learning that process."

All of a sudden, I was tired of everything. I wanted to relax a few minutes in the trailer. The heat hit me as soon as I opened the door. The trailer shook as I walked inside. "Shake and Bake" had a whole new meaning to me. It wasn't just a coating mix anymore. I ran outside and found my husband.

"The inside of that trailer is hot enough to dehydrate a camel. And furthermore, why does the trailer shake so much when I walk around inside?" I asked.

"Because we can't lower the leveling jacks to the ground while the truck is hooked up to the trailer. Normally, the jacks stabilize the trailer and stop the shaking motion."

Smiling Places

"And when do you plan to stop this shaking? When I am crispy and juicy and not pink inside?"

Doug ignored me, went inside, and turned on the air conditioning. We finally settled in to our "trailer, sweet trailer." We were hungry, so I decided to cook dinner on the cute little stove.

"I think the stove is broken," I said. "It won't turn on."

Doug checked every button known to mankind and still couldn't turn it on.

"Let's put it on our list of things for the dealer to look at," he said.

Since the stove wouldn't work, I decided to use the microwave and turned it on. All of a sudden, our whole trailer went dead.

"Now what?" I asked.

"We must have blown a circuit breaker running the air conditioning and microwave at the same time," Doug said as he headed outside.

"What else can go wrong?" I thought as I found two screws lying on the kitchen floor.

I looked up, and the screen in our kitchen roof vent was dangling overhead.

"Better get the screwdriver!" I yelled.

Doug walked back into the trailer with a sheepish grin on his face.

"I know why our stove didn't work. We forgot to turn on the gas," he said.

I sat down on the couch, propped my feet up, and wiped the sweat off my forehead.

"Oh well," I thought, "you gotta start somewhere."

10 - Frumpy Old Alumnus

Sometimes, I amaze myself with my coping skills. A few days had passed, and I was welcoming our next destination. I told Doug our cat had chewed the videotape, and he unhitched our truck and trailer. My shower was a closet and my kitchen table was a cutting board, and I wasn't concerned. My smoke alarm notified Doug in the next county when it was time to eat, and he rushed to the trailer. My refrigerator only held four items: milk, salad, eggs, and Doug's baseball cap; yet I prepared wonderful meals. Life was good.

We had no reservations. We had no schedules. We didn't have to be anywhere in particular. We unclasped our watches. We didn't care if it was Saturday or Monday. We could stop where we wanted, when we wanted, and for how long we wanted. My only order from Captain Doug was to head west. I had never explored west of the Mississippi River.

I enjoyed my new role as navigator. I had stockpiled maps, tour books, and campground directories. The backroads beckoned, as well as major attractions. My first stop was Thorntown, Indiana, and only twenty-six miles separated me from my Alma Mater, Purdue University.

In the early 1970's, when I was a Purdue college student, I observed the Frumpy Old Alumni converging upon my campus. Their gray, white or balding heads bobbed up and down in a crowd of young students headed for the stadium. They were the only fans who knew all the words to the school song. They looked like school mascot rejects, clad head to toe in baggy school colors and wearing wire rim glasses pulled halfway down their noses.

They attempted to dress like their sons or daughters—or worse yet like their grandsons and granddaughters. Let's face it: love beads never looked groovy with long gray hair and wrinkles.

They mobbed the bookstores and bought fifteen t-shirts at one time. I nicknamed them "Frumpy Old Alumni," the "wannabe college students", who returned to campus to feel young again through fond memo-

Smiling Places

ries of their own college days. What I didn't realize was I, too, had become a "Frumpy Old Alumnus."

In 1971, I turned eighteen. Richard Nixon was President. I became old enough to vote. The guys I knew received their draft cards. I could legally drink 3.2% beer. The best movie was *The French Connection*. The smiley face symbol made its appearance. And my parents enrolled me in college.

At freshman orientation, I learned that in 1869, a Lafayette civic leader named John Purdue needed to donate a large sum of money quickly, before the IRS taxed him, so he gave $150,000 to the Indiana General Assembly. The bureaucrats wanted to vote themselves pay raises with that windfall, but the good citizens of West Lafayette said, "Hey, assembly members, we'll donate some land if you build a university instead."

Tippecanoe County, not wanting to be left out of all the fun, donated $50,000 for anticipated cost overruns of the three original structures built. Classes began in 1874 with only 39 students, and Purdue University was born.

At least that is how I remember the story.

After freshman orientation, I stood on the sidewalk in front of Meredith Hall, my first dormitory, and waved goodbye to my parents. My parents waved back and switched their car radio station from rock and roll to classical music. They smiled at me and plotted to overthrow my bedroom when they got home. As they pulled away, I longed for their car keys and thought, "There goes my wheels." Their car disappeared, and I wondered how long it would be before they discovered their small TV was missing. I ran up the steps towards my dormitory room with thoughts to *party hardy* for four whole years!

I met one of the dearest friends of my life in that dorm. We lived next to each other during our freshman year and together for the next three years while we were attending Purdue. We were like Felix and Oscar of the *Odd Couple*. My Roomie was neat. I was messy. She was raised on an Indiana farm. I grew up in the suburbs of Dayton. Her mom grew green beans in a garden and canned them. My mom bought green beans at a grocery store and opened them with a can opener. My Roomie baked cookies. I ate Oreos. She sewed. I used stitch witchery. She majored in sociology. I majored in business.

I really missed her and called her from our campground. Betty would meet us on campus tomorrow.

Frumpy Old Alumnus

I knew I wanted to return to Purdue to recapture a frumpy moment of my youth. Suddenly, I realized that the second 23 years of my life had not been as kind to me as the first 23 years of my life. Armed with bags of makeup, enough hair coloring to turn Santa Claus brunette, and baggy clothes to hide my lumpy physique, I was ready to descend upon that campus. I looked like someone who had fought the battle of the age bulge *and lost*.

"Roomie," I cried, tilting my head upwards to make sure it was she whom I saw through my bifocals. We hugged and both said simultaneously, "You haven't changed a bit!"

Jim Carrey's movie, *Liar, Liar* came to mind.

Doug rolled his eyeballs.

And another frumpy moment was born.

Classes of over 39,000 students had ended that week for summer break, so we had much of the campus to ourselves. To keep my husband amused, I invented our own 1970's version of Purdue *Trivial Pursuit* that we played as we walked around our large campus.

"How did you recognize a Purdue engineer?" I asked.

"By the slide rule they carried," Betty responded.

"Correct. And what year did we buy our first electronic calculators?"

"In 1972."

"Where on campus did the Vietnam antiwar demonstrators march?" I asked.

"Down State Street," Betty said. "I sure am glad we didn't march with them."

"Me, too," I said.

Then, I threw in a trick question.

"What college did Matt Lauer from the *Today Show* graduate from?"

Betty looked at me and shook her head.

"Ohio University," Doug said. "That is where I went to college."

"Oh," Betty smiled.

We walked past the bar where our friend was thrown out for playing Merle Haggard's hit song "Okie From Muskogee" on the juke box 59½ times in a four hour period. The 45 rpm record sailed past our friend's head and missed him by inches.

"They always had such good popcorn here," I said.

"Probably Orville Redenbacher's. He graduated from Purdue you know," Betty said.

Smiling Places

"And what famous astronauts are Purdue alumni?" I countered with.

"That's a good one," Betty said proudly. Neil Armstrong and Eugene Cernan, the first and last men on the moon, and Gus Grissom from the Mercury Project.

Betty and I pointed to Neil Armstrong's fraternity house, and told Doug we had been to a party there and were shown the famous "moon rooms." We paused in front of our freshman dormitory and talked about 11 p.m. curfews, watching *Night Gallery*, and Patsy—who never stopped bragging about her fiancée back home, but never stayed in her dorm room at night.

We talked about April 3rd 1974, the day hundreds of tornadoes swept across the Midwest. Betty and I had climbed into my Volkswagen and raced to Stewart Hall on campus to seek shelter in its basement. The skies were black and the clouds swirled above us. We didn't think we would reach campus before the tornadoes struck. We were very lucky. Those storms did not strike our campus, but many places in Indiana were devastated that day.

"Where were you when the tornadoes struck?" Betty asked Doug.

"I was at Ohio University, but the storms didn't threaten us there," Doug said.

We had reached our sophomore dormitory building, McCutcheon Hall.

"Hey, Doug," I said, "The women's bathrooms had men's urinals in them because we moved in the year it went coed, in 1972. The girls on our dorm floor put green plants in them."

"And the campus guys had a panty raid, and we threw a huge pair of bloomers out our dorm window," Betty added.

"That was hilarious," I said. "We received so many phone calls from writing our phone numbers on those bloomers."

"And remember the canoe trip where I fixed you up with that guy, and you almost drowned?" I asked.

"How could I forget my canoe flipping?" Betty said. "But you and your boyfriend went under that huge tree in the middle of the Wabash River inside your canoe."

"That was scary," I said. "I was so surprised we stayed upright."

"Do you remember being covered with poison ivy after that canoe trip?" Betty asked.

"Yes, and I wouldn't go to classes for five days because my eyes were swollen shut," I said while thinking about the painful itching and

Frumpy Old Alumnus

burning associated with that malady.

When we came to the house we rented during our senior year, our eyes focused on the flatter portion of the roof where we had sat and talked for hours. We had also tried to make wine in our kitchen, and the fermentation process went berserk. The wine liquid exploded out of the bottles and went everywhere. No matter what we did, our apartment smelled like a brewery to the day we moved.

We stopped at the Sweet Shop for lunch and sat down in the wooden booth that we had called "ours" many years ago. Betty and I listed all two hundred guys that had hit upon us in our booth while poor Doug just rolled his eyeballs.

We heard that severe weather was headed towards Purdue, so we cut our visit short and walked towards our vehicles. Memories of our junior year apartment, old boyfriends, sporting events, and parties would have to wait for another day.

Betty and I had our final frumpy moment when we hugged and congratulated each other for still maintaining our youthful appearance. Who were we kidding? As we said goodbye, we both knew our college years had been some of the best years of our lives.

After my Roomie left, I aged twenty-five years in one second when I visited a bookstore to buy an alumni tee shirt before we left campus.

"Wow, twenty-five years!" the bookstore clerk gasped. That is soooo very long ago to have graduated," she said. "I just finished my freshman year, and I won't be graduating for three whole years. I just can't imagine!"

In three whole years, I would use:

—fourteen cases of hair dye,
—ten cases of extra dry skin lotion,
—sprout three hundred more liver spots on my arms.

"You certainly don't look that old," the store clerk added, trying to be nice. I knew the look she was giving me. She was trying to decide who was older, her great-great grandmother who came to their farm in a covered wagon, or me....

Smiling Places

"Well, good luck with your studies," I said, while secretly hoping she would discover her first gray hair tomorrow.

"After all, *what's one gray hair?*" thought the frumpy old alumnus

11 - Queen of the Trailer

I knew who the queen of our trailer was, and it wasn't yours truly. She ruled the moment Doug brought her inside and laid her on our couch. She was warm and cuddly, had beautiful deep blue eyes, and a purr that could soothe you to sleep. She definitely knew how to control her human servants.

"You can clean my litter now; I'm all done," she would meow.

"I'm lying in the sun, so it's time for my rubbies," she'd purr.

Like most other psychotic Siamese cats, our Sushi was fiercely independent. She had survived in a vacant city lot in Cleveland before she was rescued, and since she had agreed to travel with us, we played by her rules. Sushi insisted we sleep three to a trailer bed, and her favorite spot was on top of my feet. Her little eight pound body would become unmovable, so any ideas I had like flinging her across the trailer at 2 a.m. in the morning were out of the question. She also demanded that we use our trailer shower floor for placement of her litter box. You can imagine the inconvenience this caused me every night as I trudged up to a strange restroom to take a shower. Sushi hated cats, loved dogs, ate one kind of cat food, only tolerated distilled water from a store-bought plastic jug, and had to be groomed with a short bristle wire brush. Finicky, finicky!

So, why was I worried about her being left alone today? She was probably curled up on our fluffy white bedspread oblivious to the darkening southwest skies and chasing houseflies in her kitty dreams. Even so, I still felt a need to rush back to the campground. The Thing I now called home was nothing more than a mass of riveted wallboard and pop out windows suspended from a steel rib cage framework. A blanket of aluminum siding and a strip of rubber roof covered the entire structure. No concrete, no bricks, no basement, just four tires resting on a grassy knoll waiting to defend itself against Mother Nature's wrath. Thing would be knocked out in the first round. Our cat could go fifteen, if not inside that trailer.

Smiling Places

We left Purdue and drove toward Thorntown on what seemed like an endless stretch of asphalt highway. We didn't pass a soul for miles. My eyes followed row upon row of freshly planted corn that peaked through the sweeping rich brown soil of the Indiana heartland. My hypnotic trance was intermittently broken by two-story farmhouses and barns that were set among clusters of stately, aging trees.

We had been making relatively good time when all at once Doug firmly applied the brakes and quickly slowed to a crawl. Instantly, I became attentive again like someone had dumped a bucket of ice water over my head.

"What's wrong?" I asked.

"Look in front of the truck," Doug pointed.

Two reddish-brown foxes, mindless of our approaching truck, had darted into the center of the road. We could neither pass on the left or the right of them as they playfully chased each other in circles and trotted down the middle of the road, side-by-side. Doug blew our horn, which made them behave erratically, while still maintaining their asphalt footing. I unbuckled my seat belt.

"What are you doing?" Doug asked.

"I'm going to stick my head out the window and shout at them."

"Oh, yeah, that'll work, city girl."

I shifted my body so my head hung out the window.

"Hey, Fox! Move, Fox!" I yelled.

"Yeah, you go, Fox!" my husband added.

Both foxes looked in my direction and slowed to a walk. I brought my head back inside the truck.

"That worked about as well as the surprise birthday party you threw me!" Doug said.

"Look, I thought we weren't going to bring that up again," I said.

"What? The part about my cake catching fire or Snake Man losing the python?"

"At least Sushi found the snake."

"I think the snake found her. It took ten of us to pull it off of her," my husband said, while eyeing me suspiciously. "Wait a minute. What are you doing with my chocolate chip cookies?"

"I am going to throw one to the side of the road. Those foxes certainly eat cookies!" I answered.

"Why don't you throw it my way instead?" Mr. Chocolaholic asked.

I gave my man a cookie, stuck my head out the window again, and

Queen of the Trailer

pitched a 90 mph cookie to the side of the road. The fox kept walking. I clapped my hands. They kept walking. I banged on the side of the truck. They kept walking. I shouted louder. Nothing fazed them.

Exasperated, I pulled my head back inside. Doug took one look at me and stopped the truck. He was laughing so hard he couldn't drive. Stuck right between my squinting eyes, smack dab in the middle of my bunched eyebrows was a bug. And this was no ordinary bug, but a huge green antennaed monster with hairy, elongated legs, wiry transparent wings, and red fluorescent eyeballs bulging out the sides of its triangular head – or at least that is how my husband described it. I felt it move, either from the wind on my face or on its own. Looking cross-eyed at my nose, I grabbed it in my hand and flung it out my window with a bloodcurdling someone-is-trying-to-kill-me scream. After hearing that sound percolate from my lips, those foxes ran over each other to get the heck out of there. They both hit the adjacent field running and probably didn't stop until they reached the next county—wherever that was.

I just assumed we were in one of those severe thunderstorm-warning counties the radio kept talking about. I suppose the hazy, green-colored sky and the ominous wall of black clouds headed right for us had something to do with my brilliant observation, don't you think? Forget the green monster bug; this was serious.

You see, ever since a child, I've watched *The Wizard of Oz*, all 10,347 times it has been on TV. The thought of being carried off by a category 23 twister and landing on some unsuspecting Indiana resident wearing ruby red slippers really scared me. After all, those shoes could magically adhere to the ends of my gams, and I was clueless on how to remove them. My floppy, pigeon-toed, flat feet I inherited from my platypus ancestors just didn't do tiny slippers. And that sparkling ruby red color? A fashion nightmare with my blue jeans, I'm sure. So, when we arrived back at the trailer to search for Sushi, I double-tied the gym shoes I was wearing and calmly (ha ha ha ha) sat on the toilet with our wailing cat perched on my head while Doug manned the couch. The winds hit with a roar and, indeed, sounded like a freight train was passing within inches of where we sat. Sheets of rain soaked the ground and formed narrow rushing gullies. Our trailer leaned precariously to one side. I thought it was going to flip, so I screamed in a calm (ha ha) manner, "Our trailer is going to flip!" while a bottlebrush, pulsating tail batted me in the face.

Flying debris slammed into our aluminum siding from all directions,

Smiling Places

and a single leaf made a huge thud as it plastered itself against a window near Doug. Bits and pieces of roofing, branches, twisted lawn chairs, and witches with green teeth blew past our window. After the storm, a farmer from town drove all the way to Pennsylvania to retrieve his mooing cow stuck thirty feet up in a tree.

We never lost electricity. I know this because our weather radio announcer kept us fully informed about the storm's progress.

"Take cover immediately! The whole state of Indiana is under attack! We are all going to die!"

The more helium the weatherman sucked, the higher pitched his voice became. When the hail started, I swear I heard that man shouting,

"Aunty Em, Aunty Em, where are you?"

And then, as quickly as the storm started, it stopped. The sun came out, and the birds began singing—except those whose beaks were impaled on the wooden laundry structure. We stepped outside. Our campground looked like a hangover from Mardi Gras. Lots and lots of stuff lay strewn around the huge grassy area the trailers called home.

An older gentleman came up, clutching a string of tattered plastic lanterns.

"You kids ride out the storm in that?" he asked.

We nodded our heads yes.

"And you weren't hurt?"

We shook our heads no.

"You on vacation?"

"No, traveling around the country," Doug answered.

"How long you been on the road?" the man asked.

"About a week," Doug answered.

"Oh, that explains it. You really shouldn't stay in those things during severe weather," the man advised.

"I agree. Never want to do that again," Doug answered while mentally adding it to his list of lessons learned on the road.

I climbed back inside the trailer to open the windows and start dinner. Sushi was sitting by the door on top of the dinette seat cushion and batted my arm as I walked past.

"Hey, stop that," I demanded.

She growled when I attempted to pet her. The Queen was upset. We had violated her rule number seventy-one: Never make me stay in the trailer during severe weather.

And do you know what? We never did again.

12 - A Big Muddy Runs Through It

Whenever I thought of the Mississippi River, Mrs. Meany came to mind. Her real name was not Mrs. Meany. I changed it here to protect myself from her yardstick. She was a grade school teacher of mine a long time ago. She kept six of my classmates and me after school one day because we couldn't spell the word Mississippi. We all missed the bus, and she only allowed each student one phone call. I called my dad's lawyer.

The lawyer said I should reason with her and tell her Huckleberry Finn probably couldn't spell it...maybe Becky Thatcher could. Mrs. Meany only cackled and tapped her yardstick on the chalkboard. I tried to phonetically spell it – Miss-a-sip-pee. That didn't work either. She finally let us go home with strict instructions to learn how to spell that darn word...or else. The next morning, I could spell it backwards and forwards, while standing on my head. That old Mrs. Meany sure was a kick, wasn't she?

But that was forty years ago, and I could still spell the word "Missasippee". Unfortunately, the incessant tapping noise Mrs. Meany made with her yardstick had been stuck inside my head for years. To this day I only use measuring tapes and stay as far away from those giant wooden rulers as possible.

I'd like to say that was the only time the Mississippi River affected my childhood, but it wasn't. One day after reading *The Adventures of Tom Sawyer*, I whitewashed a portion of a wooden slat fence surrounding our back yard. I always thought the flamingo-pink paint color my mom chose for the fence clashed with our red brick home. After finishing a small section of fence, I stood back and admired my decorating skills. I could tell the whitewashed area of the fence really brought out the color of our bricks. Obviously, my parents couldn't tell, they bought more flamingo-pink paint, and grounded me for a whole week!

I suppose these childhood experiences had something to do with this

Smiling Places

need I had to head west, find a bridge, and drive across the Mississippi River. Off we went, left Indiana, and pulled our rig through the beautiful state of Illinois.

We would have been across that bridge by lunchtime if Doug had secured our sewer hose properly to the back bumper of our trailer. We thought Illinois was the friendliest state in the union when all these people drove by us honking their horns and waving their hands and fingers at us. That finger thing was such a nice gesture telling us we were number one. We really liked that. How did we know our sewer hose was flopping along behind us on the highway spewing Lord-knows-what into the faces of all those passing motorists?

At the 80-mile marker of I-74 on the western side of Illinois, we pulled into a rest area and discovered our problem. Lucky for us those sewer hoses are like giant Slinkys. We scrunched it up and shoved it into a trashcan at the side of the road. I don't think that was the smartest thing to do as the trash can lid shot five feet in the air and landed on top of an unsuspecting three pound Yorkshire Terrier. We scurried out of there quickly when the lid began running in circles and barking at pedestrians.

Our quest for the Mississippi River continued, but I have to let you in on a little secrct: It's pretty hard to miss this river, especially if you are driving cross-country. The Mississippi River nearly runs right down the middle of America's lower forty-eight. The headwaters begin as a trickle all the way up at Lake Itasca in north central Minnesota and flow almost 2,400 miles all the way down to the Gulf of Mexico. In some places it can be a mile wide, but my geographically challenged husband didn't know this. He placed me right up there with Lewis and Clark when I pointed in the direction of the "Mighty Mississippi" and said, "There she is." He thought me to be some type of navigational genius.

I estimated the bridge we used must have been built in the early 1900's, out of LEGOs. I wasn't too concerned. I could see Iowa on the opposite bank. And then we got on the bridge, and Iowa magically disappeared. Nothing was in front of us or to the side of us but a swirling mass of muddy water. We both froze when we discovered our traffic lane was only wide enough for a GEO Metro. I closed my eyes. Doug closed his eyes. Somehow, we arrived at our campground in Davenport.

A registration sign was posted outside a small white building with a wrap-around porch crowded with rocking chairs. We parked our rig in the large gravel parking area adjacent to the building and went in. The

A Big Muddy Runs Through It

office doubled as a general store, and I noticed some shelves to the side of the desk stocked with RV supplies. I walked over to browse the merchandise while Doug approached the registration desk.

An older lady stood behind the desk shuffling some paperwork. She reminded me of a dear friend in Dayton, and at once I felt right at home. I could almost smell the fresh apple pie baking in the oven.

"Good afternoon," she smiled sweetly. "My name is Linda. I bet you'd like to sign up," she said as she looked out the window and nodded her head toward our rig.

"Sure," Doug said. "We called a few days ago for reservations."

"I remember talking to you. You must be the Tomsus from Ohio. I saw your trailer when you pulled in. You have the little Siamese cat."

"That's us," Doug answered.

"And you also inquired about getting your mail delivered here," Linda continued. "It hasn't arrived yet, but maybe tomorrow. I'll keep watching for it."

"Thanks, we really appreciate that," Doug said. "Our mail delivery service said it would take 2-3 days."

Linda pushed a spiral bound registration book toward Doug and asked him to fill it out.

"Good thing you made reservations," she informed Doug. "We are almost filled up this week. A rally is coming in."

Before Doug could reply, I inquired about the sewer hoses and connectors Linda had for sale on shelves with the rest of the RV supplies.

"Funny you should ask about those," Linda answered. "Not thirty minutes ago, a couple from the rally came in and registered and told me the strangest thing. They said they were at a rest area in Illinois when a damaged sewer hose jumped out at them from a trashcan they were passing while walking their dog. I usually hear all kinds of strange stories working in here, but this one takes the cake."

"Now that's funny," I said while Doug turned ten shades of crimson.

I just couldn't believe that old sewer hose had come back to haunt us. If Linda suspected it was ours, she was too polite to ask. I chose my next words as carefully as Bill Clinton.

"We are just starting out," I said. "Our trailer doesn't have a sewer hose right now. What type of connector do we need for this hose?" I asked while pointing to a 20 foot gray sewer hose.

Linda came around the desk to show Doug and I the different hoses and connectors she had. We ended up purchasing a twenty-foot and a ten-foot hose with different connectors to accommodate the many hookup options different campgrounds had available.

"I've got your reservations for three nights. And since you are registering early today, I can put you in this space close to the bathhouse or over by those people from the rest area," Linda said as she pointed to a campground map.

"I think we'd like the first space you offered on account of their dog and our cat," I answered.

"Oh, that's right," Linda said. "Good idea."

By this time sweat was breaking out on my brow. What if that dog had picked up our scent? What if those trashcan people recognized us? What if Linda found out the Illinois sewer hose fiasco was our doing? I figured a good rap across my head with Mrs. Meany's yardstick would have been appropriate punishment for how I had just acted.

"I have one more question," Doug added. "If you had never been here before and wanted to choose two or three things to see while in the area, what would they be?"

"We are asked that question all the time," Linda said as she reached under the countertop. "Courtesy of the Quad Cities Tourism Bureau, here is a packet of information about the Quad Cities. It also includes a map."

Linda laid the plastic bag full of goodies about the area on the countertop and continued. "Now personally, I'd definitely see Rock Island Arsenal and the John Deere complex in Moline—both right across the river. Of course, you shouldn't miss East Davenport and the river cruises."

"Thanks so much," Doug said and took the package.

As we left the office, I heard Doug mutter under his breath, "Thanks to you, I have to be on the lookout for an irate Yorkshire Terrier. Nice going, Mel."

"I know," I replied quietly.

The next morning we climbed out of our trailer resembling the Griswalds in search of Wally World. We donned goofy hats and sunglasses, and carried cameras, maps, and snacks. The only thing missing was Aunt Edna strapped to the top of our truck. From Linda's suggestions and a lot more, I had worked up a thirty-day sightseeing itinerary to be accomplished in just two days. I quickly learned one major lesson early in our travels: You can't see it all, and you certainly can't do it all...at least not with my man.

The only thing that would set my man into warp speed motion was if

A Big Muddy Runs Through It

I planned a whole day of shopping. He'd be in and out of those shopping malls in milliseconds, turning a whole day of shopping into a mere 59 minutes of running away from me with our credit cards dangling from his wallet. On those days, I did not find his game of hide and seek very amusing.

But museums were a different story. Doug would turn into this touchy-feely kind of guy where all exhibits had to be read word for word, all narrative buttons had to be pushed and listened to, and all hands had to be stuck into those big black holes to feel whatever disgusting objects an insane museum curator had decided to scare visitors with. And this would take my husband hours upon hours to accomplish. With this in mind, I shoved my itinerary under Doug's nose and told him dawdling in museums could be hazardous to his marriage.

So, once again we crossed the Mississippi River, this time going back to Illinois to visit Rock Island Arsenal. The old railroad bridge we drove across was built in 1896. It had been converted from train to automobile usage and connected Davenport to this 946-acre arsenal island. In 1856, the first railroad bridge to cross the Mississippi River was built right in this same area. Well, you can imagine the steamboat companies didn't like that one bit and would say "Ooops" when they deliberately rammed their boats against the new railroad bridge. A lawsuit ensued about water right-of-ways and went all the way to the Supreme Court who decided, "Yep, the railroad bridge could stay." Abraham Lincoln was one of three lawyers who represented the railroads and won this monumental case. I was pleased no steamboats were ramming bridges the day we crossed.

But even before any railroad bridges could be built across the Mississippi, there was this *tiny matter* of the French occupying the Mississippi River Valley. By 1801, many Americans were already farming the fertile lands in this area and using the river to ship their produce. President Thomas Jefferson wanted America to control the Big Muddy so he sent some real estate agents over to France to see if they could negotiate a sale. It just so happened that Napoleon Bonaparte needed some extra cash to finance a few wars he was involved in, so in 1803, he struck up a deal with the Americans.

"Pay me $15 million dollars, and I'll give you 828,000 square miles of uninhabitable, swampy, rocky, mountainous wilderness."

"Sold!" said Jefferson. "I can nearly double the size of the United States for only 3 cents an acre. That should get me re-elected in 1805!"

Smiling Places

Thus, the famous Louisiana Purchase was made, and the Mississippi River was part of the eastern boundary of the purchase. One year later, the U.S. Government obtained Rock Island through a treaty agreement with the Sauk and Fox Indians.

So now the Americans "owned" the Mississippi River and an island in the middle of the river. They wanted to protect their waterway.

"Erect a fort," they cried, and built Fort Armstrong on Rock Island after the War of 1812.

Many years later, the Civil War shaped the destiny of Rock Island. Not only was a Confederate prisoner-of-war camp built there for more than 12,000 prisoners, but also the outbreak of the Civil War in 1861 sent Congress scrambling for new arsenals after Harpers Ferry Armory fell to Confederate forces. Rock Island's location on the Mississippi was an ideal choice for an arsenal. Congress appropriated $100,000 to build a small arsenal on Rock Island, and in 1863 construction began on the first Arsenal building, known today as the Clock Tower Building.

But when Brevet Brigadier General Thomas J. Rodman assumed command of the Arsenal in 1865, he had some very different ideas as to what this arsenal should look like.

"Small!" he shouted. "Not under my command!" And he proceeded to draw up a master plan for a "Grand Arsenal of the West." Thirty years later the building of the Grand Arsenal was complete. General Rodman was dead, and the Illinois stonecutters who cut the limestone blocks for the gigantic arsenal buildings had left a big hole in the state of Illinois.

Our truck bounced off the old railroad bridge and was swept along by the rush-hour paparazzi of Arsenal workers eager to reach their desks and get their morning fix of caffeine and sugar. We zipped right past the sign designating Rock Island Arsenal a National Historic Landmark. I always thought those Smucker's Jelly people Willard Scott portrayed on the *The Today Show* were National Historic Landmarks. When we drove down Rodman Avenue, the main artery of the old arsenal, we "oohed" and "aahed" just like watching Fourth of July fireworks, all the way down the long, straight avenue. It was simply breathtaking.

Massive u-shaped, limestone-block buildings, originally built as manufacturing workshops, had numerous, evenly-spaced windows to maximize available daylight. They lined block after block of the avenue on both sides. In my humble opinion, General Rodman was the Frank Lloyd Wright of his time. His genius was evident in the beautiful Greek Revival architectural style he chose and the outstanding symmetry of the

A Big Muddy Runs Through It

limestone buildings he planned. This stretch of our country's heritage was a most unique viewing experience.

I would have loved to see the Commanding Officer's Quarters General Rodman designed. The home was completed in 1872 but closed to the public since the current Commander was living there. The house has fifty-two rooms...yes, I said fifty-two rooms of living space. Hopefully, it comes furnished. It is not surprising that this home is the second largest home owned by the Federal Government. It ranks second in size only to the White House. Personally, if I lived in a 52-room home, I wouldn't know what to do with all that space. I would probably be running around like Jack Nicholson in *The Shining* having drinks with dead people.

Come to think of it, I was ready for a drink after Doug insisted we stay at the visitor's center for an *extra* hour to watch the locks on the Mississippi River fill with water so a hopper barge could float through. (For those of you who don't know, a hopper barge is a long flat boat filled with hoppers.) Doug also became stuck in some museum time warp thing at the Arsenal Museum. His favorite part of the museum was all of it, and they had plenty to keep him busy. Over 1,000 military firearms were on display—from those weapons developed and produced at Rock Island to the experimental and captured weapons. I thoroughly enjoyed the small display of Rock Island cavalry items (horse stuff) from the Spanish-American War in 1898. I could hear Teddy Roosevelt shouting to his Rough Riders before charging up San Juan Hill, "Boy these saddles are comfy!"

We were the last two people to leave the museum except for an employee who locked the door behind us. I couldn't believe we had spent the whole day at the Arsenal. My itinerary was a joke. It was too late to go anywhere else—including the John Deere Pavilion.

I have to tell you, I had really looked forward to visiting the Pavilion. It would have brought me great comfort and provided closure to a very trying experience. You see, I was still mourning the sale of my John Deere lawn tractor less than a year ago. I would put that blade down and go for hours, grass flying everywhere, bugs jumping out of the grass, tree swallows catching bugs jumping out of the grass—and I, catching tree swallow poop on my head. Now, I wouldn't be able to relive those wonderful mowing memories. I wouldn't be able to run my hands across that slick, smooth, green paint nor grasp that black, ribbed steering wheel. I was deeply disappointed to say the least.

My evening went downhill from there. I had an altercation of sorts

Smiling Places

while walking up to the front office to get our mail package that had arrived. All of a sudden, out of nowhere, these yapping, stringy-haired creatures with bulging eyeballs and protruding teeth came up behind me. I turned around and knew right away who they were...it was Trashcan Mama and her sidekick Yorkshire "Terror."

"It's you," Trashcan Mama said. "You, from the rest area."

"What rest area? What are you talking about?" I asked while the Yorkshire "Terror" was nipping at my ankles.

"It was your sewer hose, wasn't it Missy?" Trashcan Mama asked.

"What sewer hose?" I asked.

I was in no mood for this. My feet were killing me, and I had dinner started on the stove. All I wanted to do was go home to relax. These two were really beginning to bug me.

"Well, my little Bam-Bam was never so befuddled in his entire life when that sewer hose jumped out of the trash can and sent that lid down on top of him!" she continued

"My, my. What in the world did little Bam-Bam do with a trashcan lid on top of him? Run around in circles, yapping at people's feet?" I asked sarcastically.

"Well, there you go, you did see it," Trashcan Mama said triumphantly. "Oh, my little Bam-Bam. You knew it was this woman all along, didn't you sweetheart?" she cooed to her pet.

"Yip-yap, yip-yap, yip-yap, yip-yap, yip-yap," Bam-Bam answered as his mucous-coated tongue lolled out of the side of his mouth, and his gruesome three pound body pulsated with each yip and each yap.

And then I noticed it. Do you know how owners and their dogs look alike? Well, this woman had an uncanny resemblance to little Bam-Bam, including hair in her ears and her smelly breath permeating the air.

"Don't deny it, we know it was you," Trashcan Mama repeated for the umpteenth time.

By this time I was ready to dropkick that little yapping piece of work—and his Mama, too. But somehow I restrained myself and decided to walk away from this impossible situation. I wanted to get the last word in, so for the second time in two days, I chose my words as carefully as Bill Clinton.

"Look lady," I said and took a step toward her and that barking Bam-Bam. "I don't know who you think you are, but listen to me and listen close...I did not have sewer hose relations with that dog!"

Yep, I denied it and headed toward the "oval" office for my mail.

13 - TV, Corn, and Chocolate Mints

I wish you could have seen my husband before he bought a television set for our trailer. He was so resourceful. He washed our trailer everyday, and it sparkled in the sunlight. He wiped our windows until they were as spotless as crystal. Our truck was as clean as the day we drove it off the showroom floor. And the man terrorized Sushi by sporting a bottle of pet shampoo. Her skin turned a bright shade of scrubbed pink.

Doug was the hottest sensation to hit our campgrounds since Spam. The women campers lusted after his motivation and wanted to know how to get their own husbands off the couch. They constantly flocked to our trailer and complimented him on the great job he was doing. I didn't want to burst Doug's bubble and tell the women why the man didn't know what to do with himself. He did that all by himself in Davenport where we had our last disagreement over the television set.

I told him we should rough it, that we didn't need a TV. He told me traveling with a microwave wasn't roughing it. I said the microwave was included with the trailer, the TV wasn't. He said the microwave was optional, and the TV was mandatory to him. I said playing rummy at night instead of watching TV was fun. I also told him his rummy game stunk, and I was beating him twenty-three games to six. He said he would be winning rummy if he could watch Tom Brokaw and *The NBC Evening News*. I said what an excuse; I always beat him in Rummy. He said he couldn't play Rummy from now on because his right thumb was twitching due to TV remote withdrawal. I told him where he might stick his right thumb to keep it from twitching. He said he didn't think that was funny at all and said he was going shopping to buy a TV. I said fine, have it your way, but the TV had to be white to match our décor. He said he didn't care if it was pink polka dots and walked out the door.

He brought home an off-white 13-inch TV/VCR all-in-one combination to fit on top of our trailer's TV cabinet. I sat at our kitchen table and

Smiling Places

didn't say a word as he hooked it up. He turned the TV on, and it was black and white and fuzzy all over. "Hmmn," he muttered and reread the television instruction booklet. He messed with a couple of TV controls and wires behind the TV, but that didn't improve the picture either. Then, he went to the fuse panel underneath the refrigerator and checked the fuses. He must have decided they were in good shape because he turned toward me and said, "I have to go outside and look at some wires."

I watched him go out the door and grab one of our white plastic chairs from the concrete porch and set it by the trailer. Then I watched as he picked up one end of the wooden picnic table and then the other and walked it to the side of the trailer. Then, he put the white plastic chair on top of the picnic table, climbed up on the table, and then stood on the chair. I heard wires being shuffled about on the trailer roof. Then I made my move.

The TV was turned on and still black and white and fuzzy all over. I slowly got up from the kitchen table and tiptoed over to the TV because I didn't want him to feel the trailer shake. I reached behind the TV and pushed the antennae booster button located on the wall of the trailer by the antennae wire outlet—just as Bob, the Trailer Wizard had shown us. Voila! The picture turned all clear. I tiptoed back to the table and sat down. He climbed down off the chair and the picnic table and walked inside the trailer.

"Something you did out there seemed to clear up the picture," I told him, trying to keep a straight face.

"I knew the problem was with the outside wires," Doug answered in his macho tone of voice.

He programmed some channels in with his new thumb-twitching remote control and made sure the picture was clear before he went out the door again. He took the chair off the picnic table and set it on the concrete porch area and then, walked the picnic table back to its original position. While he was doing that, guess what I did? I got up from the kitchen table and tiptoed over to the TV. Only this time I reached behind it and turned the antennae booster button off and sat down. Now the TV picture was black and white and fuzzy all over again. When he came inside I said, "Something must have happened to the picture again."

Well, I can't repeat right here the words that flew out of that man's mouth, but believe me, those words were suitable only for premium cable TV. After his tirade, he announced he was going outside again.

TV, Corn, and Chocolate Mints

Should I have let him? Probably. But did I let him? No. Instead, I burst out laughing and told him where to go to push the antennae booster button. He said he had forgotten all about that button. He pushed it and said he didn't think this had been very funny at all. I had to disagree!

By the next day, Doug was a couch potato again, and I had removed the "I" word from my vocabulary. No longer would I speak of itineraries in this household. I had chosen only one place for us to visit today. I could close my eyes and see it. Kevin Costner riding a John Deere tractor through stalks of corn and building a baseball field. James Earl Jones sitting on the bleachers in Iowa watching a "nostalgic" baseball game. Shoeless Joe Jackson asking, "Hey, is this Heaven?" and Kevin answering, "No, it's Iowa." The *Field Of Dreams* movie set was only ninety miles north of us in Dyersville, Iowa. And since the movie, I had always dreamed of building it and having James and Kevin show up!

I suppose the day I visited the *Field Of Dreams*, I hadn't really thought about the corn being grown. I just figured Hollywood had left fields of tall, plastic, fake corn, with those life-sized picture cutouts of the actors, so movie buffs like me could really ham it up. I should have realized this wasn't Sedona, Arizona, where Hollywood has filmed over one hundred western movies and TV shows. Nature, not man, created that rugged movie setting with sandstone rock towers, windswept buttes, and singing canyons. Man had created this idyllic movie setting in Iowa, and it was the month of May where fields of itsy-bitsy corn broke through the ground in freshly plowed fields: a great place to hide baseballs, not baseball players.

The same two-story white farmhouse with the picket fence still stood on the knoll behind the bleachers. The door on the front porch slammed shut, carried by the winds. A lady named "Sue" walked down the hill from the house with a key in her hand to open up her gift-shop display stand. She didn't want to miss the two bumbling idiots from Ohio—quite possibly the only idiots she had seen all year. Even the Florida tourists knew not to show up while the corn was only four inches high. And since we were the only people there, and since Sue had made that special trip from her house down the hill, in the wind just to open the gift store for us, I knew. Doug knew, and Sue knew, that we had to buy something. There was no way out of it. She had us cornered.

We didn't mind. We were big fans of the movie. We could always buy the proverbial baseball cap to match the other 158 caps we already had in the trailer. And I, of course, had to have the VCR tape of the

Smiling Places

Field of Dreams for "my" new TV set so I could watch it and point at the TV screen and make a fool of myself as I screamed, "I stood there, and pitched to you! You stood there and hit the ball! I sat in the same place on the bleachers where Kevin and James sat!"

I also thought it might be a good idea to find out the behind-the-scenes scoop on the filming of the movie since we weren't doing anything special: except running around the baseball diamond chasing gift-shop souvenirs being blown out to left field. Sue wasn't doing anything special, either, except throwing her body across the gift countertop to stop bumper stickers and posters from being sucked down the silo.

My first clue as to what an undertaking it had been to film the *Field Of Dreams* came when Sue told us the movie had been filmed in 1988, during the worst drought ever recorded in Iowa—except for the Dust Bowl.

"They nicknamed it the 'Field of Dirt.' We never thought the directors could pull it off on account of the weather. Nothing was growing, not even the corn. They trucked in water and lots of it. They even dammed up a creek. Well, with all the irrigation going on, that corn shot up to shoulder high by mid June. In one scene they had to put Kevin Costner up on a plank to walk through the corn, so his head would stay above the corn."

Kevin walking a plank was an interesting trick, but I couldn't get over what Sue told us next. The owner had taken his tractor and plowed under the original baseball field in 1989, the year after the movie had been completed. He planted corn where the original baseball field had been. Irate movie fans made the trip all the way to Iowa to ask, "Where's the field?" It didn't take the owner long to realize he had made one huge mistake, and he rebuilt the baseball field right away, without even levying a new county sales tax! Isn't that amazing?

The big surprise was the last scene of the movie. Remember the hundreds of vehicles driving down the road with their headlights turned on? I really hate to disillusion you, but 1,500 motor vehicles were sitting on the road with their engines turned off. They weren't moving. The vehicles gave the appearance they were moving because the drivers kept switching their headlights from dim to bright...dim to bright. A helicopter captured that terrific scene.

We ended up buying enough souvenirs from Sue to jump-start the local economy. Some White Sox baseball players were messing around in the *Field of Dreams* baseball field so we walked over to see what was

TV, Corn, and Chocolate Mints

going on. A player crawled out of the cornfield on his belly and apologized. "It's May and the corn is short," he said as he brushed off his uniform. The team invited us to take a few practice swings at the plate and then posed with us for some great camera shots. I couldn't wait to tell my friends and get the pictures developed. But a funny thing happened to the pictures at the photo lab. The White Sox players never showed up in our photographs. The lab technician told us it happened all the time. Perhaps it was better that way. We still had our dreams.

It was after 1 p.m. by the time we started home. Sue suggested we take the back roads to Davenport. "The picturesque towns and the checkerboard roads crisscrossing Iowa's agricultural countryside are so pretty," she emphasized.

Sue was right. We drove along traffic-free roads almost in a dreamlike state. The farms spread out before us on gently rolling hills, and seemed to meander for miles. No fences cluttered the land, except where livestock was concerned, and not one piece of trash littered the ground.

Iowa is home to an astonishing number of farms—over 97,000. And here is something to think about: Just one Iowa farm family can grow enough food to feed 279 people. Imagine setting a table for that many folks. They owe this blessed abundance to their fertile soils and arable lands, once part of the great grasslands that covered much of the state. And Iowa farmers love to grow soybeans, corn, and raise hogs—they rank first in the country.

If the farms were hypnotizing, the small towns were tantalizing with manicured lawns and inviting front porches with rocking chairs that practically begged you to come and sit a spell. We discovered one more treasure that Sue hadn't mentioned: beautiful churches with tall spires reaching up to the skies and unique stained glass windows of different shapes and designs. We couldn't resist jumping out of our truck and taking pictures, often three to four pictures of the same church, from different architectural angles. In our joyous moment, we nicknamed Iowa "The Land of Heavenly Churches."

We had been so caught up experiencing our country's rich, rural heritage, it was somewhat of a shock to reach the outskirts of Davenport and "civilization" again. We were tired from our day's journey; We needed to pay bills from the mail package we had received yesterday, eat anything, pack, and go to a visitors' center. I had procrastinated, shirked my responsibilities, and fallen down on my job; whatever you want to call it, I didn't know where we were going tomorrow. Our reservations

Smiling Places

were up, and there were no vacancies.

By the time we asked for directions to the nearest visitors' center and started heading in the right direction, I was famished and sharing multiple personalities with Henry VIII and Hannibal Lector. We stopped at a newly built visitors' center sitting high on a bluff, overlooking the Mississippi River. I went in.

"Welcome To Iowa! Can I help you with something?" a robust woman with red cheeks asked. She was standing behind a large, circular counter eating chocolate mints and wearing a name badge with Jenny scribbled on it.

"Well, Jenny, yes, you can," I answered eyeing those mints. "Can you tell me what the number one tourist attraction is in Iowa?" I asked.

"Certainly I can," she laughed. She had the most beautiful white teeth I had ever seen.

"Just step right over here to this section of the counter."

I walked over and could see those mints lying by some brochures. My saliva glands were working overtime. There was an Iowa map laying flat on the countertop under a sheet of plastic that she pointed to and said, "Now look right here, just west of Iowa City off I-80. See all those cluster of towns with Amana in their name? That's where you should go. Over one million people visit there each year."

"One million people. Now that's a lot of visitors! It's not too far from here, is it? I asked.

"No, it certainly isn't. I'd say it's only about 80 miles or so."

"Is that where they make the Amana appliances?"

"The factory is right down the road from the villages," she replied. "The villages were settled in the 1850's by a group of German settlers seeking religious freedom," she said.

"Are any of the villages still around?" I asked.

"Oh yes. There are over 475 historic structures and sites here."

"Do you have any literature on Amana?"

"Right behind you Sweetie, on that rack right there."

I turned toward the rack and picked up a brochure that said, "Come for the food. Come for the shopping. Stay for the experience." On the front of the brochure was a sketched picture of an historic building, crafts, and a smiling girl holding a tray of fresh bread, wine, and meats. I almost drooled on the brochure.

"Jenny, is this Heaven or what?" I commented.

"No, Sweetie," Jenny smiled, "it's Iowa."

14 - Extreme Eating

In the early 1840's, the first covered wagon trains headed west through millions of buffalo chips to settle California and Oregon. At the same time, European immigrants boarded boats and sailed for America, eager to start a new life in the land of the free—and even more eager to get off those heaving, pitching seafaring vessels with stomachs intact.

The Community of True Inspiration, who later settled the Amana Colonies in Iowa, felt they, too, should come to America. Years of economic hardships and religious persecution by government officials in the German Provinces had taken its toll on the members. In 1842, a small committee of Believers boarded a ship and made the arduous journey across the Atlantic Ocean and landed in New York City. Still delirious with bouts of seasickness, they bought 5,000 acres of land near Buffalo, New York so other members from Germany could eventually join them to fight the blizzards. The founders called their new village Ebenezer and established a communal way of life.

"Give the Community all of your stuff, including your snow shovels, and we will give you a lifetime of food, shelter, jobs, and tall boots," the elders told their followers. "Of course, we will all share the same religious beliefs and wear similar clothing," they added. Thus the village of Ebenezer prospered and grew to 1,000 hardy souls who braved thirteen snowy winters.

Thirteen years and 133 days after the founding of Ebenezer, a woman cooking supper in one of the many communal kitchens in their village threw up her hands and exclaimed, "Ich nine da ya ya! How can I be expected to feed our people when there are communal pots and pans all over the place, and I don't have enough counter space to make my noodles?"

On the same day, a man driving a team of oxen hitched to a plow, tilling a field of wheat in Ebenezer stopped his team, pushed back his wide brimmed black hat, and wiped the sweat from his brow. He said, "Oy yoi yoi ya ya! How can I be expected to harvest enough wheat for

Smiling Places

bread to feed our people when many of our acres are covered with storage barns of communal property?"

Thus, in 1855, a small group of Believers left Ebenezer and headed west in search of more land. They eventually traveled all the way to the Iowa River where their leader told them, "This is far enough. My boots and clothing are still wet from crossing the Mississippi River a few days ago. I am not crossing another river today."

So, they settled in this gently rolling, fertile region of eastern Iowa, and called their new village Amana, which means to believe faithfully. Then they built another village close-by and called it West Amana, which means to believe faithfully from the west. And then they built another village close-by and called it South Amana, which means to believe faithfully from the south—until 26,000 acres of land had been purchased and a total of seven villages had been established, so everyone believed faithfully from all directions.

Now, much to the chagrin of the real estate agents, the communal villages were built with numerous residences that each housed four to six families but didn't contain any kitchens. Several separate kitchen facilities were erected in each village so forty people could eat together at one sitting. The real estate agents scolded the Amana Elders and said, "You must think resale, resale, and resale! We cannot sell without a kitchen!"

But the real estate agents didn't need to worry back then because it wasn't until 1932 that the followers voted to end the communal way of life, divided up their assets, and formed a corporation known as the Amana Society. Many followers stayed in the villages and called plumbers to install new kitchens. Some structures were sold to outsiders who came to the area and stayed a lifetime. A new business was founded and became part of the restructured Amana Society—Amana Refrigeration—whose sales soared supplying all those new kitchens with appliances.

Then, one day in 1932 ½, a weary traveler ran out of gas and asked a kindly resident for some food. He feasted on bowls filled with home-grown vegetables, loaves of freshly baked breads, and meats so tender they melted in his mouth. And while he ate, he noticed a beautiful hand-crafted clock hanging on the wall.

"Is that clock for sale?" he asked his hosts.

"No, but I can make you one just like it," the owner answered.

The owner kept his promise and built a clock more beautiful than his own to sell to the weary traveler. In turn, the weary traveler told everyone he knew about this "undiscovered" community where the simple life

Extreme Eating

of the Old World was still preserved. Tourists began flocking to the Amana Villages to taste their foods and wines, experience its historical values, and cherish the quality handmade crafts. Restaurants and shops sprang up across the villages to cater to the tourist trade, and the Amana Society Corporation grew into a highly sophisticated business.

So, how did I feel about visiting Amana for the first time? Well, very excited I'd say, but I'm almost embarrassed to tell you why. You see, ever since my first spoonful of strained peas, I had been hooked on eating. No "here comes the choo-choo train" for me! I was the train depot, where all the food cargo was deposited. My mouth had always been open for food—until we hit the road, that is. Then I began to eat better: smaller portions, and less fat. But let's face it, my stomach had been growling like an old bear since we had left Dayton, and I was more than ready for a really big meal, or two, or three.

When my husband noticed how hard I was trying to lose weight, he realized I had resisted many goodies on the road. Yet, all he could talk about from the moment we pulled out of Davenport to the instant we pulled into the Amana campground was how hungry *he* was. Can you believe that? Didn't the man have any sense?

"What did you say?" I asked.

"I'm hungry," he replied.

"You're hungry? What about me? I have munched enough celery sticks to give myself lockjaw. I have worn strong magnifier glasses so my food portions look larger. I have watched you eat your way through Indiana, Illinois, and part of Iowa, and did I say anything? Did I ask you for one little bite of that huge gooey donut you ate the other morning?"

"No, you ate your own donut," Doug said.

"That was my breakfast *and* mid-morning snack," I replied.

So, armed with maps, and a list of 101 Things to Do In the Amana Colonies (I figured ninety-three of them were food related), we descended upon this community of 1,700 residents on a warm, sunny day.

"Hurry up and unhitch the trailer," I said to Doug while drooling on the maps. "I can't wait to try some ice cream, then hit the meat and cheese store, find some fudge, and try a family style restaurant tonight."

"I thought you were dieting," Doug said.

"Dieting in this gastronomical paradise? Are you nuts?"

"Oh, c'mon," he laughed. "You can't eat all of that food in one day."

"Wanna bet a dollar?" I asked.

By the end of the day, I was one dollar richer and four pounds heav-

Smiling Places

ier. "Four pounds," I gasped as I stood on our scale. "Well, this just can't be. The trailer must not be level; that's why this scale is off."

So, I did what all desperate dieters do in times of weight gain—I put most of my weight on my left foot—watched the dial instantly make me two pounds lighter. Unfortunately, I was totally out of control. I had only eaten my way across the village of Amana. I still had six villages to go.

The next morning, I raced to the village of Middle Amana to buy streusels and breads from a bakery that used an original 1860's stone hearth oven to bake their goodies. The ten x ten oven could hold up to one hundred and forty loaves of bread. When the day's baking was sold, the bakery closed for the day. I got there early and was first in line. The luscious smells permeated the air as I stepped up to the counter.

"I will start out with 12 streusels," I said to the baker.

"Two streusels," the baker replied.

"No, twelve," I said again.

"A dozen?" she asked as her face crinkled up like a Chinese pug.

I nodded, and as I did, I got the distinct feeling that she knew the streusels were all for me—well almost, since Doug would eat a few. She removed the streusel tray from behind the glass counter and put twelve warm streusels with overflowing fruit fillings in several small bags.

"Is there anything else?" she asked. She smiled as I asked for three loaves of bread.

"Family reunion," I muttered as she grabbed for more bags.

"Lots of family reunions come through this bakery," she said with a twinkle in her eye.

Ten minutes later, and almost as many bags, I exited the bakery only to confront a disenfranchised crowd of people, waiting not-too-patiently in line, and contemplating bake rage. I saw them eyeing my baked goods and decided to leave in a hurry. Once inside the safety of my truck, however, I couldn't resist my tasty treats. While I drove the truck back to the campground with one hand, the other hand was clutching a bent streusel, dripping with fruit filling that dropped on the steering wheel and slid down my wrist and arm. But believe me when I tell you—that streusel was one of the best streusels I had ever eaten.

The rest of my day was filled with epicurean delights. After downing three more streusels and two huge slices of bread, I descended upon the meat and cheese shops in different villages to polish off their free sample platters of meats and cheeses. I also visited every fudge shop in the villages, not only to devour all their free samples, but also to deter-

Extreme Eating

mine who made the best fudge. The salads, soups, and sandwiches were delectable, and before I knew it, it was time for dinner.

"Doug, let's go," I said. "It is almost five p.m., and I don't want to be late for opening."

"Where are we going?" he asked.

"To that family style restaurant our campground host recommended," I said.

"Family style? You aren't going to pig out again, are you?" he asked me suspiciously.

"Now why would you say that?" I laughed as I took his hand and led him to our truck.

Little did he know the restaurant closed at nine p.m., and I planned on being the last person out. Doug and I were seated at a corner table in the back of the room.

"Welcome to our wonderful restaurant," our waitress smiled, while sizing us up.

But behind that smile, I knew she was thinking, "I bet these two will get their money's worth tonight."

"I'll take that bet", I thought and smiled back.

After the main course is brought to your table at a family style restaurant, the first rule of restaurant management is for the food servers to stare at you while you are eating, so you won't eat as much. After twelve serving bowls of vegetables, slaw, fruits, mashed potatoes, and gravy, not only was our waitress staring at me, but the whole restaurant was also looking my way. My husband kept asking me if I was done yet. I just kept shoveling it all into my open mouth.

At 8:10 p.m. Doug grabbed my fork. He announced we were leaving.

"Can I at least ask for a rain check?" I cried as he led me out.

"Don't you dare," he growled.

And our waitress was thinking, "Honey, where did you learn to eat like that?"

The next morning my eating binge came to an end when Doug stepped on my day old bags of streusels and breads piled on the floor inside our trailer. The fillings from the streusels squished out between his toes and stained our carpet.

"I think this has gone far enough," he said.

"What do you mean?" I asked innocently, eating a chunk of cheese.

As he stuck his gooey covered foot in the kitchen sink balancing on one leg, he asked, "How many streusels and loaves of bread are in this

Smiling Places

trailer?"

"There were 8 streusels and 2 ½ loaves of bread left until you stepped on them," I said.

"That is exactly my point," he said. "You have filled this trailer with so much food; there is no place to move. I even made a butt print in your cheese last night when I sat on our kitchen bench."

I quickly spit out the cheese I was chewing on.

"So, what do you want me to do, stop eating?"

"Now that's an idea," he retorted.

I knew he was right. My walk had turned into a waddle, and my stomach held a sixty-day reserve of food.

"I would be far from skin and bones on the last night of *Survivor*," I thought.

"OK, you win," I said. "So what do you want to do today?"

"Just like that? I win?" he asked like a doubting Tomsu.

"Yep, I'm all done. No more binges. I really need to lose weight."

"Are you sure?"

"Yes, I'm positive."

"Well then, would you like to go look at some craft and furniture stores?" Doug asked.

My husband sure knew how to pull my chain. Just when I thought he was the most wonderful man in the world by asking me out on a shopping date, he added a few stipulations to his generous offer.

"Now, you know we don't have any room in the trailer, so you really must be careful when you shop. And we can't store any gifts you might be buying for Christmas, either. It's only spring."

The man had read my mind. How did he know sweaters from the Amana woolen mill would make perfect Christmas gifts?

For several hours, we shopped till he dropped. I dragged him through basket shops, candle shops, glass shops, ironwork shops, clock shops, furniture shops, gift shops, art galleries, and of course, the woolen mill. I did end up buying some Christmas gifts—with the Captain's approval, of course—that we stored under our bed.

Then it was Doug's turn. Remember when I told you I was married to the King of Facts? My little tour guide had done all his homework and decided to take me on a walking tour of the villages. I was surprised at how skinny the sidewalks were.

"The sidewalks were built narrow so there would be more space for gardens," Doug explained. "See the trellises on the sides of the build-

Extreme Eating

ings? They support grape vines. Lots of wine is made here."

We stood outside the gate of a graveyard that was still in use. Fir trees planted on the perimeter of the graveyard represented everlasting life. The gravestones were all the same dimensions and faced east. The trees and the gravestones were eerily erected in perfect straight lines. Doug informed me that residents were buried in the order that they died. There were no family plots.

"I was told only one husband and wife are buried next to each other because they died so soon after one another," the King of Facts said.

At another village, Doug pointed out that the settlers quarried their own sandstone and made their own bricks for their dwellings.

"They also cut their own timber, but no, they didn't make vinyl siding," he said sarcastically when we passed a wooden frame house that had been covered with siding.

"I bet the Historical Society is none too pleased," I said.

I thoroughly enjoyed his tour at first. I found the historical aspects of the villages fascinating, but the more I walked, the hungrier I became. The more fudge shops we passed by, the more I wanted to eat. At the agricultural museum, Doug saw corn-planting equipment, and I saw hot buttered corn on the cob. At the Community Church Museum, Doug learned about the religious history of the Colonies, and I dreamt of church socials with homemade pies and cakes.

Finally, we reached the communal kitchen museum.

"Who would prepare all the food?" a lady from Illinois asked our group guide.

"As soon as the young ladies left 8th grade, they would be assigned to work in a kitchen. There was no further education for the women back then. That all changed in 1935 when they were allowed to attend high school."

"That's a good thing," the lady from Illinois said.

"Amen to that," someone else retorted.

Our historian continued, "Many of the older ladies would be assigned to work in the communal gardens where food was harvested for the community. This was no small tasking as each community's garden was quite large and generally ranged from 3-5 acres."

"Now that's a lot of hoeing," someone quipped.

"The last communal meal was served in 1932," our historian concluded.

All this talk of food had taken its toll on me. I was surrounded by

Smiling Places

cookware, a huge table with many place settings, menus describing the foods they used to serve, but no food was anywhere to be found. As soon as we left the Communal Kitchen Museum, I dragged Doug back to the same restaurant where we had eaten the night before. I promised him I would behave, and this time I meant it.

But when we arrived, a tour bus was parked behind the restaurant. We walked around to the front of the establishment and noticed a large line waiting on the front porch.

"I bet you ten bucks I can down five bowls of mashed potatoes," one Rugby player said to his teammate.

Well, that's all we needed to hear. We could just see us sitting next to a table brimming with hungry Rugby players in a family style restaurant. It would be like sharing your food with a pack of Alpha Males. So, we decided to go back to our trailer and eat the foods I had stockpiled there over the last few days. A smile crossed my face when I glanced back and saw our waitress from last night seating the Rugby team.

"And you thought I was a porker," I muttered. "Just wait until you serve these guys!"

When we arrived home, I opened the large picture window spanning our kitchen table and a nice breeze blew in. I lit two small candles and set out paper plate platters of meats, cheeses, fruits, and bread I had bought from Amana merchants. Doug popped open a bottle of Amana quality wine and poured us each a bit in two small plastic cups. (Sorry I can't be more romantic, but we don't travel with glass or plates.)

We both sat down at our table and gazed outside at the beautiful countryside.

"Life doesn't get any better than this, does it?" I said as I reached for my cup of wine.

"Wait a minute," Doug said as he took his cup of wine. "I have a toast."

He held up his glass and I held up mine:

>"Here's to Amana,
>A place with great food,
>Whose streusels stained my toes,
>And filled my belly, too!"

We laughed and drank our wine. What a wonderful meal we enjoyed that evening.

15 - A Visit from Murphy

The first time we noticed our trailer wasn't riding smoothly, we were pulling it along a wind-swept portion of I-80 between Amana and the western edge of Iowa. It was mid-morning and we were headed towards Desoto National Wildlife Refuge. I was busy sampling some leftover cheese and crackers. That's when we both heard the noise.

"KEROP, KEROP, GREE, GROP! GLUMP! GLUMP! GLUMP!"

Usually, we could associate a sound like that with my stomach growling, but this particular noise was coming from behind the truck. So we pulled over to the side of the highway, and just as we stopped, my cheese and crackers slid off the console into our cat's litter pan. Now normally, I wouldn't think twice about it, but this was *Amana* cheese and crackers. What a shame!

"Mel, can you come back here and look at this?" Doug asked.

"I'm mourning the loss of our cheese and crackers."

"Forget the cheese and crackers, we sheared a bolt holding our sway bar."

I walked to the back of the truck and looked at the towing hitch.

"We sure did. Do you have a spare bolt?"

"No, I didn't think to carry one with us."

"Well, we better call roadside assistance then," I suggested.

"I don't think we need them."

"That's what you told me when we had that flat tire in Ludington,"

"Look, don't worry. The trailer is drivable. There are five more bolts holding the sway bar in place."

"What, me worry about pulling a 5,200 pound trailer down a bumpy, pot-holed highway and only being stabilized by five bolts instead of six?"

"That's exactly my point."

"What's your point?"

Smiling Places

"The safety factors."

"What do you mean by safety factors?"

"Well, picture this. Let's assume the Leaning Tower of Pisa had six bolts—one bolt sheared, and then there were five. But it's still standing, isn't it?"

"But the Leaning Tower of Pisa doesn't have rubber tires that roll down highways at speeds of 55 mph or more."

"OK, so what is it that you want to do?" he asked.

"Well, I guess since you don't want to call roadside service, we can drive it, but only if the trailer doesn't lean precariously to one side, like that Tower thing you talked about."

"It won't."

"And please, let's drive at the minimum speed limits."

We limped along the highway looking for a Bolts R Us. Doug was hungry so I gave him some cheese and crackers to munch on. No, not those crackers and cheese. How could you think such a thing? Forty-five miles later, we found our spare part. Doug replaced the bolt and bought three others, just in case. It was that "just in case" thing that got to me. First the bolt, then the cheese. My intuition told me our fun was just beginning.

We arrived at the wildlife refuge on the Iowa-Nebraska state borders, and had the entire adjacent campground to ourselves, which was a nice surprise. The simple things in life now meant so much to us—a peaceful place to spend the night, a clean shower, and good water--things I took for granted while living in a house, and things that my intuition loved to play havoc with. The campsites in the park were spacious and accurately level. Each was surrounded by several shade trees and a picnic bench—a great convenience to us—since we didn't travel with a folding table and chairs.

When we had settled into our spot, a park ranger strolled over to talk to us.

"So, how are you folks doing today?" he asked.

"Well, pretty good, except we sheared a bolt on the way over here today," Doug answered.

"Did you get it taken care of?" the ranger asked.

"We sure did."

"I see you're from Ohio and have a Wright-Patterson sticker on your truck. I was stationed there many years ago for a couple of years when I was in the military. Nice base."

A Visit from Murphy

"Yeah, I worked there in Civil Engineering for 25 years. I just retired, and we are living in this trailer and traveling around the country."

"Now that's the way to do it. For years, I tried to get my wife to travel like you all are doing, but she just wouldn't leave the family," the park ranger sighed.

He stared wistfully at our trailer, and for an instant he was rolling down the open roads with his wife at his side.

"The thing I wanted to tell you about is they are excavating over that hill, about a mile from here," the park ranger said. "Oh, about two to three times a day, they do a little blasting with dynamite. Didn't want you folks to be scared. Just listen for the warning bell, and you should be OK."

"It's OK to camp here, isn't it?" I asked, somewhat unnerved.

"Sure it is. The ground will shake a little bit, that's all," he responded.

I prepared a light lunch and set it out on the picnic bench. As we ate, our audience of three rabbits ran wide circles around our campsite. I heard a bell ringing in the distance, and then silence. We stopped eating, and I put my hands over my ears expecting a loud "KABOOM!" What we actually heard was a soft, muffled "pop." The ground shook a bit and then stopped.

"Is that the best they can do?" Doug said, and we both laughed. And then his expression changed from a happy face to a surprised face, like one of those swimmers in *Jaws* right before they went under.

"Did you hear that?" Doug asked suddenly as a loud SNAP echoed across the empty campground.

"Y-yes, what is it?" I asked.

I don't remember much of what happened after that. Doug recalled that after I heard the "CRACKLES" of what sounded like several exploding strings of firecrackers, I jumped up off the picnic bench and began doing an Irish jig while screaming about some fringe, radical group shooting at us from behind the trailer. Doug explained his reaction was much more calculated. He had picked up our plastic salad spinner bowl and held it menacingly in one hand, ready to protect us against the mob of chimpanzees he thought had escaped from the local zoo.

"Well," he said, "a large tree shading our campsite was violently shaking its treetop. What would you have thought was up there?"

And then, according to Doug, the shaking tree sneezed and expelled a massive chunk of wood, limbs, and leaves that fell to the ground, not

Smiling Places

ten feet from our trailer. He said my bloodcurdling scream of "Sushi" started a rockslide over by the excavation site.

I must tell you; we were lucky. The fallen tree chunk didn't touch our trailer or make kitty pancakes out of Sushi, but Murphy didn't want to hurt anyone. He was just plain devious, and he had come to visit us once again. Now don't look so puzzled. I am sure you all have met Murphy at one time or another. He's the guy whose name got stuck on that old *law* that has been around since Adam and Eve: "If anything can go wrong, it will." Remember when Adam took a bite of the forbidden fruit?

Why Murphy liked to hang out with us, I have no idea. A few years back, Murphy sent an eighty-foot red oak tree crashing through the roof of our house, right into our laundry room. I was standing in the doorway, and a leaf tickled my nose as the tree landed. They said the black streak on the stump indicated lightning was the culprit, but I knew something was up. Two weeks later our well pump was fried. They said lightning was the cause of that, too. I don't think so.

But what really perplexed me was why Murphy coaxed those bees into my mom's new hair-do when she came to visit us. OK, I'll admit her hair-do was a little high—maybe three feet straight up from the top of her forehead. It stayed like that because she sprayed her "do" with a gallon of some sweet-smelling sticky stuff. But don't you find it strange that the poor woman only had to go ten feet from our driveway into our house, and the bees attacked her anyway? How did those bees know she was there? Why were they congregating on the windshield before she opened the car door? And how did they know she was sporting a new "do" called a beehive?

Unfortunately, those bees couldn't hold a candle to the biting deerflies that chased me up and down our 200-foot driveway when I ran for the mail. Or those raccoons that broke into our great room after tearing a hole in our sliding screen door. That old Murphy sure was a hoot!

So, you can see why I concluded Murphy had found us at this beautiful campground in an isolated part of Iowa, and I was betting he planned to stay awhile. We had parked our trailer in a site near the Missouri River, perhaps in the same spot where Lewis and Clark had camped when they came through here in 1804. Lewis and Clark navigated a huge part of the Missouri River during their famous expedition. Surprisingly, the Missouri, not the Mississippi, is the longest river in the United States and flows some 2,540 miles from Montana to St. Louis where it

A Visit from Murphy

empties into the Mississippi River. Some people call the Mississippi "The Big Muddy," others use that name for the Missouri. As far as I am concerned, they were both big and muddy—but fascinating.

Of course, the 7,500-acre refuge wasn't here when Lewis and Clark came through, and even the course of the Missouri River was straightened out around 1960 when the refuge was created. Just a few years back, the Missouri River had flooded this campground. The waters had come right up over some stop signs in the park. The rangers took a motorboat in and out of the park for 2-3 weeks, until the floodwaters subsided. But there was little chance of it flooding today. The Missouri was at its lowest level people around here had seen in years.

Perhaps the low river level had something to do with our next Murphy. The campground did not have water hook-ups but had free drinking water at the camp office. So we piled in our truck with some empty plastic jugs, eager to receive anything that was "free." I guess a bumbling idiot from Ohio is born every thirty minutes because as soon as I turned on that spigot to fill the plastic jug, a rotten egg smell from a high concentration of sulfur in the water was everywhere. It made Florida swamp gas seem like a walk in a botanical garden. Needless to say, we spent the afternoon looking for the nearest place that sold bottled water.

The next morning the smell of that water followed us right into the campground showers. No matter how much soap I used, the smell would not leave my body. I swear when I reached our campsite, two rabbits who happened to be downwind of me, stopped dead in their tracks, and twitched their noses frantically in the air. All at once they ran for their lives. My theory is they caught a whiff of my rotten-egg odor. But, no matter, because Doug smelled the same way I did, and pretty soon our olfactory senses became stupefied to the whole thing—just like our cat Sushi. I caught her sleeping peacefully in a corner of the trailer with her paw over her nose.

I did discover one very important use for our body odor in the refuge. If we stood upwind of tall grasses and brush, animals would voluntarily flush themselves out from their protective cover, sniff the air, and then run away. Deer, coyotes, rabbits, and other small mammals were popping up all over the place. Even the carp were jumping out of the waters. We didn't meet up with many human beings, though, which was probably a good thing. We almost had the entire refuge to ourselves. The humans we did make contact with were either real polite because they didn't stick their noses up in the air and run, or we all smelled alike

Smiling Places

because they took showers, too, you know.

The only creatures that seemed totally oblivious to our strong odor presence were the birds. Over 240 species of birds had been spotted in this refuge over the years. I wish we could have been here in the fall with our umbrellas to watch over 500,000 snow geese migrate over our heads. And while we didn't see any snow geese, the Canadian geese were plentiful, and all their little goslings were fun to watch. We did manage to identify seventy-two different species of birds, according to the Tomsu Field Guide to Birds. Our entries were described as Mel's relatives (six turkeys that crossed the road), the bird with the yellow throat and black eyeliner, or the small one with the purple and white poop I know this because a gift of poop was left on my sleeve one morning as I watched thirty-two white pelicans with wingspans of seven to nine feet flying in a V-formation over the impressive 750-acre Desoto Lake.

When Lewis and Clark explored the Desoto area, excerpts from their diaries show, they saw thousands of white pelicans in the area and collected them to (you won't believe this)…carry water in.

> "August 08, 1804", John Ordway (a member of the Lewis and Clark team) wrote, "We saw the sand bars covered white with pelicans this afternoon Capt Lewis Shot one which had a bag under his neck and bill which held 5 Gallons of Water."

I'm sure you are probably thinking, "Icky! I would no sooner drink water out of a pelican's fishy mouth than I would kiss a toad with warts. And by the way, what are pelicans doing in Iowa? I thought they hung out on the coasts around oceans."

Well, you are partially correct. Brown pelicans like the coastal waters. White pelicans mainly hang out on the inland lakes of the west in summer.

And since summer was right around the corner, we needed to find a place to spend Memorial Day weekend. We had heard that most parks were crowded during Memorial Day. We needed to arrive at our destination a few days early and claim a campground space. Murphy had an exciting action-packed holiday weekend planned for us at Lake McConaughy State Park located near Ogallala, Nebraska in the west central part of the state—but first we took a detour.

16 - Murphy Takes a Hiatus

One of the joys we realized from traveling about in our beautiful country was every new bend in the road brought fresh experiences to our lives in ways we never thought possible. Almost daily, we would stumble upon these magical "somewheres" that we had only glimpsed for a brief moment while reading a passage or sitting in a classroom. But to actually be at this "somewhere" was a different story. To stand where a President played as a child or walk among waves of colorful grasslands demanded we dare not leave this wonderment without first reliving its history or absorbing its natural beauty. Such was the case with Nebraska—a state rich in history and seemingly untouched.

When Doug announced we had crossed into Nebraska, I was excited and felt adventuresome. The Nebraska I wanted to know was chocked full of pioneer history—from the first prairie schooners rushing across the prairie grasses toward Utah, Oregon, and California to the later settlers or "sod busters" who lived on the Great Plains. We would take Interstate 80 to Grand Island, Nebraska and stop to see The Stuhr Museum of the Prairie Pioneer. Further west on I-80 we would visit North Platte and then follow US 26 to Lake McConaughy, where Murphy was deviously plotting our arrival. Thank goodness that little "Beetle Juicer" was out of our hair.

It was 150 miles to Grand Island. We had not particularly planned to stop there. In fact, we may have pulled all the way to Lake McConaughy if it had not been for our camping neighbors in Amana. It just so happened that Nebraska was their favorite state to vacation in.

"The pioneer landmarks will astound you," they told us. "Visit the museum and follow the Overland Trails. You can still see wagon ruts that are over 150 years old!"

After speaking with them, I was ready to jump on a covered wagon, grab the reigns, and yell, "Wagons, Ho!"

We chatted with everyone we met while traveling. We learned early

Smiling Places

on that a simple "Hi There" could lead to a wealth of information—and in some cases prevent life and death situations. A story we heard involved a retired husband and his wife who were pulling their fifth wheel in Idaho. These "greenhorns" were not familiar with the area and didn't ask anyone about the road conditions. The husband mapped out a scenic route in a mountainous region of the state. Up they went, pulling their trailer, higher and higher, until they were barely hugging a precipitous drop, hundreds of feet below. They did get off the mountain safely, doing five mph on some stretches. The man's wife vowed never to ride in their truck while pulling that trailer again. She did not, and they sold the fifth wheel. In our case, we would have missed some significant historic sites. Not a life and death situation, but disturbing just the same.

Now, I do not want to confuse you because many westward trails crisscrossed our nation during the 1800's and were used by Indians, explorers, trappers, traders, settlers, and the Pony Express. But meandering in an east-west fashion through central Nebraska were two famous overland trails: the Oregon (California) Trail and the Mormon Trail. Both of these trails followed the Platte River and became collectively known as The Great Platte River Road. For the most part, the Mormons used the north side of the river, and the pioneers traveled on the south. Today, Interstate 80 and US 26 parallel much of the Oregon and Mormon Trails. When we hopped on I-80 around Omaha, it took us two to three hours to drive to Grand Island. The same trip would have taken the pioneers seven to eight days and a healthy dose of determination.

But determination was only part of the story. The eastern United States was in a tizzy in the middle decades of the 1800's. President Bullheaded Jackson didn't listen to his financial advisor, Alan Greenspan Sr. Sr. Sr. Sr., and in 1837 our country ended up in a major financial crisis with many banks shutting their doors but leaving their ATM's operating so people could buy wagons and head west in search of free land.

The Center for Disease Control (CDC) had no employees at this time, so all these germs named Dysentery, Cholera, Yellow Fever, Scarlet Fever, and Tuberculosis were running around and killing people. Other people were infected by greed and hate and practiced slavery and religious persecution. The one bright spot came in 1848 when a man mistakenly identified as Fools discovered gold in California.

Murphy Takes a Hiatus

I certainly can't blame all those people for packing their bags and escaping that tizzy of events; 350,000 of them hit the Oregon Trail and traveled through Nebraska seeking a better life in the far west. But some of the more crazy ones actually tried to settle in Nebraska. Now, don't get me wrong, I have nothing against Nebraska, but you couldn't have paid me a million bucks back then to live on the vast plains in houses built of sod with "blowholes" in their roofs and walls…and floors made of dirt. I couldn't have tolerated the "Honey, can you give me the hoe so I can make up our bed?" or "Please get me the shovel. I must scoop the three foot snowdrift off our table!" For the more hardy readers out there saying, "So what?" How about those unrelenting howling winds that sounded like fifty hoot owls on hooch? How about those super-sized grasshoppers that ate your crops and tried to eat your cows?

When you were one step away from a straight jacket—and we all would have been eventually—you would pack up and leave a note on your door like this man actually did:

> "250 miles to the nearest post office
> 100 miles to wood
> 20 miles to water
> 6 inches to hell.
> Gone to live with wife's folks."

Not only did one man go back "home," others followed. And the one vital piece of information that I believe is missing from our history books is: How many pioneers started out, traveled some, turned around, and high-tailed it back to the east? I came up with this compelling question because that is exactly what I'd have done. I'm not proud of this, believe me, but there is only so much a product of the baby-boomer generation can take. According to my precise calculations, I figure I would have lasted exactly ten hours on one of those trails in the 1800's. The following is a so-called account of my so-called ordeal:

Hour One
Me: "Man, my bare feet are killing me from all this walking alongside our overloaded covered wagon. I think I'll throw our "Lazy Boy Sleeper Couch" on the side of the trail and make more room in the wagon.

Smiling Places

Hour Two
    Me: "I'm hungry. Hey, where are all the trees in this prairie? I need firewood to cook with! What do you mean there are no trees? You use *what* for fuel? Did you say dried buffalo chips? You mean those things that look like giant brown cinnamon rolls? Eeewww!!! Gross me out!!! I'm not picking those things up!"

Hour Three
    Me: "Where's all that thunder coming from? The skies are blue. Buffalo, you say. Millions of them? Each weighing 2,500 pounds and headed right for our dinky little wooden wagons…

Hour Four
    Rumble…rumble…rumble…rumble.
    Rumble…rumble…rumble…rumble

Hour Five
    Rumble…rumble…rumble…rumble.
    Rumble…rumble…rumble…rumble

Hour Six
    Me: "Those wooly-headed creatures sure kicked up a lot of dust. I need a bath. Why can't I have a bath? No clean water? I have to wait how long? *A month?* Are you kidding me?"

Hour Seven
    Me: "Would you look at those Indians and that make-up they are wearing! What do you mean, don't worry, they come in peace? Then why are they sporting those human hair scalps on their belts and waving those tomahawks in the air? And why is that arrow sticking out of your ear?"

Murphy Takes a Hiatus

Hour Eight
Me: "Don't you dare trade me for that smelly old buffalo hide!"

Hour Nine
Me: "Are we there yet? You mean to tell me we've only gone eight miles? Just how long is this going to take? Five to six months! 2,000 straggling miles! Are there any Super Wal-Mart's on the way?"

Hour Ten
Me: "Pee You! The flatulence from those oxen is killing me. What's in that prairie grass anyway? Can we ride our oxen back to Ohio and ditch the wagon?"

My so-called account describes just some of the hardships faced by the pioneers. Mother Nature delighted in crafting more peril and was known as a "female dog"—lightning bolts and prairie fires that turned pioneers into crispy critters—rattlesnakes and Dracula-inspired mosquitoes—hail, tornadoes, flooding, and dust storms—and merciless heat that drove livestock to foam at the mouth and run in circles. As if that wasn't badly enough, guns would fire by accident and take out a few hapless pioneers (what safety latch?), and people would slip under rolling wagon wheels or be washed away in raging river currents.

Timing of the pioneer's journey was another critical issue. If they left too early in the year, the prairie grasses would not have grown enough to feed their livestock, which would then starve. And if they arrived too late towards the end of the trail, then some unlucky person could end up as the main course in a pot of soup. I say this because in 1846, the Donner Party became trapped in the snows of the Sierra Nevada Mountains bordering California and spent a harrowing winter up there trying to survive. Need I remind you of what their "rigor mortis" soup consisted of?

But the worst fate that befell anyone traveling those trails was cholera. It killed more pioneers than any other single cause. And it was deadly. In a matter of hours you could be gone. Some poor souls were left by the side of the trails with their bedding and died alone. Others watched as their graves were being dug. Nobody knew that contami-

Smiling Places

nated water caused the disease. And sadly, with so many using the Platte River on their journey west, it was not in too good of shape. One pioneer described the Platte as "bad to ford, destitute of fish, too dirty to bathe in, and too thick to drink." I'm sure you can imagine what that river must have been like with everyone, including the livestock and buffalo, using it for everything.

But the day we arrived at Grand Island, no perils awaited us, and Mother Nature was in a good mood. The weather—sunny, a gentle breeze, 79 degrees—was perfect. We had just missed the thousands of migrating Sandhill Cranes. Our campground was surrounded by the rich fertile farmland of eastern Nebraska and seemed tidy and well-kept. Up close, we were delighted to find immaculate bathrooms and a well-maintained laundry room. Our campsite was across from two wall-mounted pay phones with large, comfortable chairs shoved underneath. I would deplete my 180-minute phone card by the end of the day.

The local newspaper headlines for Grand Island weren't that much different than any other U.S. town with 40,000 residents. Firefighters from across Nebraska were attending State Fire School this weekend and learning dive rescue and forced entry techniques; gasoline prices had jumped five cents to $1.59 forcing some residents to "empty their wallets"; the men's Big 12 Track Meet results had Missouri in first place and Nebraska in second; an area Habitat for Humanity chapter, consisting of all female volunteers, was building a home for a local family.

I never expected that newspaper to drive me to tears. The hometown flavor, families helping families, the smiling faces of happy Nebraskans plunged me into a homesick funk. I was two steps away from grabbing our truck keys and heading east. I could be home in a few days. Besides, I didn't have to be out here. Nobody was forcing me to do this. But instead, I literally ran to the payphone, which at that moment served as my security blanket. I needed a quick fix of family, friends, anyone who would listen.

My mom was home. Her friend had an operation and was still in the hospital due to complications. My mom missed me. She wanted me to bring her a quart of milk—we laughed at that one. Her feet were bothering her. Did I like the shoes I was wearing? We said a tearful good-bye and hung up. My niece had been dating her boyfriend for eight months. She was starting a new job next week. Did I like being on the road? She missed me and would tell her sister I had called. My dear friend's mother had a stroke last week. She was doing fine and starting rehab

Murphy Takes a Hiatus

tomorrow. My aunt and uncle wanted to know when we were coming to New Jersey to visit them. My other dear friend was cleaning out a bedroom and getting boxes ready to take to Goodwill. Doug's sister was not at home and neither was another friend. But that was O.K. because my phone card only had four minutes left, and my own "pioneer spirit" now felt renewed.

By the time I woke up the next morning, I followed my nose in the direction of outside our trailer where my husband was fixing a luscious ham steak on the grill. Inside, the cutting board was covered with diced onions, green peppers, and plum tomatoes ready to be sautéed. The eggs were already cracked in a bowl, and the frozen blueberry waffles were inside the toaster oven just waiting for someone to push the toast button down. The table was set, the maple syrup was out, and the orange juice was poured.

When Doug saw me through our kitchen window, he asked if I would get back in bed. Sushi and I curled up in bed and let the chef do his thing. Oh, those smells were so yummy. I think we woke up the whole campground. People were floating past our grill asking Doug if we wanted any company for breakfast. My own gastric juices were all churned up by the time Doug called me to the kitchen table. We thoroughly enjoyed our scrumptious breakfast while fourteen campers pressed their faces against our kitchen picture window and watched us eat. Just kidding. After I washed the dishes, we left for the Stuhr Museum. I couldn't eat another bite of food and was more than ready to walk off breakfast. Surprisingly, by the end of the day, we had walked off breakfast, lunch, and dinner.

I was shocked when we arrived at the museum. It was huge. Joel B. Stuhr had the right idea when he donated land and money to preserve Nebraska history. And this was no ordinary museum. The museum complex, which opened in 1967, was spread out across 200 acres. More than sixty buildings had been rescued from different parts of Nebraska, including Henry Fonda's birthplace. And here they all were—clustered in groups of recreated towns or rural settlements dating from 1850-1910.

This gem was a step back in time as each building had been painstakingly restored to its original condition. We stood inside a Pawnee Indian earth lodge, representing one of the oldest inhabitants of Nebraska. The Pawnee dominated the area until the 1850's and built communities of large circular homes with walls of dirt and a roof of sod supported by large tree trunks. We walked through a veterinary infirmary for sick and

Smiling Places

ailing horses containing a large operating table and medical instruments. It was obvious to us that the recreated Railroad Town had prospered when the transcontinental railroad came through. The train depot and steam locomotives were located on the edge of town.

Costumed interpreters brought the history alive as they scurried about their daily activities. Oftentimes, they might ask you for a helping hand with their chores or invite you to participate in an old-fashioned recreational past time. Beware if you were a single lady. The hotel clerk in town wouldn't put you up, but a man could pay twenty-five cents to sleep upstairs on a bed or floor with perhaps five to six other men in the same room. Dinners were thirty-five cents back then that today would cost eight dollars.

We spoke with one interpreter who was the town's telephone operator. She had a huge switchboard in her living room.

"Some people are still scared of these telephones," Susan said. "They get frightened when they hear someone talking out of the other end of a machine. Oh, well. I try to tell them not to be frightened. You know, I almost didn't have this job," she continued as we looked around her house. "At first they hired a man for my job, but he didn't last long. Do you know why?"

"Because he was irresponsible?" I blurted out. Doug shot a disparaging glance my way.

"Not exactly," Susan whispered, "because his language was so bad. And you know, I don't get to leave the house that much either because I have to be here twenty-four hours a day. If I want to go to the store or go visiting, I have to find a substitute. So, I taught my daughter how to run the switchboard. She sits in when I want to leave. Do you know what? We are both sworn to secrecy about what we hear. Don't ask me anything about the town gossip."

"I thought other people could listen in on phone calls back then," Doug said.

"I don't know about back then, but some people have gotten used to the phones now. If they pick up and someone else is talking, they can listen in. We call them Rubbernecks. And there are some folk who just sit with that phone in their ear all day long. Imagine that!"

"I know someone who would have made a good Rubberneck," Doug said and looked my way.

Many of the costumed interpreters had ancestors who had helped settle Nebraska.

Murphy Takes a Hiatus

"I remember my grandpa stored ice all year to use in an ice box that kept the food cold at his farm. He dug a huge pit, like a root cellar, to put the ice in and would layer it with straw in among the ice blocks. And since the ground stays a constant fifty-five degrees, that would keep it cold enough."

"My grandma had a washing machine just like this one," another lady said while standing next to a washing machine on a back porch. "I used to agitate it by pulling a lever back and forth that would turn a wooden stave and churn the clothes. Then, we would put the clothes through a ringer to dry them."

After our stroll through railroad town and the separate museum buildings, where hundreds of artifacts were displayed, my feet were tired, and the mercury was pushing ninety degrees. Now, I am sure you remember yours truly, my Mr. Museum Man. With breakfast long forgotten, he said he just had to walk to every one of those remaining buildings and on every square inch of the remaining 200 acres, even though a road circled around the museum grounds specifically so visitors could drive to the sites. I objected to his lack of logic, but, of course, followed Mr. Museum Man anyway—to my destiny. And, my destiny was *blisters*.

The man I had promised to love, cherish, and abandon had given me blisters the size of "Appalachian Trail hiking-in-brand-new-boots-for-a-week" blisters. Now, you might wonder why I was so quick to blame him. It was definitely those socks. Ever since we had been married—which, according to my calculations, might not be too much longer—the man has insisted on going outside in socks. He never puts on his shoes if he is just going to hang around the outside of the house or trailer or whatever. So, then, he gets holes in his socks—or our socks because I wear them, too. That morning, I made the mistake of putting on some holey socks, and—wouldn't you know it—every one of those peeling, raw, wet, patches of epidermal skin on the bottom of my feet were sticking through the holes in my socks. The rest of my feet were fine—except where those holes were.

Now, you might be wondering why I don't just sew the socks instead of complaining about them. Well, I tried that once, but ended up with that little material-fold thing from stitching together both sides of the hole; every time I stepped on that little material-fold thing, it felt like I had a stone in my shoe. So, no—I don't darn socks. I just can't imagine how the pioneers tolerated those fold things!

Smiling Places

When we returned home that evening, I immersed my burning feet into a plastic pan filled with tepid water. Immediately, relief spread throughout my being.

I thought about the scrumptious breakfast Doug had prepared for me and looked the other way when he went bounding out of the trailer door in what else—but his socks. I guess you can't teach an *old, gray horse* new tricks, can you?

17 - Murphy Overstays His Welcome

As we proceeded farther west into Nebraska, the farms became fewer, and the land more rugged. Fields of corn and wheat gave way to grazing cattle. And a stretch of Interstate 80, near Kearney, Nebraska, contained a giant winged horse and an alien spacecraft. Believe me; I hadn't been puffing those prairie grasses. It comes out of nowhere. One minute you are driving down I-80, alone out on the plains with nothing around you for miles, and the next minute, you slam on the brakes. There it is, this monstrous, fortress-like structure built of logs larger than any found in Nebraska—or possibly this world, for that matter—with a 309-foot archway spanning the entire width of the highway. The top of the arch has these floating, metal-like "finger things" protruding out of it with a giant, winged sculpture of a horse sitting eight stories high.

Now, if that doesn't send your freckles into the next county, just travel a few miles west of there and stop at the rest area beyond Kearney. Get out of your vehicle and slowly proceed to the pond. A small, alien spaceship with finger-like protrusions—looking suspiciously like the mother ship a few miles back—is docked there. A ramp to an entrance/exit door keeps moving up and down, up and down, as if to beckon you inside. Move over, Richard Dreyfus! The aliens have landed in Nebraska!

By the time we pulled into North Platte, I was a wee bit leery about this part of Nebraska. It sure made me feel better when I found out human beings, not aliens, built the arch to commemorate The Great Platte River Road. In fact, the entire structure is a visitors' center, built right over the highway. The winged horse represents The Pony Express that galloped through the area. The small alien space ship is really a 7,200-pound wind sculpture that (what else?) moves in the wind. You certainly could have fooled me—until we heard about the two-headed stuffed calf in North Platte—but that is another story.

So, our visit to Scout's Rest Ranch, the home of Buffalo Bill Cody, went well with no alien sightings. Being a native of Dayton, Ohio, I was

Smiling Places

especially interested in Annie Oakley, who was born in 1860 only a few miles from my hometown. "Little Sure Shot" worked in Buffalo Bill's Wild West Show for many years with her husband Frank Butler. She entertained audiences around the world with her fine marksmanship abilities and would often shoot the ashes off of cigarettes her husband held in his mouth. Now, there's a good reason to quit smoking.

I suppose in our hurry to get to Lake McConaughy, we rushed through Buffalo Bill's Homestead and left North Platte all too quickly. By doing so, we missed an opportunity to meet the wonderful people of North Platte and to thank them for the many kindnesses and compassions they bestowed upon millions of Americans a long time ago, and we didn't get to see the old photographs and exhibits displayed around the town. If only we had known about "The Miracle on Front Street," we would have stayed awhile. We do want to go back someday, but for the moment, I will share this truly inspirational story with you. This is about a small town with a huge heart—the true meaning of being an American.

During World War II, many troop trains came to North Platte for a short stopover. From 1941 to 1946, the trains rolled in every day and every night, from 5 a.m. until after midnight with at least 2,000 to 3,000 soldiers each day. The 12,000 citizens of North Platte wanted to know what they could do to help the war effort; so, they changed the railroad depot on Front Street into The North Platte Canteen. They made sure the canteen never closed until the last troop train of the evening had come through. And when the trains did arrive, the citizens were there to greet them all with homemade goodies, foods, gifts, and a big "thank you" to the soldiers for serving our country.

Communities from all over Nebraska and beyond helped with this effort. They prepared sandwiches, baked cookies and pies, and collected magazines and chewing gum; and they asked for nothing in return. Everything was donated during the entire 4½ years this massive undertaking took place. The government did not provide any assistance, and the truly amazing thing—this was accomplished in spite of food, gas, and tire rationing during the war.

By the end of World War II, more than six million troops had come through the famous North Platte Canteen and left with memories that would last a lifetime. Many years after the war, concerned citizens attempted to save the famous Canteen building. They were unsuccessful, and the fate of the Canteen was sealed. A wrecking ball came through in 1973 and demolished the building. I find that part of the story very dis-

Murphy Overstays His Welcome

heartening.

Doug's father and my uncle were discharged from the service in 1945. They both hopped on trains in California and traveled back to their hometowns of Detroit and Philadelphia. Whether they came through North Platte or not, we may never know. They both have passed away now and didn't talk much about the war. Doug and I would like to think they came to the Canteen. Perhaps they enjoyed a fresh boiled egg while they were there. After all, we did hear many complaints about powdered eggs over the years.

We stopped our truck and trailer at a pull-off area on top of a huge dam. I had to pinch myself. Were we still in Nebraska, or was I dreaming? As far as my eyes could see, crystal blue water filled the horizon. White sails far below us glistened in the sunlight while a motorboat skipped across some waves leaving a jet stream behind. Hundreds of swallows dipped and dived over our truck and disappeared under the bridge. Recreational vehicles of every type imaginable were stacked like Cracker-Jack boxes along expansive sandy beaches. If ever there was an oasis in Nebraska, we had found it—along with half of the state's population. Welcome to Lake McConaughy on Memorial Day weekend!

Time stood still for us on top of that dam.

"Oh, sure," you say, "aren't you getting a bit flowery here in the description department?"

"No, not really," I respond. "We crossed over into Mountain Time somewhere between North Platte and here. We set our truck's clock back an hour once we reached the dam. It was two p.m. all over again for us."

"Oh, now I understand," you reply.

I had never lived in a Mountain Time Zone before, and it felt strange. We were now operating two hours behind Dayton time. The nightly news came on at four-thirty p.m. The stock market opened at seven-thirty a.m. The birds started singing at four-thirty a.m. The sun came up at five-thirty a.m. And I was ready to eat dinner at three p.m., and go to bed by seven p.m. I bet the farmers and ranchers loved it.

But getting used to the time difference didn't worry me as much as the crowds that were camped along the beaches. I really didn't want to spend the long weekend on top of a hundred other campers on a sandy beach, broiling in the hot plain's sun. I wanted all the comforts of home and that meant air conditioning. I know, I sound spoiled, but living full-time in a small travel trailer was stressful. We needed to live as com-

Smiling Places

fortably as possible so we wouldn't burn out and quit traveling. In our case, we always checked first for creature comforts, and we were even willing to pay for them—if they weren't too much more. Believe me, it's a lot different from taking your pop-up camper out for a weekend, "roughing it," and returning to your spacious, comfortable, home a few days later.

From the top of the dam, we saw a treed campground situated next to a small lake and pulled our rig down to check it out. I was relieved to find electric hook-ups. We had filled our water tank before we left Grand Island in anticipation of limited camping facilities, so we were in good shape with our utilities. Now, if we could just find a space.

This campground did not accept reservations and looked spooky to me. Many of the sites were already occupied with recreational vehicles, coolers, bikes, and grills, but where were the people? Were we getting into a *Twilight Zone* situation? My husband assured me we weren't. He figured the working folks had driven over early in the week to claim their space, left their stuff, and returned home. They would come back for the weekend after they got off work. I still thought I'd keep my eyes open for anyone with a vacant stare on their face—just to be on the safe side.

Call us lucky or unlucky, whichever you prefer, because Murphy (remember him?) had saved us a wonderful site adjacent to an open field on the fringes of the campground, and he was there to greet us. I know this because as soon as we turned down the road to our campsite, a horrid noise as obtrusive as fingernails on a chalkboard, emulated from our hitch area. A few campers standing nearby threw their hands over their ears and scrunched up their faces as our noise permeated their lives. I, too, put my hands over my ears and glared at my husband. I was in no mood for another trailer problem today.

"Now what?" I asked as the man tried to maneuver quietly the truck and trailer into a backing position.

"I don't know," he shot back with a clenched jaw. "Will you please get out of the truck and see if anything is in the way?"

I jumped out of the truck and walked around the campsite and ended back at his driver's window.

"I don't know what is causing that noise, but it's coming from the hitch again."

"Is the campsite all clear?" Doug asked impatiently.

"You shouldn't hit the picnic table. It's over far enough. Then, if you avoid the two trees and don't flatten the tent in the next space, we

Murphy Overstays His Welcome

should be O.K."

"Hey, keep the snide comments to yourself! Just direct me into the space," he barked.

I saluted—not in a very professional manner, I might add—and took my position by the left rear side of the trailer. A group of five had gathered to watch and make faces at our noise.

I pointed to the right. Doug's wheels turned to the left, and the trailer swung to the right. I pointed to the left. Doug's wheels turned to the right, and the trailer swung to the left.

"What are you doing?" he yelled out the driver's window.

"Just checking!" I yelled back.

I waved him straight back and then motioned with my arms for him to stop. He slammed on the brakes and then burned rubber going forward. What was the man doing?

"Stop!" I yelled to him while running after the trailer.

"What do you mean, stop? I thought you wanted me to go forward, that something was wrong," he said.

"I didn't tell you to go forward, that is my signal to stop," I said.

"No, *this* is the hand signal for stop," he said as he held up a fist.

I really didn't understand that man. Wasn't frantically waving your arms the universal signal to stop? I mean people, do it all the time to stop cabs in New York City, don't they?

"OK, let's do this again," I said exasperated. I retraced my steps to the side of the trailer and waved him back again.

"C'mon, come straight back, keep coming; that's it, you have another four feet to go…".

Doug slammed on the brakes. "What does that mean?" he yelled after I had put my hand over my nose and mouth.

"I sneezed," I said.

Finally, Doug turned off the ignition and got out of the truck. It had taken ten *long* minutes to park our rig with ten *agonizing* minutes of listening to that noise. I didn't know how to shed this Murphy character, but I knew he wasn't done with us yet. The weekend was just beginning.

The group of five campers, who had been watching us, disbanded since the amusing show was over. A man and a boy from the group walked toward our campsite.

"Hey there," the man said.

"Hey there," Doug answered.

Why is it people act like parrots when greeting other human beings?

Smiling Places

You say, "Hi," I answer "Hi." You say, "Good morning." I answer, "Good morning."

"My name is John and this is my son John, Jr."

"My name is Doug, and this is my wife Melodee."

"Glad to meet you, Doug and Melodee," John said, and the men shook hands. "We heard that noise when y'all were parking. We think we know what the problem is."

"What's that?" Doug asked.

"You ever use any hitch grease on your ball and coupling?"

"No, I haven't."

"Well, that's what would cause it, metal rubbing against metal," John explained.

"Hey, thanks. That makes sense," Doug answered. "I'll have to pick up some."

"Don't worry. I've got some I can give you. I carry it with me since I started pulling," John said.

Then John, Jr. added, "The same noise happened to Dad one of the first times he towed something."

"Well, if you hadn't noticed, we are pretty new at this trailer thing."

"Oh, we noticed all right, didn't we, Dad?" John, Jr. said.

We all laughed, and our next few days were filled with big John and little John.

They lived north in Valentine, Nebraska, and just the two of them camped together every Memorial Day weekend. They always brought their fishing rods. John, Jr. was twelve now. He had just had his birthday last week, and John, Jr. loved homemade potato salad. Could I make him some if he shared some of his fish with me? And could he drive on the beach with us since we had a four-wheel drive truck? And would Doug play catch with him? He had brought two baseball mitts. Did Doug like to fish? Could he go with them?

So it was settled. Early the next morning, Doug would go fishing with them—but just to watch. We couldn't afford to buy fishing licenses in every state we stayed in. I would take the truck to a little store up the road for potato salad supplies and other fixings, and tomorrow night we would feast on the catch of the day.

That afternoon we went exploring. We ended up halfway around Lake McConaughy at a place called Ash Hollow—the pioneer's Garden of Eden. Large ash trees provided the first shade the pioneers had felt in weeks, and flowing springs provided fresh water, a welcome respite from

Murphy Overstays His Welcome

the contaminated waters of the Platte River.

A sign posted by the springs explained that an emigrant named Madison Moorman had traveled through this area in 1850 and described the springs:

> "Low down near the mouth (of Ash Hollow) a number of springs of cold and crystal water gushed forth from under the high and barren bluff, of which without ceremony, and with common consent we all partook most freely—the best and purest ever drank—a beverage prepared by God Himself."

Another sign was also posted at the springs. It said,

"We do not recommend that you drink this water."

Go figure!

It took the pioneers about forty days to reach Ash Hollow. But first, they had to negotiate a treacherous hill called Windlass Hill, a few miles down the road. We also negotiated it and hiked to the top on a paved footpath so as not to disturb the wagon ruts that had eroded into ravines. The hill was so high that our truck looked like a Matchbox truck. I could see why so many wagons had crashed to the bottom. Wagon brakes didn't work on this steep hill, so the pioneers locked their wheels and used metal spurs and ropes to lower the wagons—and this was no easy job. Some of those wagons weighed 2,500 pounds. I wish Doug could have lowered me down the hill on a rope. My ankles and knees felt stretched and jammed by the time we reached bottom. Why was it? Climbing up a trail always seemed easier than coming down.

The next morning I found the little store and bought the food I needed. On the way home, I pulled into a yet-deserted parking lot and walked down to the water. Lake McConaughy was a man-made reservoir, and everything about it was big—twenty miles long, four miles wide, and 35,000 acres of surface waters. It was situated on the edge of a great expanse of sandhills, and the beaches here rivaled many of the public beaches we had been to on the Great Lakes. I pulled off my shoes and walked along the water's edge. The white sands melted beneath my feet as the cold water lapped at my toes. I could see that the lake bottom was sandy smooth, just like the beach. Oh, swimming in this lake would

Smiling Places

be such a joy! I was glad we were here at the end of May; someone had mentioned the biting flies had not yet arrived.

But I'm sure if Murphy could have figured out a way to send a plague of flies my way that day, he would have. As it was, he almost did away with me while I was alone in the trailer, preparing dinner and exercising in advance of the caloric avalanche that I anticipated that evening. By the end of the day, my right foot was bruised, my head had a small knot, and my arm had a one-inch red mark. I was lying on the couch with two pillows, a heating pad, and two ice packs when my man returned from his day with "the two Johns."

"Did they catch anything?" I asked him.

"Oh yeah. There is plenty for tonight. Little John is all excited."

"I'm glad you had a good time," I said while sitting on my pity pot.

"Hey, you don't look too good. You didn't have an accident, did you?" Doug asked, finally noticing my condition.

"No, I didn't have an accident." I replied. "Your truck is fine."

"Great! Well then, what happened?"

"Oh, not much," I began. "I went to the store and picked up the food. I put the potatoes in the microwave and the eggs in a pot on the stove to hard-boil them for the potato salad. I started doing my trailer Tae-Bo and slammed my right foot into the wall. Have you ever dry-walled a trailer? Then, my potatoes were done, and I opened our wall mounted microwave door to get them out. Well, I must have leaned wrong on my bum foot because I pitched forward and knocked my head good on that open microwave door. The microwave is fine by the way. And as I pitched forward, I flailed my arms wildly in the air and grabbed at the stove to keep from falling. I didn't fall, but my arm touched the hot pot the eggs were boiling in. It gave me this red mark. So, what do you think about all this?"

"I think I better get my tool chest and fix the wall," my husband said and ran out of the trailer.

I "felt" Murphy smile.

Our dinner was glorious, even though my right foot kept telling my left foot to slow down. The fish was succulent and coated with cornmeal, herbs and spices. I loved that it was baked and not fried. I wish I had asked for the recipe. The two Johns loved my potato salad. I didn't tell anyone I had created a new low-fat recipe that afternoon. To the potatoes I added a variety of minced veggies—green onion, celery, green pepper, carrots, and pimentos, a few hard-boiled eggs, pickle relish, and

Murphy Overstays His Welcome

a small amount of low-fat mayonnaise. I even added a dollop of yogurt. I was learning to "cook healthy" while on the road and it was beginning to show. I did have many more pounds to shed, but just how much—I am too embarrassed to say.

We ended the evening sitting around a campfire. Little John opened a package of marshmallows. We toasted them until they caught fire and ate them when they became black and gooey. Big John brought out his guitar and started playing songs we all learned as youngsters. Soon, other campers joined us. We sang to our heart's content under the starlit skies.

The next day little John decided to go four-wheel driving on the beach, with or without Doug and his dad. My right foot decided I would stay home with a plateful of fish to keep me company. I knew Murphy and I had been in the trailer too long when the fish pieces jumped up on the plate and began singing to me like Billy Bass.

"Take me to the river," they crooned in harmony.

I quickly put a stop to that nonsense. I ate them.

I sure was glad when Doug got home. I smelled like fish.

"Can you drive me to the showers?" I asked him.

"Sure. Let me get a change of clothes, and I'll take one, too."

The minute I stepped into the ladies shower room, I should have known to turn around and leave. There was a blood-curdling scream from shower stall number four, and then a tiny voice that pleaded, "Ouch! Mommy, Turn It Off!"

I stepped into shower stall number five. My fish smell was overpowering. The stall was clean and spacious, but the showerhead was huge and suspicious. A push button had replaced the entire shower faucet. Shower stall number four was quiet now. The people had left in a hurry. I was scared. I didn't want to push that water button. How did I know what would pop out of there? Cold water? Hot water? I stepped back into the little dressing area attached to my stall, reached all the way across, and pushed.

"Ah, a nice warm shower," I thought as I stepped under the stream of water. I lathered my hair with shampoo, being careful of the knot on my head. Was I imagining things or was the water pressure increasing? I began to rinse off. The water pressure was getting harder and harder. It was hitting the knot on my head so hard that it was pulsating in pain from a showerhead gone berserk.

"Ouch! Mommy, Turn It Off!" I cried.

Smiling Places

The button popped out, and the water stopped. I dried myself off with my towel, soapy hair and all. There was no way I was going to push that button again.

When I went outside, Doug was against the truck waiting for me.

"Is that a new hair-do or is it Halloween already?" he asked me.

"Didn't you feel it?"

"Feel what?"

"The water pressure."

"I don't know what you mean," Doug replied.

"The water pressure in your shower," I stammered. "Mine was hard enough to blow me and the knot on my head clear to Wyoming."

"The water pressure, huh? Let us see. No, I don't remember any discomfort at all."

"Didn't the water start out nice—then increase into a raging stream?"

"No, I don't think so."

"So, then, you're not sure?"

"No, I'm sure," he replied.

"Murphy," I muttered and got into the truck.

Well, I am sure you have all enjoyed Murphy's antics and would love him to stick around, but after my daunting shower scene, he left us and found another family to have fun with. The wife apparently did some type of work for the Board of Elections. They had an adorable baby son named Chad. As they were pulling away, we saw Murphy in the back window. He turned and waved good-bye to us. I think the license plate on their recreational vehicle said Broward County...*Florida.*

"Murphy," I whispered, "you wouldn't, would you?"

It was very hard saying good-bye to Big John and Little John. Kind of like Dorothy saying to the Scarecrow, "I think I'll miss you most of all." Big John assured us the hitch grease would do the trick and stop the noise. He was right. Little John said they would probably be back next year on Memorial Day weekend. He really wanted us to come back, too. For some reason, I didn't think that would happen. And as I hugged little John good-bye, I wiped away a tear that was running down my cheek.

18 - This is the Oldest I've Ever Been

On June 1st, I awoke to my husband dancing in our trailer, wearing nothing but his gym shorts and a funny pointed hat. He had an old Beatles song blasting away on the CD player, "They say it's your *Birthday*.... We're gonna have a good time...".

A huge blueberry muffin was sitting in the middle of our kitchen table with a box wrapped in newspaper. Sushi was wearing a funny pointed hat around her midriff and hiding under the table.

It was my forty-seventh birthday, and I have to admit: If anyone in Scottsbluff, Nebraska had walked into our trailer at that very moment, we all would have ended up in a loony bin wearing straight jackets with our appendages tied in front of us, including Sushi. Even so, the scene was hilarious, and I really appreciated it—if it had been anyone else's birthday but mine.

I felt like a dinosaur. The Beatles had recorded the "Birthday" song in 1968, fifteen years after I was born. Sir Edmund Hillary and Sherpa climber Tenzing Norgay had just reached the top of Mount Everest a few days before I was born, and Eisenhower was President.

So, I sat at our kitchen table, put a birthday hat on my head, shared a blueberry muffin with my husband and cat, and tried on a pair of blue fuzzy bedroom slippers that Doug had bought for my birthday because I told him my feet were cold in the trailer. Whatever happened to perfume and flowers? I guess practicality comes with age.

"I've got an exciting day planned for us," Doug bubbled.

"At my age? I don't know how much more excitement I can stand than this," I bubbled back.

"How does hiking by the Oregon Trail sound?"

"Like too much work. How about a nice soak in a tub for these old bones?"

Smiling Places

"You might as well get dressed because I am taking you to Scott's Bluff," he said triumphantly.

"You mean that 800-foot high rock across from our campground? That giant formation somebody called 'Nebraska Gibraltar?' The landmark the pioneers spotted days before they reached it? You want me to hike to the top of *that*?"

"Don't you think it would be fun?" Doug asked.

"No-no-no-no-no-no. I think I need to give my right foot a few more days to rest," the dinosaur replied.

"Oh, I forgot about that. They do have a road to the top."

"Now, that I might be interested in," I said relieved.

My prince whisked me off to the big rock. The first thing I noticed at the visitors' center was a pamphlet entitled "*Snakes of the Prairie*". It was very interesting indeed—especially the part that talked about prairie rattlesnake bites. I am not joking here. It said prairie rattlers could bite you *after they had died* through a reflex action.

So, I asked the park ranger if this was true.

"Oh yes, they can strike after they are dead," he assured me. "Another thing about prairie rattlers is they are shy. Usually, if they are coiled up, just walk carefully around them, and you should be OK."

"Now you aren't just saying that because you saw our Ohio license plates are you?"

"Of course not," he answered somewhat irritated.

"So... if we get bit by one, what should we do?" I asked the ranger.

"First and foremost remain calm. Don't exert yourself. Send your hiking partner for help. It's very important to keep the bitten part still, below the level of the heart."

"And what if I am out hiking by myself?"

"Then walk, don't run, to get help."

Armed with all the precarious information I could gather for the moment, we hiked for a short distance from the visitor center on the Oregon Trail. The wagon wheels had cut ruts into the earth where we walked, and the ground rose up on both sides of us. Erosion had created a ravine affect on the trail over the years. Wagon trains would normally fan out when traveling to minimize the dust being kicked up on the trail. But once they reached Scotts Bluff, they would come together and create wagon jams because the pass they used, Mitchell Pass, was so narrow.

This is the Oldest I've Ever Been

This being my birthday, I realized all this had happened a mere hundred years before I was born. One hundred years is not a very long time, *dinosaur*!

The other thing I kept thinking about was my right foot. Once we drove to the top of Scotts Bluff, we hiked on additional trails. My foot did surprisingly well for my age, I thought, and it carried me close to all the lookouts. But it stopped short a good distance from them. I attributed that to its DNA makeup consisting entirely of Ohio flatlander genes.

"We aren't going anywhere near that drop-off," my right foot said and stopped.

"But I want to see what's down there," I pleaded.

"Not in this lifetime," my right foot answered while my left foot agreed.

Doug, who had the fortitude of a mountain goat, stood precipitously close to the edge of the lookouts and took pictures. I saw the wagon swales in the valley, the towns of Gering and Scotts Bluff, and even Chimney Rock, on video. He told me the views were spectacular and he could see twenty miles or more. I just hung on to the closest rock outcropping until he was finished.

We didn't see any rattlesnakes on my birthday, dead or alive, but we discovered our first prairie dog town. I couldn't tell you where. We were somewhere in Nebraska. Doug wanted to reach two other pioneer landmarks, Courthouse Rock and Jail Rock. We could see them towering over the plains from where we were and guessed they were "five miles up the road." It seemed we drove from here to eternity to reach those rocks.

Our brain functions that dealt with distances were totally distorted as we left our truck to hike on a trail we saw leading to the base of Courthouse Rock. And whatever was left of our brains at that point was blown out between our ears by the gale force winds that kicked up dust in our eyes, mouths, and every other human orifice. I believe that was the shortest hike we had ever taken. Ten feet from the truck and then hand signals to turn around because we couldn't hear each other screaming into the winds.

"Those poor pioneers, how did they manage?" I thought, as we recovered in the safety of our truck.

Smiling Places

It was much easier finding Chimney Rock since it stands near major highway US 26. I was happy as a bear standing in salmon infested waters to be there. Nearly every story I had ever read about the westward trek of the pioneers had mentioned Chimney Rock. The pioneers saw the landmark days before they reached it. I had imagined standing next to the 370 foot rock weeks before I reached it.

But surprisingly, the visitors' center was built a long way from the rock. I had presumed there would be a hiking trail to the base of the rock. There wasn't.

"Go up the road and veer to the right. You will find a small parking lot at the end. There is a hiking trail leading into some brush, but I wouldn't recommend using it—lots of snakes," someone told us.

I do believe they were kind in their account of the beginnings of that trail. I feel a more accurate description would have portrayed a thirty foot deep ravine with a narrow animal path disappearing into thick, woody foliage, probably laden with prickly cactus and slashing yuccas. Snakes (and who knows what else) were patiently waiting down there for their next victim.

If you were lucky enough to clear the ravine, a long hike awaited you across the plains to the rock; that is, if the buffalo didn't charge you. Supposedly, they were wandering around out there somewhere, but we didn't see them.

We wondered if we were in the right place, if there wasn't an easier way to experience our national heritage. Needless to say, the two bumbling idiots from Ohio didn't venture into the ravine but enjoyed the moment from the parking lot.

For the rest of the afternoon we drove on sand-packed roads, kicked up mountains of dust, but never saw another human being. Many cattle grazed the hillsides, and every once in a while a sign posted by a long dirt drive would point to a cattle rancher's home. There were no side roads to speak of. A secondary sand road seemed to run for miles, connecting one asphalt highway to another. Sometimes, colorful patches of blooming wildflowers would cover acre upon acre of gently rolling fields. At other times, we were intrigued by the dry, desert-like conditions of the terrain. All in all, we felt not much had changed since the pioneers had traveled through. And that was just fine with us.

This is the Oldest I've Ever Been

When we returned to our trailer, my husband surprised me and said we were going to a chuck wagon cookout that evening.

"Really? That is so sweet of you, but please don't tell anyone it's my birthday," I begged him.

"I guess I won't, if that's what you want," he answered.

"Do you promise?" I asked again.

"It's your birthday," he answered.

I'm sure you can relate to my dilemma. I didn't want clapping, off-key food-servers singing "Happy Birthday" to me in front of an audience of strangers. So what if it was my birthday? Strangers certainly would not care. They would want to finish their meals before they got cold. But everyone, whether they know you or not, feels obligated to join in and sing. And they sing along until the "Happy Birthday, dear whatever-your-name-is-part." Then, the room quiets down just for that split second. Nobody knows your name except for your guests and the frenzied food-servers. And to add to your humiliation, a teeny tiny birthday cake with one skinny candle is brought to your table. All your guests look at you with hungry eyes. They expect you to perform a biblical miracle—divide the cake into enough pieces to feed the masses. No thank you. I'll just enjoy my birthday dinner in peace.

When we arrived, the parking lot was thick with pickup trucks wearing Nebraska license plates. It was early in the season. The tourists had not yet invaded. Tables were set up outside under wood-covered roofs. Anvils held large cast iron pots swinging over open pits, while a huge grill lay suspended over a substantial wood fire. The "watering hole" was busy with laughter. Everyone had congregated there. Our appetites were charged up from the day's activities.

"Welcome to the Oregon Trail Wagon Train," a friendly voice said.

I turned around and looked at a man who had stepped back into the 1850's.

"How are you folks doing?" he asked.

"We're great and real hungry," Doug answered.

"Well, I can guarantee you, you won't leave here hungry," he said. "By the way, my name is Pete. I'm the cook around here."

Pete shook our hands. At that moment, Pete, the cook, was the most important man in my life.

Smiling Places

"We're gonna have a small covered wagon trek. Why don't you go on up and get yourself something to drink," Pete continued. "Meet back here in a few minutes."

We "moseyed on up to the bar" and met some wonderful Nebraskans from the GW Sugar Company. I had bought the blue and white bags of GW sugar many times from the grocery store in Dayton—never knowing GW stood for Great Western. I also never knew sugar beets were grown in Nebraska. In fact, one of the largest sugar beet processing plants in the U.S. was down the road from our campground in the town of Scottsbluff.

Almost every part of me loved the covered wagon trek—except for my butt. No shocks, no springs, no nothing between your cheeks and the hard, jostling ground.

"I flew from here to Oregon," our wagon master told us. "From the plane, I could see the wagon swales carved into the earth."

When he turned our wagon around to head back to the chuck wagon, Chimney Rock was close-by.

"That's why so many wagons rumbled through this very area; they came to see the rock," our wagon master explained. "Even the Pony Express came through here and delivered mail to the wagon trains and outposts on the frontier," he ended.

"Howdy, Pardners, You've Got Mail!" Doug said with a smile.

Our thirty-minute wagon trek was enough for me. The pioneers had endured six to eight months of such travel. We had no canvas cover during our small wagon ride. Temperatures during the day soared to 115 degrees under the canvas covers of the pioneer's wagons. This dinosaur sure was glad she didn't have to use her old bones to climb down off the wagon. The nice chuck wagon people had built a wooden staircase for us *older* folks.

I was more than ready to indulge in food when we returned, even though the high cholesterol alarm was ringing in my head. The steaks were sizzling, the pots were boiling, and some people were seated at the long tables, carefully watching Pete grill the steaks. Finally, the iron triangular dinner bell clanged, so we grabbed a huge plate and took our turn with Pete.

"How do you like your steak?" Pete asked me.

"Well done," I replied.

This is the Oldest I've Ever Been

Suddenly, there was a hush throughout the line. You'd think I had spoken a bad word. "Easterner," they thought. "Shoe leather steaks."

OK, so "well done" out east is a lot different from out west. Pete's well done looked like medium to me. But once I cut into that thick slab of Nebraska-raised steer and tasted that melt-in-your-mouth meat, I wouldn't have wanted it any other way. It was absolutely delicious!

Our plates were loaded—a huge baked potato, green beans, sourdough bread, relishes, and for dessert, homemade ice cream. We both wrapped up a large remainder of our meals and took home the leftovers. We were stuffed!

The next morning I pulled the *beast* from its resting place against the wall. I carefully stepped on its belly and watched its face roll through a range of numbers.

"Six pounds," I said in disbelief. Was the scale right? Had I actually lost six pounds since we had left for the road?

"The scale is my friend today," I thought as I shoved it back against the wall.

Our new lifestyle certainly was healthier than it ever had been. We had completely eliminated the fast food visits and opted for grocery stores instead. We brought our own lunches for our day-long excursions—low-fat crackers, raw veggies and fruits, and plain turkey or chicken that we packed in a cooler on our truck's backseat. We also kept a well-stocked salad spinner in the refrigerator. I felt much better and thought I might be gaining some muscle from all the walking and hiking we were doing.

But, starting this increased exercise regime at forty-seven years of age brought its own set of hurdles for me. My muscles seemed to ache all of the time. My increased activity made me hungry. My decreased fat intake made me ravenous. I craved fat more than sweets, and when five o'clock rolled around, I was ready to eat—from five p.m. to nine p.m.— non-stop. I had two voices fighting in my head all the time: one, the complainer, telling me this was too hard, and two, the cheerleader, saying I could do this.

Today was no exception. I was hungry right after we crossed into Wyoming and arrived at Fort Laramie, an important frontier outpost in the 1800's. We walked for two hours, climbing up steps and going through buildings. Some were refurbished and others were in ruins. The "post trader" who ran the General Store at the outpost was fun to speak with.

Smiling Places

"This general store was the Wal-Mart of the West. All the migration trails came together in this area. In June and July, two-thousand people a day came through this store and purchased goods. And I'm not going to fool you; we didn't charge the pioneers army prices." The post trader added, "We ripped them off!" He held up a "newfangled can" of peaches at a pioneer price of $1.25.

Many famous people had transacted here—a "Who's Who of the Old West": Buffalo Bill, Annie Oakley, Crazy Horse, Brigham Young, Kit Carson, Red Cloud, Sitting Bull, Doc Holiday, Wyatt Earp—and quite possibly, even Sam Walton.

"Here, touch this original countertop, and you are touching history," the post trader said.

In 1890, Fort Laramie was abandoned.

When we got back to the truck, I was hot, hungry, and tired. Doug started the engine and the air conditioning flooded the front seat. I took turkey and tomatoes out of the cooler, and Doug opened a box of low-fat crackers.

"I think tomorrow will be a day of rest," I told Doug. "I need to do some paperwork."

"And I think I'll do the laundry," Doug said. "Let's just drive to the last two places we planned for today. They aren't far at all and should be very interesting."

"OK, but this is kind of sad," I said. "Our last day following the pioneers. I found their journey fascinating."

"I know. I never realized how difficult they had it, but I think we both agreed we wanted to see South Dakota and Montana. You aren't changing your mind, are you?"

"No, but someday I would like to come back and follow the remainder of this trail all the way to Oregon. I still can't believe we are only one-third of the way there," I answered.

With that, Doug pulled out of the parking lot and continued west on SR 26 to Guernsey, Wyoming. When we arrived, we were surprised to find an army base and National Guard unit there. We were even more surprised to meet a lady who had been stationed at Wright-Patterson in the late 1990's. We played the "do-you-know" game, but didn't come up with any matches. It sure is a small world.

We climbed a short path up to the wagon rut site. Other wagon rut sites we had seen were carved into the soils. These were carved into rock. I just couldn't believe it—thousands upon thousands of wagons

This is the Oldest I've Ever Been

had cut through sandstone rock to create this trail—an amazing five-foot deep gully about four to five feet wide. I stood in the gully—the rock walls up around me. What traffic jams there must have been on top of this hill with people trying to squeeze every single wagon through the trail in the rock.

I touched the sides of the gully where so much history was made. I didn't know if I would ever see wagon ruts this prominent again.

Our last stop, Register Cliff, was equally inspiring. This place could be compared to a modern day rest area. The pioneers would rest here, by the Platte River, where a trading station was located. And like some welcome centers today, this place had a guest register; only this register was located on the side of a rocky cliff. Thousands of pioneers clambered up the cliff and inscribed their names in the soft sandstone rock.

Today, many of the signatures are still legible. Those that stood out had been signed under ledges or in corners where they were somewhat protected from the elements. I carried my notebook and pen with me and wrote down some of the signatures that I could read. Do you know any of these brave souls?

J.W. Rogg 1857 U.S. Post   G.O. Willard 1855 Boston

T. Parker   T.F. Goodwin   IMD Hatwood 1864

R. Nesbit August 2, 1855   Jo Taylor P.A. 1859

Tex Seppa 1889-The Oregon Wagon Train-Wagonmaster

Family Kuprel Aug 18 1862

TB Marker 1872   JN. Elliott 1850

CW Bryson 1855 KY   LN Breed 1868

H Boles 1859

James Huge   I.N. Cotton 1852

W. Lovatt   LJ Marsh 1864 M. Colliage Ohio

Smiling Places

After the forty-seven year old dinosaur rested for a few days, we left Scottsbluff and headed for the Nebraska Panhandle. We came upon a little sign that I followed to my own fountain of youth. In the remotest of hills, we hiked to a quarry where an archeological dig had uncovered fossilized bones. Now, these weren't just any bones but nineteen million year-old bones. Suddenly, I didn't feel like a dinosaur anymore and welcomed my youthful forty-seven years. And as I stood at the top of the world at Agate Fossil Beds National Monument, I had a revelation.

"This is the oldest I've ever been. No wait! *This* is the oldest I've ever been. No wait! *This* is the oldest I've ever been....". The echo rebounding through the hills could be heard as we left.

19 - Tickphobia

They waited for us on tall blades of grass. Their backward-pointing teeth were sharpened and ready to feast. They could not run, hop, fly, or move quickly, but they sensed our approach. Our warm-blooded bodies reeked of carbon dioxide, and the ground vibrated as our big feet climbed higher and higher into the Nebraska pine forest. We stepped over fallen tree limbs and shuffled through overgrown vegetation, as the trail had not been used for quite awhile. That by itself should have clued the two bumbling idiots from Ohio that something was amiss.

All of a sudden, one of them stretched out her rear legs and reached for my knee. Ah, success was in the air as she snagged my blue jeans, and started her ascent toward my blood-laden flesh. Another, seeing the huge shadow that I cast upon her vantage point, quickly attached to my white sock. Again, and again, these blood-sucking parasites grabbed at us as we passed them. Soon our bodies were crawling with these silent, hungry critters. I was covered from head to toe. Doug, however, was only covered from head to ankle (even ticks were smart enough to stay away from Doug's offensive foot odor).

We had been hiking for twenty-five minutes. Doug followed me on the narrow trail that wound up a steep hill.

"Hold up for a second," he said in a calm manner.

I stopped and felt his finger flick something off the back of my short-sleeved white t-shirt.

"Just a small bug," he said, and we began hiking again.

Abruptly, he asked me to stop again. This time I wasn't as composed as before.

"What is it?" I asked and turned around to face him.

"We have a *small problem*," he said. I knew the way he emphasized the word "small", that this was something big, something major—something excruciatingly gigantic.

Smiling Places

"Now, don't panic on me," he continued, "but there are a few ticks on your back."

"How many?" I asked as my heart ricocheted around my chest.

"Several," he answered, "but don't run; you could hurt yourself...."

He didn't have a chance to finish his sentence. I had already run over him and flattened him like a tortilla as I headed down the trail at top speed. What took me twenty-five minutes to hike up only took me seven minutes to race down—the best sprint I had accomplished in years. By the time Doug found me in the trailhead parking lot standing alongside our truck, I had cast all modesty aside—well almost. I had flung my clothes toward the back bumper of the truck and stripped down to my underwear. I was even contemplating removing those intimates until Doug stopped me.

"Wait a minute," he commanded.

"Get these horrid ticks off of me," I yelled and thrashed my arms about like Tippy Hedron in Alfred Hitchcock's *The Birds*.

"Here, put this around you and please calm down!" Doug ordered as he handed me a beach towel we had in the truck.

The only witness to our ordeal was an older gentleman in a white pick-up truck. He drove past us at a most inopportune time. I was holding the beach towel in both hands spread full-width in front of me. Doug knelt on the ground with his head and torso popped up in that beach towel with me. The older gentleman only saw Doug's hiking shoes, blue jeans, the beach towel, and my head from the road. He slammed on his squeaky brakes, and backed up to where we were positioned.

"Forty-seven, forty-eight, (He missed.), forty-eight (He got it.), forty-nine," I counted as Doug flicked those troublesome ticks off my body.

"Are you all right?" the gentleman asked my head, which was staring at him from above the beach towel.

Doug answered, "Yes" from under the towel, and then picked that exact moment to exit his cover. He backed out on all fours, and stood straight up in the parking lot with a face as red as a cooked beet. The gentleman looked right past Doug, and again addressed his question to me.

"Are *you* all right?" he asked my head again.

"Oh, yes sir. It's ticks; my husband and I got ticks from that hiking trail," I said to the gentleman. "There's a whole bunch of them and we are trying to get them off of each other."

Tickphobia

Somehow, I don't think the gentleman believed me. His eyebrows furled, and he gave Doug the thrice over. Did I detect a hint of recognition in that gentleman's eyes? Was he thinking, "Didn't I see that red-faced character on *America's Most Wanted* last week?" Speechless, he drove away, slowly at first, and then his white truck disappeared around a bend in the road.

I was already unnerved from forty-nine ticks taking up residence on my body. Now, I was watching the road for those bad-boy retina-scorching flashing lights to appear. I certainly didn't want to explain this perplexing situation to Bubba and Barney Fife. So, we finished our examinations, put on clean clothes, triple-bagged our infested clothing and shoes, and got out of there.

We drove through the Nebraska National Forest and headed toward Chadron State Park. I knew more pin-head-sized ticks were riding back with us to our campsite. I had already found another that I flitted out the truck window as it creeped up my forearm. The one that crawled out on Doug's neck had gotten away from me. It was still on him—now hidden. I couldn't fling the third one out of the truck; it was on my bare foot, and I stomped it into the truck's carpeting.

Looking back, I had never given much thought to ticks. I had spent much of my life tromping around outside, and had always considered mosquitoes and biting flies—especially biting flies—more of a problem. Several times, I had ventured into the woods and ventured out with blankets of flies chasing me into a frenzied dance of sorts—like a disco hokey-pokey.

I think my nonchalant attitude about ticks was caused by a tick encounter I had had several years ago. Doug and I owned a small farm with an old wooden barn. We loved to go out there on weekends and putter around after being imprisoned at work all week. One day, I was in the barn raking some hay off the dirt floor, and unknowingly became a host to a tick for a few days. Back then, we didn't use spray or check for ticks. How that particular tick survived my showers is still a mystery to me.

I discovered that blood-sucking infidel when the nape of my neck itched. I reached back to scratch it and felt a hard lump. After feasting on me for a few days, that tick had grown to about 500 times its normal size—the size of a peanut M&M. Doug gave me a few swigs of whiskey and a stick to bite on before he removed it. I wasn't bothered by it too much. The very next weekend, I returned to our barn and finished my

Smiling Places

raking while buckets of sweat poured off of me. Those hip-wader boots and the ski mask I wore the rest of the summer sure fooled the ticks at our farm.

Nevertheless, telling you this story today was not a good idea. Doug and I had too many spooky tick thoughts going through our heads; and *spooky tick thoughts* can make normal people do strange things. When we arrived at our campsite, I watched Doug empty a Tylenol bottle he found in the glove compartment. Then, he held the bottle and probed my fully clothed body.

"What are you doing?" I asked.

"I'm searching for another tick."

"Now, why are we doing this again?" I asked as he scooped a tick from my arm to the bottle.

"I read somewhere, but can't remember where, that you should save a live tick in case you get sick."

"Maybe you read it in that *Space Alien Handbook* you keep tucked under your pillow," I said.

"Very funny."

"So, why did you put a wet tissue in the Tylenol bottle?"

"Well, it said to keep the tick hydrated and alive so it can be identified."

"Oh, silly me, of course," I said while backing away from the man.

Unfortunately, I was acting stranger than my husband was. After my third shower, I saw Sushi scratching her whiskers. Sushi scratches her whiskers everyday. But on this particular day, I reached ten feet across our trailer, grabbed Sushi and her whiskers, and threw her under our outside shower hose—all within eight seconds.

That poor cat didn't know what hit her. Her body tensed in the throngs of rigor mortis, and goose bumps covered her wide-open eyeballs. She managed a gurgling sound from deep within her throat. No doubt about it: That cat was out to get me for this injustice. When that tick shampoo hit her, she flew out of my hands and raced up a pine tree shading our campsite. It was an amazing feat since Sushi has no claws. She clung to a branch about fifteen feet up and shrieked in "god-awful," high-pitched sounds that got everyone's attention within a one-mile radius of that tree.

"Shush, Sushi. Shhh," I pleaded with her.

"Well, maybe you should have thought about this before you dragged me out of the trailer," she screamed.

Tickphobia

Doug came racing out of our trailer with a piece of turkey and stood under the pine tree.

"Treats, treats," he said as he dangled the turkey over his head.

Turkey is Sushi's favorite food; so, it didn't take her long to quiet down and exit the tree. Doug finished bathing her.

I stayed away from that cat for the rest of the day. I still think she had it in for me. So, my next strange tick maneuver had to do with our truck. I found a "sticky-paper" mousetrap and put it on the passenger seat of our truck. I made sure I placed it right-side-up because we all know how quickly those traps can stick to things. Then, I ran my hand back and forth over the upholstery, and chased four ticks into eternal Sticky Hell. My idea worked so successfully that I put the same sticky trap on the driver's seat. It was way past lunchtime now, and I was thinking only of a turkey sandwich on whole wheat bread with lettuce and tomato. So, I stopped what I was doing with the full intention of returning after lunch to finish the job.

About the same time, Doug was thinking of vanilla ice cream and chocolate sauce. He thought it would taste great on a ninety-degree day. He stuck his head inside the trailer and told me he was driving to Chadron to pick up some ice cream. I was totally engrossed with my turkey sandwich and forgot to tell him about my little sticky truck project.

Well, the man didn't see the trap and sat right on it. He didn't feel it, either. The trap clung to his shorts like a thong on a fat man's derriere. He told me he didn't understand why people at the gas station were staring at him. Only when the clerk at Wal-Mart laughed so hard that she had tears running down her face did he discover his little butt warmer.

Doug was none too pleased with his number one wife. When he walked into the trailer and turned around to show me his shorts, I tried—I really did—try to hold in the laughter. After a few moments, though, I lost it. I laughed so hard I almost fell off the couch.

"I don't think it's funny at all," Doug said with the most serious expression. Then he took off his shorts, looked at the rear end, rolled his eyeballs, and pitched them into the trashcan. When he rolled his eyeballs, I howled again. He quickly dressed and took a long walk around the campground. He came back and had three bowls of ice cream.

I had expected Doug to be upset with me the next morning since I had mutilated his shorts, but actually, he was quite agreeable. He made us breakfast—a fruit salad and cereal—and poured me hot herbal tea.

Smiling Places

When I straggled out of the bedroom looking like I had been floating on a piece of the Titanic for three months, he asked if I felt OK.

"I tossed and turned all night."

"Thinking about those darn ticks, I bet."

"What else."

I suddenly remembered to check for those telltale tick rashes and looked down at my arms.

"I didn't see any rashes on you or me," Doug said as if he read my mind. "And Sushi seemed fine."

"When did you check me out?" I asked.

He just smiled, and continued to crunch his cereal.

"I do want to apologize for yesterday. I am so sorry. I truly forgot to tell you about the sticky trap in the truck," I said.

"There aren't any sticky traps placed anywhere else, are there?" Doug asked.

"Nope, that was the only one."

"OK, then. Apology accepted, but you owe me a pair of shorts."

"With or without the butt warmer?" I snickered.

"Hey, that's not funny, you know. By the way, we ran out of water. Want to help me fill the water tank?"

"I guess. Probably ran out because of all that tick commotion yesterday."

"Probably."

"I guess you'd rather fill it manually instead of moving the trailer, right?"

"It's a lot easier that way."

I got dressed while Doug gathered some empty plastic water jugs. We walked up the road to a water station, about 200 feet from our campsite. I felt like time had stood still for a hundred years. Here I was in the Great Plains "fetchin' some water." Life sure was different living on the road.

Doug turned on the water spigot. He turned it off in a hurry. The water pressure could have blown us both down the road a few thousand feet. So, he turned the spigot on again, ever so slightly, and it made a noise that sounded like the mating calls of ten rambunctious bull elks. A rabbit that was nibbling grass looked at us and decided humans make the strangest mating calls. It darted under an overgrown shrub. Nearby campers laughed and waved. Obviously, they were familiar with the water station. We made several trips and partly filled our water tank using a

Tickphobia

large funnel that slid into the opening on the back of the trailer. Thank goodness, a restroom/shower facility was right up the hill from our campsite.

Near lunchtime, we took a pleasant drive to Fort Robinson State Park, just west of Crawford, Nebraska. Finding a parking space was not an easy task. The place was packed. Vendors and artists had set up booths surrounding the small fairgrounds and sold food and crafts. People had squeezed into the bleachers and watched intently as Native Americans shared their culture and traditions with the audience. Other people were standing, and we found spots to stand quite a distance from the performers. Since we had never seen a pow-wow before, I struck up a conversation with the lady standing next to me in hopes that she could shed some light on my ignorance. It just so happened that she was an eighth-grade school teacher from Iowa. While she had never seen a pow-wow, she had read about them; and she was pleased to share what she knew.

"What beautiful outfits," I said. Native American women had taken their places in the field and begun to dance. They moved their feet to the beat of the drums and kept them close to the ground.

"Their dance outfits are called regalia. Each outfit is different and expresses the life of the individual dancer. The Dakota craft theirs of vibrant colors, like a rainbow, and use beautiful geometric designs. This represents the Great Plains."

"The songs they chant: Are they sung in their native tongue?" I asked.

"Yes, so they may teach their children, and their children may teach their children about the old ways and their rich heritage."

I noticed a man was signaling for her to leave.

"Is that your husband?" I asked.

"Yes, I have to go. My kids are in the car."

"Just one more question…why do they dance in a circle?"

"The circle represents the cycle of life, and the dancers follow the pattern of the sun. It was nice meeting you," she said and hurried off.

As if on cue, the constant beat of the drums stopped, and the dance was over.

It was sizzling hot standing in the ninety-five degree sun. I felt like a giant piece of fried chicken—extra crispy on the outside and juicy on the inside—so, Doug and I left the pow-wow, and bought some sodas. We walked to the edge of the horseshoe-shaped parade grounds, and found

Smiling Places

refuge under some tall shade trees.

Surrounding the grounds were meticulously restored buildings—old barracks, officer's quarters, the post headquarters, stables, a blacksmith shop, a veterinary hospital. We noticed a person lugging a suitcase into the restored, present-day lodge. Everywhere I looked, I saw historic markers. There was even an archeological dig going on across from us; I figured the whole place was a historic treasure chest.

I didn't want to leave here without learning about its history. I did have a problem, though; I didn't know the first thing about Fort Robinson. So, I took it upon myself to walk the grounds of the old fort, to read every historic marker I could, to grab any brochures I saw, and to compile a historical "account according to Mel". Now, I must apologize in advance: I was in the throngs of heat stroke, and may have gotten some of my facts confused. Here goes:

>It all started in 1874 during the turbulent times of the frontier Indian Wars. Over 900 soldiers came here with one hammer, one saw, and one gun. The hammer and saw were for protection while the gun was used to build sleeping quarters. About a mile down the road, the Red Cloud Agency was having all kinds of problems. Chief Red Cloud, a famous Oglala Sioux warrior and statesman, was complaining about the quality of food and supplies that the agency was issuing to the Indians. The U.S. Census Bureau listed thirteen-thousand Sioux, Cheyenne, and Arapaho Indians camped at the agency. The latest Gallop Poll found that 12,995 didn't want to be there. Better yet, they didn't want *us* to be there. But the wise officials in Washington told them they had to live there. As you can imagine, tensions were high; and from this time forward, poll-taking took its place in American Politics.
>
>Now, about this time, a man named George Armstrong Custer ventured into the Black Hills. He wasn't supposed to because the treaty said the Black Hills were sacred Indian lands. Then, Custer said, "There's gold in them there Black Hills," and gold fever struck the white man. Washington political leaders threw up their hands and said, "Treaty? What treaty?", and the soldiers from Fort Robinson protected the prospectors.

Tickphobia

A few years later in 1877, Little Big Man, who was having a psychological identity meltdown, decided to become an agency policeman to help find "renegades." Before that, he had fought the white man, and during all that time, he had been hitting the bottle pretty heavily. So, when Crazy Horse—one of the greatest Oglala Sioux warriors who ever lived—was arrested and brought to Fort Robinson, Little Big Man was by his side as a foe, not a friend. Crazy Horse struggled when shown to the guardhouse, and another soldier killed him. The guardhouse has since been reconstructed on the exact spot where it once stood at Fort Robinson.

Then in the mid 1880's, the railroad arrived, and Fort Robinson became really important. When a government installation becomes real important, it expands because Washington sends it money and more troops. So, the famous black soldiers (called "Buffalo Soldiers" by the Indians) from the Ninth and Tenth Cavalry units came. They were paramount in maintaining order in the region for eighteen years.

When World War I rolled around, Fort Robinson "remounted" horses for the cavalry units. When World War II rolled around, the fort "demounted" horses, and surplused them (gulp). Now, I don't know about you, but when I hear the word "surplused", I think glue factories and dog food. Hey, the dog food could have been used to feed 14,000 K-9 Corps dogs that were trained here during World War II. I know, that last remark was not in good taste. I blame it on my heat stroke symptoms. Anyway, they even constructed a German prisoner-of-war camp here in 1943, and in 1948 the military post shut its doors.

Needless to say, I was hot and tired after figuring all this out. And Doug was muttering something about a museum that struck fear in my heart. Remember, this is the man who can spend hours in a single exhibit museum. I made him a deal: I would buy him a buffalo burger from the fort's restaurant, if he stayed out of the museum. Of course, the man was hungry; so, it wasn't long before we carried two buffalo burgers to our car. We were going to have a car-picnic-kind-of-thing while we

Smiling Places

drove around the 22,000 acre state park.

We had never eaten buffalo burgers before, and I thought mine was delicious. Buffalo meat has the advantage over beef of being lower in fat, cholesterol, and calories. I liked the leaner, less greasy taste of my burger. Doug craved the fat of beef. I wrapped up the rest of my sandwich for later when we came to a buffalo herd grazing by the road. I couldn't eat them while they were all staring at me. We arrived back at our campsite at dusk. We fell into bed almost immediately.

It was our last day in Nebraska. Tomorrow we would head to South Dakota. So, we took off for one last Nebraskan adventure and drove to the extreme northwest corner of Nebraska, where Wyoming, South Dakota, and Nebraska all come together—where badlands meet grasslands.

"Pretty remote out here," I told Doug as we headed toward Toadstool Geologic Park. It seemed like we had been driving for hours over gravel and dirt roads to reach these lunar-like rock formations. We had not seen a soul for miles.

"The park ranger told me this was a long trek, but well worth the visit," Doug said.

I was beginning to doubt we were actually heading anywhere. "Remote" was not an accurate description of this area. The road just rambled on, and on, and on.

Then, we saw them—rock hills that looked chalky white in the distance. Scattered about those rock hills were the most unusual rock formations. They looked like giant mushrooms with their caps cocked in precarious positions. Some had already fallen and crumbled. Others were in the process of being formed. The sculptured "toadstool" affect had come from wind and water erosion. The soft clay stem of the rock "mushroom" eroded quicker than the harder sandstone cap.

We parked and stepped out of the truck. A barren, lifeless landscape greeted us. The ground was hard and cracked in places, and it was littered with fossils. We noticed this place seemed hotter than our campground, which had been pushing ninety-one degrees at high noon. A hazy dust filled the air as the wind splashed around us, and it was dry—exceedingly dry. The atmosphere made it somewhat hard to breathe; so, we stayed close to the truck, although we would have loved to explore.

Reaching the fields of the 95,000-acre Oglala National Grasslands was a joy to us. We filled our lungs with the heavily scented, perfumed air of blooming flowers and native grasses. A dainty yellow flower covered miles and miles of the prairie—for as far as the eye could see. A

Tickphobia

purple flower that looked like foxglove and a white "primrose" type flower had begun to bloom, and patches of white and purple intermixed with the plush yellow carpet. The entire prairie seemed to sway as one in rhythm with the breezes, while songbirds flittered and perched on the tips of the taller grasses—just like those nasty ticks. We had been so preoccupied with Fort Robinson and toadstool rocks, that I had completely forgotten about those parasites. There had to be a hundred-million-zillion of them in this endless prairie, waiting to feed on any warm-blooded mammal that came their way. "Dinner," one tick called to his fellow ticks when a group of pronghorn antelopes walked out from some tall grasses adjacent to our truck.

An adorable baby antelope was being nursed by its mother. What a Kodak moment! Doug grabbed the camera and quietly left the truck. I don't think I would have done that. As far as I was concerned, once Doug left the safety of our truck, he became "contaminated man." I pushed the automatic door lock button, and looked at Doug through the windshield—the prairie grasses and ticks whipping all around him.

When the antelope in charge stuck his head straight up in the air, his horns formed a big "U" above his head. The pop of the door locks had spooked him. The white hairs of his rump seemed to stand up, and signal the others of danger with a bright white flash. All at once, the fastest mammals in North America took off running. They can reach speeds of sixty miles-per-hour; I figured this group, including the baby, were doing about eighty-two miles-per-hour when they "high-tailed" it out of there—so to speak.

My husband was a bit perturbed when his Kodak moment ran away. He mouthed for me to open the door. I shook my head no. He said, "please". I shook my head no. How could I possibly let "contaminated man" in the truck? Lord knows how many were still left in here from yesterday. I rolled the window down partway and told him I would hand him the tick spray. He glared at me, as I fumbled through our console, and found the can. As he got close and reached for the can through the window, I screamed. The tips of his fingers had turned black.

"What tick malady is *that*?" I wondered as I did a quick brain scan of tick diseases. Now, if I had been thinking clearly, I would have remembered the two newspapers we had read at our campsite late that morning—the newspapers with the cheap black ink. I wasn't thinking clearly, so I screamed even louder when I looked at my own blackened fingertips.

Smiling Places

The next few minutes are somewhat fuzzy to me. I know I jerked my neck back in time to escape strangulation. The tick spray can was yanked from my hand, and flew through the air by accident. It landed with a thud by the edge of the road, as its plastic top rolled under the truck. The tiny nozzle that controlled the spray was nowhere to be found. Vultures circled overhead eyeing Doug. A small car drove by, fairly quickly, kicking dust into Doug's face; he then coughed and rubbed his eyes. In my delicate condition, staring at my fingertips, I am surprised I unlocked the doors and let the unsprayed, "contaminated man" back into the truck. It must have been those circling vultures. They were right overhead and licking their curved, pointy beaks.

When we arrived home, I flopped on the couch and turned on the only TV station we could receive from this campground—a show about mothers needing makeovers. Let me tell you, Betty Crocker had packed up and left this woman, years ago. She wore a skimpy two-piece, black leather outfit with high-heeled boots and chains. This was AFTER the makeover. The woman looked like a reject from a 1960's Sturgis Biker's Rally. Of course, everyone was screaming on the show, which gave me a headache; so, I turned off the TV and went looking for a Tylenol.

I opened our truck's glove compartment and found my Tylenol bottle. I popped open the plastic lid, and peered inside. I did not see any pills, just a slightly damp tissue stuffed inside. My little pea-brain processed this familiar moment—Tylenol bottle, damp tissue—LIVE TICK!!! Now I remembered, but, I didn't see the tick. It had to be in that bottle somewhere, or in the truck, or *on me*. Just then, the pea-brained woman emitted high-pitched shrieks from inside the truck. Her shrieks went unanswered. The man lay inside the trailer surfing the one TV channel with his remote. He burst out laughing—a booming, sinister laugh. His eyes glowed red, as he rejoiced in hearing his woman's shrieks. He got off the couch, and spoke aloud, "Paybacks are so sweet, aren't they, Dear?" Then, the man locked the trailer door and went back to surfing. Sushi smiled and went back to sleep.

20 - Driving Mrs. Flatlander

In 1953 Sir Edmund Hillary and Sherpa Tensing Norgay climbed to the top of the world. As they stood atop Mount Everest and gazed 29,028 feet below, Sherpa Norgay saw a small section of flat terrain in the far-far-far-off distance. It took oxygen-deprived Norgay four agonizing minutes to raise his arm, and point toward it.

"What's that, boss?" he wheezed.

Sir Edmund, who was sucking on an oxygen bottle, was able to answer Norgay's question in sixty seconds.

"That's Dayton, Ohio in America," he gasped, as they started their downward trek off the mountain. "Flatlanders live there."

And, three days later, amidst all the fanfare of this mountain-climbing achievement, I was born—in the flatlands our heroes saw from the top of the world.

I spent my formative months crawling on flat floors, bouncing along flat sidewalks in my carriage, and riding on flat streets in my parents' car. No wonder I thought the world was flat—then, we moved across town to a new home, and I discovered "Dayton" hills. As a youngster, I raced up our neighborhood's seventy-five-foot "suicide hill," dragging my Radio Flyer sled behind me. I squealed with delight as the flying snow stung my cheeks while I rocketed down the snowpacked pathway. Only the bales of hay at the bottom of the hill stopped me from tumbling into the icy creek.

In warmer weather my friends and I grabbed our roller skates and scurried to the top of the steepest driveway in our neighborhood. We tightened the metal skate sides against our hard-rimmed saddle shoes with keys we wore around our necks. We waited for the spotter at the bottom of the driveway to yell, "*All clear*!" Then, we crouched down and pushed off with our hands. We sailed down the concrete hill, past the spotter, and over the curb to the opposite side of the street. We sprawled on the lawn, and grass stains soiled our clothes. What fun we had! So, when Doug and I decided to visit the Black Hills of South Dakota, I was

Smiling Places

excited! I loved the hills of my youth, and couldn't wait to explore our new destination.

Only one hundred miles separated us from The Black Hills. The next morning we broke camp and pulled into the Chadron Wal-Mart—Thing in tow. The smell of freshly-baked donuts permeated the store, so we bought a month's supply of RV chemicals, and a month's supply of the biggest, gooiest, delectable donuts you could ever imagine. Pangs of both guilt and hunger stabbed at our stomachs when the cashier tallied our purchases.

We left Chadron and headed north on Highway 385 in quite agreeable moods. We were high on sugar, and couldn't be happier. Doug threw in a Willie Nelson tape, and I babbled about how many pounds each bite of donut was adding to my derriere.

"Pretty soon, I won't fit into the front seat, let alone my jeans," I said as I bit into another jelly donut oozing with a red, sticky concoction and loaded with white, sugary icing that collapsed the middle of the donut. "I'd better weigh myself tomorrow."

Doug turned to me with chocolate icing-speckles hanging off his three-day growth of face stubble.

"Look over to your left on the field," he said with a huge smile on his face.

Two ATV's, driven by teenagers clad in cowboy hats and boots, were racing over pastureland chasing a herd of twenty cows: To where, I have no idea. What I couldn't get out of my mind, was the crazed look in those cows' eyes as they glanced over their shoulders when the ATV's gained on them.

"Are those the new steer in town?" one mooed. "Lord, help us if they catch us!"

We drove across the northern edge of the Nebraskan panhandle into South Dakota, our seventh state. Fields of petite yellow flowers stretched to the horizon in the Buffalo Gap National Grasslands. Soon, the yellow fields yielded to hills—small at first—and pockmarked by pine trees and grazing herds of pronghorn antelope. In the distance, huge, black, forbidding obstructions popped out of the prairie floors and created a looming wall of terror. Believe me, I sobered up in a matter of seconds when I realized those were the Black Hills—the very place we were headed to. Mountains of craggy rock piled thousands of feet high and covered by pine trees, emitted a dark, ominous glow from afar. Those Black Hills were as tall as any mountains I had ever seen east of

Driving Mrs. Flatlander

the Mississippi River.

I gulped, and then I gulped again, as my throat turned as dry as a salt lick. I quickly realized my honeymoon was over. I had met the challenge of the Nebraskan terrain, but today I was getting into some major elevations. My first thought was of the lunatic who called these mountains "hills." My second thought was how this flatlander would survive for three whole days and nights in the Black Hills. Forget that "survival-of-the-fittest" stuff. "Survival-of-the-Smartest" became my motto.

I looked at my husband. He smiled, as he effortlessly guided our truck and trailer to the campground, and lovingly caressed his four-wheel drive button, as he parked our trailer on a sheer hill. There was no way to level our trailer, except with a bulldozer. Our leveling blocks hid in their zippered cloth bag, afraid to come out when they saw our campsite. The nose of our trailer pointed downward at a 45-degree angle, ready to plummet onto the roof of the rig parked in front of us. "What if…"

"No, now don't think like that, Melodee. Zen, yes, that is it, Zen… Zen…Zen. Relax. Now that's better. Don't let the man see you upset. Do you know why? Because if the man knows you are scared, he will do everything in his power to make you fearless—over, and over again— until he breaks you. Be smart, and hide your fear from him. You must play along with his mountain fantasies: No matter how dreadful they might be."

I calmly opened our trailer door, and it almost swung me down the hill.

"Here, let me close that for you," Doug said.

"Thank you," I said sweetly, and pulled myself into our trailer doorway while holding the interior grab bar.

"I could check with the office and try to get another space," Doug suggested.

"Oh no, this one is fine," I lied. "The campground looks full. It would be a lot of trouble."

Doug looked at me quizzically, shrugged his shoulders, and handed me a bag of brochures he had picked up when he registered. Then, he shut the door and began to set up our campsite.

I made my way to the couch, and propped pillows between my body and the wall I was plastered against.

"What have I gotten myself into?" I wondered as I opened the bag and began reading. The area was enormous and full of adventure, not a good situation for a flatlander hiding her fear of heights. I was sur-

Smiling Places

rounded by 1.2 million acres of pine-tree clad "hills." From a distance, the trees gave the hills their black appearance. The entire range covered an area sixty-nine miles wide by 125 miles long. A small part extended into northeastern Wyoming. Seven "hills" were more than 7,000 feet high. The tallest, at 7,242 feet, was Harney Peak—the highest point east of the Rocky Mountains. Hyperventilating views of waterfalls, rock formations, streams, and cliff walls awaited me   Zen…Mountains are nothing but flatlands at an angle…Zen...Zen.

The next morning, Doug and I decided to visit Mount Rushmore. We ran downhill from our bedroom to the kitchen to plan our route. I would say the only thing that separated us from plunging headfirst through the front window was our kitchen table. We sat pinned against the table edge as it dug into our ribs like Scarlett O'Hara's corset. I held a South Dakota map up to my nose.

"Now, where did you say that road was?" I asked.

"Look in the upper dark green area."

"I am. I still don't see it."

A finger floated in front of my eyes.

"Look right here, by my finger. Can't you see that tiny gray squiggly line?"

"That's a gray squiggly line? I thought it was a crinkle in the paper."

"No, that's Iron Mountain Road, part of the Peter Norbeck Scenic Byway," Doug said.

Chills cascaded down my spine. Peter Norbeck was well-known in flatlander circles as one of those "Hill" huggers. I heard the man came to The Black Hills in the early 1900's and befriended a mountain goat. Together, they roamed the area and forged the Mother of All Byways (MOAB). Today, these byways are consistently listed in the Top Ten Scenic Drives in America. Unfortunately, to a flatlander, "scenic" means one thing…diapers. So, with that thought in mind, I asked Doug if he was sure the teeny-weeny gray, squiggly line took us to Mount Rushmore?

"It gets us close," Doug answered.

It got us close all right—from a bird's eye view. I saw the tops of the four carved President's heads and their noses protruding from the side of a mountain.

"Isn't this view something?" Doug asked me, after stopping inches short of Thelma and Louise's final maneuver.

"I can't quite put my finger on a word for this view," I answered, as

Driving Mrs. Flatlander

my flatlander genes went flat-line.

We encountered hairpin turns, and pigtail bridges that looped over themselves, compliments of Mr. Norbeck and his friendly goat. Long, narrow tunnels swallowed us whole, and framed Mount Rushmore like a painting. I prayed to the Mountain Gods to delay oncoming vehicles. When we came to the only place wide enough for a restroom in the entire seventeen miles of this scenic nightmare, I shouted, "Stop the truck!"

I collected my bulging eyeballs, and staggered to the restrooms, my every move watched by the four sculptured Presidents. A posted sign said the restrooms were closed due to vandalism.

"Vandalism, way up here? Is this a joke?" I thought as

I kicked and clawed at the padlocked door. My Zen was completely out of whack as was my mind. I saw George Washington turn his carved head toward Abe Lincoln and say,

"We got us another tourist, didn't we, Abe?"

Then, Abe laughed and replied, "Sure was a good idea of yours, George, closing those restrooms."

"Oh, I agree," Thomas Jefferson added. "Relieves the boredom up here."

Teddy Roosevelt smiled, and nodded in agreement. I ran back to the truck, and didn't look back.

"The restrooms are closed," I told Doug. I didn't tell him the *Talking Stoneheads* had closed them.

We left the rest area, and twisted and turned down the mountain for another agonizing forty-five minutes. My husband was such a card. He stopped at every scenic overview on the way down. I was totally not amused by his antics. At one point, I contemplated dangling the man off the side of the mountain on a 500-foot bungee cord. Lucky for him, we finally emerged from the staggering heights to a fairly level highway.

"This highway should take us to Mount Rushmore," Doug said.

"I have a pocket knife for the bungee cord if it doesn't," I said to myself.

A short while later, we pulled into the main entrance.

I was elated! There was Mount Rushmore—gloriously above us—sitting on top of (where else?) 6,800-foot Rushmore Mountain. I looked up and could see all the President's nostrils—seemingly big nostrils—on sixty-foot tall faces carved from a giant outcropping of granite. The four faces did not speak nor move this time—but remained positioned at different angles—giving the sculpture a most unique three dimensional ef-

Smiling Places

fect.

"I made it," I thought, and removed my feet from the scuffed dashboard. (I had assumed a fetal position to handle my flatlander scenic crisis.)

"Well, that was a lot of fun," Doug said, and wiped the perspiration from his upper lip.

Oh, I bet it was fun, you male macho super-freak! Ah, ha! You are sweating! Serves you right! Not used to driving those scenic routes, are you Mister? Well, you can count on one thing, there is no way that I am going back the same way we got here. You'd better be getting out that map of yours, and figuring out another way home, if you want to stay married to me for another twenty-four hours! And no teeny-weeny gray squiggly lines either! I want a thick, black line—a real thick, black line! Do you hear me, you silly man? Well, do you?

Of course, he didn't hear me. I was screaming at him in my head; instead, I turned to Doug and patted his hand. Yikes! I caught my reflection in the mirror. I bore an uncanny resemblance to Carrie on her prom night—*after the bucket had been dropped.* Zen...Zen.

As you can see, I need to take some time to compose myself. Hey, I'm sorry, but I've had a rough morning. In the meantime, how would you like to hear my take on the history of Mount Rushmore? Excited? I bet you are!

Before we begin, however, I want to get two things straight. Alfred Hitchcock had a replica of Mount Rushmore built at MGM Studios in Hollywood. Cary Grant and Eva Marie Saint used the replica in the 1959 movie thriller *North by Northwest.*

Second, Mount Rushmore was not named after anybody who had anything to do with the carving on that mountain. A lawyer named Charles E. Rushmore, from New York City (of all places) just happened to be taking a stroll with his friend in the Black Hills in 1885. Of course, adding a little hooch to this story wouldn't hurt. So, when Charles looked up, and asked his friend what the name of a mountain was, his friend took a swig and said, "Let's call it Mount Rushmore, after you, Good Buddy." Of all the dumb luck, the name stuck—and 42 years later, the mountain carving began.

Now, the real story of Mount Rushmore begins around 1924, when State Historian Doane Robinson was sitting at his desk in South Dakota reading a newspaper article about the creation of Stone Mountain in Georgia. At that very same moment, American Sculptor Gutzon Bor-

Driving Mrs. Flatlander

glum, and his crew, sat atop Stone Mountain in Georgia chiseling Robert E. Lee's face.

"It's not fair," Doane pouted and put down the newspaper. "How come they got Gutzon? I want Gutzon Borglum to carve figures in our Black Hills."

So, Doane went to his friend, South Dakotan U.S. Senator Peter Norbeck (yes, *that* Peter) who, by this time, had held every political office in the state of South Dakota.

"Peter," Doane said, "I think my idea would put South Dakota on the map."

Peter agreed because South Dakota wasn't on any maps. (OK, maybe, a few.) So, Doane invited Gutzon to South Dakota.

"Where's South Dakota?" Gutzon asked.

It just happened that Gutzon was not a happy camper at Stone Mountain. He was a flamboyant kind of person who didn't get along with too many people—let alone the daughters of the Civil War. Funding shortages only compounded the problems with the Stone Mountain Project. So, he left Georgia temporarily, hopped on a 747, and parachuted into the Black Hills since there was no airport around. (Hey, I told you I had a very trying morning.)

When Gutzon met Duane he said, "Man, those local yokels back in Georgia are driving me crazy. I can't take much more of this. I'm sick and tired of this regional hero stuff. If you want regional heroes carved in the Black Hills, you can find another sculptor!"

Well, Duane had already spent his entire 1924 budget on a 747 airplane ticket for Gutzon, so he really had no other choice.

"OK, so what do you have in mind?" Duane asked.

"We need something big…something huge…something where history is timeless and my paychecks are endless…something dedicated to our country and 'yours truly'…something that…that…"

It was right on the tip of Gutzon's brain, but his vision was clouded. He needed to clear his mind with a walk in the Black Hills. It was a cloudy day. He strode to the place where Charles E. Rushmore had stood and looked up. Just at that moment, the sun tore through the clouds, and lit up the side of Mount Rushmore with a brilliance never before seen by any man.

"That's it," Gutzon cried, "I will build a Shrine of Democracy right here, on this mountain. Who better to embellish my shrine but famous Presidents! Wow! Just look at that igneous (granite) rock. It only

Smiling Places

erodes one inch every 10,000 years. My work will live on forever!"

Then, Gutzon returned to Georgia and the Stone Mountain Association Board fired him a few months later. Well, to say the least, Gutzon was enraged.

"Nobody puts Gutzon in a crevice," he screamed.

Gutzon raced up Stone Mountain and flung his models of Stonewall Jackson's head and Robert E. Lee's shoulders off the side of the mountain. Then, he fled Georgia under a barrage of gunfire from Georgian officials, who chased him clear to North Carolina. Eventually, Borglum returned to the Black Hills, and began planning his new undertaking.

In the meantime, the summers in Washington D.C. were hot and muggy—simply stifling. In June of 1927, President Calvin Coolidge and his wife, just happened to spend their summer vacation in the Black Hills. What a coincidence! The formal dedication of Mount Rushmore was slated for August! There was only one problem: how to keep the President there until August?

"Teach him to fish," someone whispered, "the South Dakotan way."

Wire was run across the creek, above and below the President's vacation quarters in Custer State Park's Game Lodge. Each night, more fish were secretly dumped into that stretch of creek. Even a two-year-old could have fished that creek. The President was so pleased that he extended his vacation—either because he loved to catch big fish in three seconds, or he thought a fifth head (his own) might look good carved on the mountain. On August 10, 1927, President Coolidge rode horseback to the site and *formally* dedicated Mount Rushmore while 1,000 onlookers listened. Gutzon Borglum climbed up the mountain, and *formally* drilled the first six construction holes, and, Peter Norbeck *formally* smiled at all the big bucks the President had promised.

There you go. Interesting, huh? Well, I think I'm a bit more relaxed now. My Zen has now returned like a zap from a stun gun; I have to run. Doug is waiting for me on Grandview Terrace, Mount Rushmore's main viewing area. See ya there!

People come to Mount Rushmore to take pictures. Many wander around this mountain for decades trying to take the perfect picture. I am here to tell you: there is no perfect snapshot. The Faces don't line up right. I had not noticed this until I reached the Terrace, and tried to use my camera. Back and forth I walked, surrounded by a group of camera deadheads. If I stood in one spot, I had a clear view of Washington's face, but Jefferson's was partially hidden. If I moved to another spot,

Driving Mrs. Flatlander

Roosevelt would be front-and-center, but Washington and Lincoln were to the side. I quickly concluded Mount Rushmore had many great photographic opportunities. So many, in fact, that I felt like the photographer for the *Sports Illustrated* swimming suit issue. OK, George, let's work it. That's right, You're Number One! How about a profile of that cute hair-do? CLICK. Hey, Teddy, give me that Rough Rider look. Oh, you BAD BOY! CLICK. And Thomas, my main man, four cents an acre! Better than The Donald. CLICK. Yeah, that's it, Abe, Show-Me-Your-Pennies. CLICK.

My last snapshot of Abe put me near a group of sophisticated photographers, whose tripods and super-sized camera lenses lined the stone wall facing the mountain. Now, this group acted like they knew what they were doing. When in reality, they were clueless as to how to get the perfect picture. These sophisticates did have a plan, however. Every few minutes or so, they picked up their tripods in unison, walked a few steps, and set them up for a new picture. It was as if a Marine drill sergeant was there barking out that snappy little tune to his recruits.

"Pick your tripods off the ground,"
Answer, "Pick your tripods off the ground,"
"Walk four steps and put it down,"
Answer, "Walk four steps and put it down,"
"One, two,"
Answer "three, four"
"One, two,"
Answer "THREE, FOUR!"

Personally, I think we ought to give these photographers a challenge. My suggestion is to carve ALL the President's faces in the Black Hills. I mean, why stop at four faces? Every carved face could be positioned in a different direction—for virtually, trillions of photo opportunities. Just think about it! We could have our own shutter-crazy Survivor series right here in the Black Hills. And the winner is: the last person out in a straight jacket.

I found Doug sitting on a bench watching me do all the camera work. I handed him the camera, and we followed the half-mile Presidential Trail to the base of Mount Rushmore. Now, I have learned over the years, when you hand a man a camera, you can expect some strange pictures. In this case, Doug became curious, or should I say obsessed, with

Smiling Places

the Presidents' eyes.

The stone eye sockets of The Faces have been hollowed out, and a large piece of wood (perhaps a railroad tie) inserted in the center— like a wooden eye to give The Faces depth and realistic expressions. Kind of neat, until you develop the pictures, and have 50 different shots of eyeballs staring at you.

The same goes for the smooth rock surface to the left of Washington. Gutzon had originally put features of Jefferson's face there, but flaws in the rock prevented him from finishing, so—BAM! Jefferson's original face was obliterated. Thirty pictures of the same smooth rock surface get boring after awhile.

Then, Doug took one set of pictures in Gutzon's workshop and museum that I could not figure out. Let me explain. Gutzon had built a model of Mount Rushmore in 1936, midway through construction. This very model was on display, and scaled to one-inch equaling one-foot on the mountain. Gutzon incorporated the upper torsos of the Presidents in the model hoping to carve their bodies, as well as their faces, on the mountain. Gutzon's dream was never realized. He died in 1941 from complications after surgery. His son Lincoln spent another seven months on site, but the sculpture was left largely to the degree of completion Gutzon had directed. When Doug's pictures of the model were developed, I found that he had only taken the lower half of the model. Now, we had pictures of clay torsos but no heads. I was curious as to why Doug did this, so I asked him.

"Well, you had taken all those pictures of the real Faces on the mountain. Why did I need to waste film on the model faces?" he answered, seriously I might add. (Oh, to get inside a man's brain for just a day!)

By the time we reached the gift shop, we were starving. I had smelled the bacon and eggs, and my stomach juices started singing. I quickly purchased a few gifts, and we ended up at the Concessions area, sitting next to a glass wall overlooking Mount Rushmore. Our plates piled as high with food as the mountain itself—scrambled eggs, bacon, hash browns, biscuits, gravy, fruit, and a huge piece of chocolate cake for the man. Our delicious meal was low calorie—and fat free, of course!

We returned to our trailer via a very pleasant "thick black line." When we pulled into the campground, a truck and Airstream trailer were parked in the check-in lane. Suddenly, Doug hit the brakes, and I tasted my breakfast all over again.

Driving Mrs. Flatlander

"Aaahhh," I screamed. "What's wrong?"

"Ohio—Greene County! Look at the license plate," Doug said as he pulled the truck over.

"Yeah, great, but did you have to stop like that?"

"Sorry," he apologized.

We watched two people walk out of the registration office.

Doug smiled.

"Can you believe it? I know them," Doug said excitedly. "They both work in contracting at Wright-Patterson, and handled some of my projects."

We both exited our truck, eager to speak to them. It was wonderful seeing folks from back home, even if they were only business acquaintances.

"Doug, is that you? What in the world are you doing out here?" Ellen asked.

"I retired, you know. So we left Dayton, and are traveling around the country."

"That sounds like what I want to do, but I still have to work on him," Ellen said and nudged her husband. "Roger, you should talk to Doug."

Then, Doug introduced me to the couple. When I shook Roger's hand, our flatlander eyes met. Now I understood why Roger was hesitant to travel.

"So, whatever happened to Joe Wertz?" Doug asked, and old home week began.

Unfortunately, these nice people were only staying overnight. They had to be in Montana the next day for Ellen's father's 75th birthday celebration. So, we decided to spend the rest of the day together. Ellen got into the driver's seat of their truck and pulled the Airstream into their overnight camp spot. Doug found that strange. I didn't. Roger was just practicing his flatlander survival skills.

After Ellen and Roger had settled in, the four of us climbed into our truck and headed for Custer State Park, just down the road. Encompassing 73,000 magnificent acres, Custer is one of the largest state parks in the nation today. And, yes, Peter Norbeck helped establish the park in the early 1900's by setting aside the huge tract of land and restocking the area with wildlife.

"You ladies doing OK back there? Doug asked.

"It's a little cramped, but we're managing," I answered. Our Tundra's backseat was not known for spaciousness.

Smiling Places

"So what would you all like to do? Mel and I aren't too familiar with this park," Doug said.

"Oh, we've been through here quite a few times on the way to Ellen's family." Roger said. "I think we should stay on this road. Eventually, it winds through the park and is quite beautiful with gently rolling grasslands and awesome wildlife. It's definitely one of my favorite drives of anyplace I have visited."

A flood of relief came over me. My fellow flatlander had just told me in so many words that the road we were on was safe. I smiled at Roger.

"So what wildlife have you seen here?" I asked.

"Bison!" Roger answered. "Lots of them."

"It's one of the biggest herds anywhere. They have around 1,500," Ellen added. "Now, when I grew up in Montana, ranchers had private herds, but nothing like this."

So, that's why Ellen was driving. I knew she wasn't a flatlander.

"Yeah, one year we were in a buffalo jam here," Roger said.

"A buffalo jam?" I said. "Is that like a bear jam?"

"Well, not exactly," Roger answered.

Just then, Doug stopped our truck.

"Have you guys ever been up there?" Doug asked and pointed to a narrow gravel road that seemed to go straight up the side of a mountain.

"No," Ellen said excitedly.

"No," Roger said quietly.

"The sign says it leads to a look-out. Want to try it?" Doug asked.

"Yes," Ellen answered enthusiastically.

"No," Melodee answered just as enthusiastically.

"I don't think we should take…."

Roger's words were lost to the sound of gravel crunching under our tires.

"Don't worry. If the road gets bad, I can always turn around," Doug assured us.

"Oh yeah, I've heard that one before," I thought rolling my eyeballs.

Well, by the time we reached the top, not one of us was in the mood to see the view. Roger had turned pasty-white and my face was sickly-green after tasting my breakfast for the third time that day. Even Doug and Ellen were subdued. You see, Doug could not safely turn around on that road; so, he shifted our truck into four-wheel drive, and we crawled up a winding ridge at a steeper grade than our parked trailer. Nothing

Driving Mrs. Flatlander

separated us from a cliff but scattered Ponderosa pine trees. Roger drummed his fingers on the truck door, but nobody spoke a word—until we met the other car, that is, speeding down the middle of the road. In all the commotion, I remember the fast-moving car braking on gravel and traveling sideways toward our truck. I heard a man scream, but it wasn't Doug because Doug shouted, "I have to back up." He threw our truck into reverse, floored it, and just avoided the sliding car and the sheer cliff drop-off. Frozen with fear, Ellen and I watched the whole thing from the back seat. Thank goodness, nobody was hurt.

After that incident, Doug agreed not to take us on any more wild excursions—at least for the rest of the day. So, we took Roger's suggestion and followed the eighteen-mile Wildlife Loop Road that wound through the park. Doug and I were amazed at the abundance of wildlife—especially the large mammals—that roamed freely throughout the area. By the end of the day, we both had a pocketful of new experiences to add to our lifetime list of firsts.

Our first wildlife encounter happened as soon as we turned onto the Wildlife Loop Road. Four bighorn sheep—all Rams—walked down a rock-studded hill and crossed the road, right in front of our truck. They sauntered over to a grassy area, swinging their fat white rumps as if they didn't have a care in the world. We pulled over and could almost touch their massive horns that curled back over their ears and extended down past their cheeks. Horns that would be used for butting, not goring. They paused to look at us—the bothersome humans—and disappeared down a hill. I was thrilled! We had never seen bighorn sheep in the wild before…nor the mule deer that stood silhouetted against a cave's opening at the top of a hill.

Further down the road, I spotted a most interesting footpath that wandered over a grassy knoll. Roger flipped back the passenger seat and shut his eyes while Ellen, Doug, and yours truly explored the area. Two fairly large birds made quite a racket, and then eluded us by hiding in the grasses adjacent to the path. Every so often they popped their periscope-shaped necks up to keep us under surveillance. Mottled-brown in color and sporting ling, yellow beaks and legs, I concluded they were Upland Sandpipers, endangered in Ohio, but holding their own in South Dakota.

A little ways down the trail, we rounded a bend, and fourteen Pronghorn Antelope stood stoically between the remainder of the trail and us. In a split second, the antelope shed their stoics and took off running as if the starting gates at the Kentucky Derby had just rung open. A short dis-

Smiling Places

tance later, they stopped, and all heads turned to watch us. Soon, they lost interest—apparently satisfied we meant no harm. The adults feasted upon the rich grasslands while one baby antelope dashed in and out of the herd. Another baby slowly approached its mother, in a submissive posture, with its head hanging toward the ground. Then their noses touched and Mom gave her baby a lick on the face. Now, how cute is that?

Baby buffalo are cute, too, but I really didn't want to see one, nor its mother or father for that matter, on a desolate footpath leading to nowhere. I became a tiny bit concerned when we found a fistful of buffalo fur lying next to the path. I became a little more concerned when we came upon a buffalo wallow—a large dirt spot where buffalo wriggle on the ground to take dirt baths. I became a lot more concerned when we wandered further, and found—how do I say this—steaming, fresh buffalo chips. However, I can't *begin* to tell you just how concerned I was when we heard the unmistakable breathing—the "Humpf, humpf, humpf," of the bison's emphysema ward.

"Buffalo!" Ellen mouthed to us with a look of terror on her face that rivaled the kid in the water with Jaws.

"Where?" Doug mouthed back.

Ellen shrugged her shoulders. Doug looked at me. I shrugged my shoulders. Nature was playing a cruel trick on our ears. We couldn't tell if they were in front of us, behind us, or to the sides of us, but there was no doubt in our befuddled minds that they were close-by.

We did know that our truck, our only safe haven, was behind us. So, we turned around and walked quietly, but quickly, down the footpath which suspiciously looked more and more like an animal path to me—a buffalo stomping ground, in fact! And Doug, who claims that chivalry is not dead, brought up our rear, ready to sacrifice himself to save the women. Now this, our only line of defense, did not give me any warm fuzzies. A 2,000 pound bull could make mincemeat out of my 180-pound man in a matter of seconds.

But the longer we walked, the fainter the "Humpfs" became. Soon, the "Humpf" sounds disappeared all together. It seemed like an eternity, but we finally rounded our last bend in the path and saw Roger pacing back and forth in front of our truck.

"I was so worried about you when I saw all the buffalo come down the path!" Roger said. "Surely you must have seen them?"

The three of us looked at each other.

Driving Mrs. Flatlander

"We heard them,' Doug answered.

"Can you believe 25-30 of them just came out of there a few minutes ago and crossed the road in front of the truck?"

"I guess we were lucky they didn't cross our path," Doug responded.

We never did figure out how the buffalo got behind us, or did they get in front of us? Well, no matter, because a few minutes later they were all around us—1,500 of them, according to the park ranger—in the road, on the grass, under the pines, on top of hills, each weighing up to 2,000 pounds. Now, if I figured correctly, that's some three million pounds of iron pumping, steroid-popping chests, biceps, calves, and necks, all in one place...reminded me of a Mr. Universe convention—except participants were on all fours and had a bit more hair, but just a bit.

Now imagine, if you will, contending with three million pounds of muscle. We sat in a line of several vehicles on the Wildlife Loop Road. A sign posted by the road read:

"Buffalo can be dangerous. Do not approach."

I searched for part two of the sign—the part that said what to do if they approach you. The buffalo must have stretched a quarter mile or more. At every pause in the flow of brown furry bodies walking amongst our vehicles, we crept along at zero miles an hour to advance a few feet down the road. The buffalo were not bothered by the vehicles, but seemed to enjoy them, and used them for their own vices such as scratching and rubbing. The car in front of us did not fare well with one rambunctious bull's itch. He used the passenger side mirror as a scratching tool for his wooly head. The lady in the passenger seat dove for cover as the buffalo's horns clicked against the metal mirror, just a pane of glass away from her head. The bull finished his scratch and left their car's mirror dangling by one screw. Believe me; the humans did not get out of their car to fix that mirror.

The babies, or calves, were most active. They leaped about like little lambs. Often they waged battle with another formidable calf by challenging him to a head-butting dual—pushing their strong bodies back and forth to prepare for their manhood. Then, like most men, the calls of their stomach outweighed the calls of the wild, and they tore around looking for their mother's milk, often nursing within inches of vehicles.

But pound for pound, I'd lay my money on the begging burros as the

Smiling Places

park's most dangerous mammal.

"Oh my," you are thinking, "those adorable little pointy-eared, fuzzy creatures that the park service encourages tourists to feed? Now, how could they be dangerous?"

Well, first of all, their genes are strong, my friend. Their donkey ancestors used to haul people to the top of 7,242 foot Harney Peak, until the park service let them go wild. Today, the donkey *gang members* hang out in "the hood" around a feeding station on Wildlife Loop Road—just waiting for you and me to drive by. The Alpha Burro, the strongest and biggest of the bunch, stands in the road and blocks your vehicle so you have to stop, just like we did.

Like the rest of the gullible tourists, Ellen and I exited our only safe haven and at once were surrounded by the toe-stomping, finger-chomping eating machines.

"What cha got to eat lady?" the ringleader burro asked me. Maybe it was the half-burnt cigarette hanging out of the side of his mouth, but he reminded me of Humphrey Bogart—in a weird sort of way.

"I have some delicious cereal," I answered and pulled out the large box.

"Cereal? Is that all you tourists think we eat? Where's all the good stuff like the fresh veggies and fruits? I bet you have them stashed away in that picnic cooler. Well, are ya gonna hand it over?"

"Yeeess," I stammered while the other gang members pinned Ellen against our truck.

I emptied the cooler's contents on the ground away from the truck, and Ellen and I made our get-away.

Needless to say, we arrived back at the campground too tired for conversation and coffee. Unfortunately, Ellen and Roger were "leaving at the crack of dawn," so we hugged like old friends and promised to email. When we pulled away from their campsite, I, again, felt sad for all the old friends and family we had left behind. But then I gazed upwards, and a million stars twinkled back. Even my trailer—parked precariously at the side of a hill—could not overshadow this beautiful moment. As I climbed uphill to our bed and laid my head on the pillow, way above my feet, I composed a little prayer, just for me.

> Now I lay me down to sleep
> The blood is rushing to my feet
> If nature calls me during the night
> I hope the seat is still upright.

Driving Mrs. Flatlander

Hey, it was a bit difficult moving around our slanted trailer, and, yes—for those of you who care—my prayer was answered.

The next morning we slept in until eight a.m.—late for us. Usually, the morning bird chatter would wake us. This particular morning, the scrumptious smells of Texas cuisine floated into our trailer from an adjacent campsite. Now, I wasn't about to stick my head out our door without weighing myself first. After all, that cuisine would have to wait if some unsightly blubber had not magically fallen off my body. So, I slid the scale to the middle of the bathroom floor and stepped on, leaning downhill of course.

"Doug," I screamed, "I've lost ten more pounds!!! No wait, make that thirteen...fourteen....seventeen pounds!"

Who was I kidding? The pitch of the trailer enabled me to lose as much weight as I wanted in a split second. For a fleeting moment, I was in hog heaven—so to speak.

"Maybe I should find a doctor's office built on a hillside," I thought.

Pitch or no pitch, I jumped out of the trailer to investigate the intoxicating food smells.

Well, those Texans sure knew how to cook! They were frying up a huge batch of breakfast burritos. I was invited to share their goodies almost as soon as my feet touched the dirt. I ran back inside and grabbed some fruit salad and my husband. Other neighbors had already gathered around the Texan's campsite. So, we had ourselves an impromptu morning potluck. Those burritos were so exquisite that my mouth is watering right now just thinking about them. And for all you food gurus out there, those nice Texans did share the burrito recipe, but not on paper I am afraid. So, the recipe I am about to divulge may or may not be exactly what we feasted on that morning, but it is close:

Texan Breakfast Burritos
>Dice red peppers, green peppers, green onions, sweet onions, and celery; fry up with spicy, crumbly, breakfast sausage. Add some spices: I use garlic, paprika, salt, and a little cumin. Now, add shredded hash browns, and fry up with the sausage mixture. Add some fried scrambled eggs to mixture, and put a serving into a warm burrito. Serve with sour cream, shredded cheese, and fresh salsa.

Smiling Places

I do have a word of advice however—only eat breakfast burritos after two hours of strenuous exercise. We barely survived all that food and fell into a senseless state of overstuffed malaise. We chastised ourselves for our overindulgence and seriously considered lounging about in the trailer for the rest of the morning until we realized that sadly, this was our last day in the Black Hills.

So, with our tummies quite full, and our waistbands fully extended, we set off for Deadwood, that decadent, gold-rush boomtown of the late 1800's era. We parked in a trolley stop station at the edge of town—a town with only one main street, affectionately known as Deadwood Gulch. It was lined with renovated saloons, active gambling halls, and yesterday's houses of ill-repute. Other structures clung to steep rock, walls on both sides of the gulch, giving me a feeling of vertigo as I stared at the town's layout.

Deadwood was just beginning to liven up for the day when we arrived. Main Street was partially closed for Wild Bill Days with staged gunfights (my ears are still ringing from those blanks.) and sweet country music performed by the Oakridge Boys. A few props used in the skits were scattered about, including a small jailhouse and wooden wagons. Not too long ago, wagons had to be lowered into the gulch with ropes and windlasses. This was before the first train arrived in 1890.

But today, the two bumbling idiots from Ohio had arrived by truck, and we were ready for some action. We descended upon the casinos like two gambling aficionados. We each carried a crisp new $5.00 bill that burned holes in our pockets. In a matter of minutes—quite possibly seconds—Doug lost his money in the bowels of a greedy little poker machine. I was a bit more conservative and scouted out a warm, nickel slot machine that a lady had just vacated; it was strategically placed adjacent to a busy aisle.

I sat down with my cup of nickels at my side and talked to the machine. Then, I carefully massaged each nickel before I placed it into the slot.

"You have got to be kidding me," Doug said while standing behind me. This is going to take all day."

"C'mon, Baby, Come to Mama," I cooed putting another nickel in the slot.

All of a sudden, my machine started singing and belching nickels like there was no tomorrow!

"Put your cup under the hole," my man advised, now taking a sincere

Driving Mrs. Flatlander

interest in my gaming strategy.

Now, in the olden days, if you won some money, you were kind of expected to stick around for awhile and lose it again. Not me. I always quit while I am ahead. So, I cashed in my winnings—all $10.00 of it—and rushed out of the casino like I had just won a million.

Many gamblers like Wyatt Earp, Doc Holliday, and Wild Bill Hickok frequented Deadwood in its hey-day. Wild Bill's luck ran out in 1876 when he was shot and killed while playing poker just a few doors down from where I had seduced that slot machine. Supposedly, Wild Bill was holding a black pair of aces and a black pair of eights—now known as the dead man's hand—when killed.

They laid poor Wild Bill to rest in Boot Hill Cemetery on top of a monstrous hill overlooking his favorite hangouts—the gambling halls. Calamity Jane, Preacher Smith, and Potato Creek Johnny are all up there, too, keeping company with Wild Bill. Now, we really, truly wanted to pay our respects to these colorful characters, so we stood on Main Street and stretched our necks until our protruding veins ran blue—just to see to the top of that cemetery. It was one of those defining moments in our lives when our heads said, "Yes, yes, yes, you can climb up there," but our breakfast burrito said, "No way, don't even consider it!" We listened to the burrito and stayed in the gulch.

We left Deadwood a whole $3.85 richer—not a bad day's wages—for the year 1876, that is. But our winnings and more flew out of our pockets just thirty minutes later when we paid admission at our next destination—an ongoing work-in-progress to create the largest statue in the world—The Crazy Horse Memorial. When I say ongoing, I mean ongoing. The statue's dedication took place in 1948, a few years before I was born, and we all know that I am older than dirt (but not stone, I guess). OK, bad pun, but five of nine survivors of the 1876 Battle of Little Big Horn attended the dedication ceremony. Now that's old!

And Korczak Ziolkowski, the genius who created this conceptual masterpiece, was no stranger to rocks and chisels. Korczak had worked under the guidance of Gutzon Borlum on the Mount Rushmore project.

"Wow!" the Lakota people exclaimed while reading Korczak's resume. "Let's hire him for the Crazy Horse Monument. He will do a swell job."

So, the Lakota drew up a five-year contract, with option for another five years, and another five years, and another five years until they stopped counting.

Smiling Places

And Korczak said, "Okey Dokey. I want to spend the rest of my life hanging off the side of a mountain hammering stone."

And thus, the world's largest sculpture was born.

Now, very few people at that time knew what Crazy Horse had looked like. Crazy Horse himself forbade any and all photographs or sketches to be made of him. But the Lakota people wanted to honor Crazy Horse, their greatest warrior, whose skill in battle and loyalty to his people was unsurpassed by no other man. So Korczak created the model of the monument in the likeness of all North American Indians. He also determined the monument would extend out and wrap around the top and sides of a mountain—for 642 feet. This concept became known as an "in-the-round" sculpture and Korczak was satisfied.

Each day, Korczak dutifully climbed the mountain and meticulously chiseled another half-inch of the face on the monument; however soon he realized that he was a slow sculptor and that he needed help. So, with a *tiny* bit of help from his wife, they raised ten children, who were also slow sculptors. And when Korczak died in 1982, his family continued the project. Fifty years later, in 1998, the face on the Monument was finally finished. It is huge—nine stories high and big enough to fit all four heads of Mount Rushmore inside, but they still have a large portion of the monument left to carve—the body, hair, arms, hands, and horse.

This brings me to my next point. (It struck me as I looked back and forth from the finished model to the unfinished mountain carving…from the model to the mountain…model-mountain….model-mountain….Oh, it was downright dizzying!) So, I have something very important to say to anyone involved with the monument project. "WOULD YOU PLEASE HURRY UP? MY BIOLOGICAL CLOCK IS TICKING! I DON'T HAVE 250 YEARS LEFT TO WAIT FOR YOU TO CARVE THE REST OF THAT MONUMENT! Can't you procure like a million sticks of dynamite to blast the heck out of what is left on that mountaintop, PLEASE? I mean, when this sculpture is complete, it is supposed to be taller than the largest pyramid—even taller than the Washington Monument! I sure would like to see that, WOULDN'T YOU?"

Whew! Glad I got that off my chest! Now I can go shopping at the beautiful Crazy Horse Memorial visitor and cultural center, museum, workshop, and gift shop—all rolled into one, and I am here to tell you this was one impressive structure! The building was newly constructed, and more than 20,000 quality works of art and artifacts were on display for sale. I could not resist purchasing a few pieces of one-of-a-kind tur-

Driving Mrs. Flatlander

quoise jewelry, but Mr. Kill-Joy put his foot down when I longingly gazed at an inspirational painting that an artist was creating right before my eyes.

"You know you don't have room to put that in the trailer," he whined as he led me out of the door.

"I don't think that was very nice," I snapped as we walked back to our parked truck.

"You were digging through your purse to see how much money you had, weren't you?"

"So, what if I was?"

"We can't travel with a painting. You know that."

"Oh, all right. So, what do you want to do now?" I asked the man who was now on Letterman's top-ten list for why husbands are annoying.

"Well, since this is our last day here, I want to go back to Custer State Park."

"Yeah, that was neat," I said thinking about the wildlife, but then I became suspicious. "Why do *you* want to go back?"

"Well, the wildlife was awesome, and the scenery was outstanding," he answered.

Had I heard the word scenery? What was this man up to?

"OK, Mister. Quit beating around the bush. What is it that you want to do in Custer State Park?"

"I want to take the Needles Highway—part of that Peter Norbeck Scenic Byway."

"Instead of Byway, how about Noway," I said as my flatlander genes bristled. "I am not going up there with you today. I have had it with scenic roads. You can just leave me right here if that is what you are planning to do."

"My, my…touchy, aren't we? I thought you liked our ride to Mount Rushmore."

"About as much as I like eating squiggling earthworms," I said.

"Please? It is supposed to be one of the best scenic drives in America."

"Nope!"

"I'll give you a nice foot-rub tonight."

"Double nope."

"How about if we pick up some ice cream on the way home?"

Now, that was hitting below the belt. "Nope, nope, and double nope. But maybe if you bought me a painting."

Smiling Places

"No painting! Oh, all right. I won't go on the Needles, but can we go to the park anyway?"

"OK, if you promise no Needles!"

"I promise," Doug said.

Well, it wasn't the Needles, but it was the Thread. When he said, "I can turn around if it gets too bad," I should have stopped him then and there, but I didn't. Hadn't I learned anything from yesterday with Ellen and Roger in the truck?

So, when we came to a very wide—and I emphasize *very wide*—dirt road, Doug got this innocent look on his face. "Let's take this road through the park to the visitors' center instead of going around."

"OK." I agreed for some reason that now escapes me, and I did this willingly, knowing that the road was not marked on the state park map.

The first thing we saw should have clued me to ask my husband to turn around. A lone buffalo stood in the middle of that wide dirt road and posed for us. Then, we drove on for a few more miles and saw more buffalo taking dust baths. We took another intersecting road and started climbing straight up—like The Beast at Kings Island—slowly chugging up that first hill where terror awaits you anticipating the drop down. It was at that point where the road became exceedingly, excruciatingly, extraordinarily narrow—almost too narrow for our own truck, let alone another oncoming vehicle. But I didn't have to worry about that. There was only one fool in this world who would deliberately drive on a mountain goat path.

"Tor run," I said from underneath the coat now draped over my head.

"What?" Doug asked. "I can't understand you."

"TOR RUN," I said louder.

"I still can't understand you."

I pulled my coat off my head and screamed, "TURN AROUND, YOU IDIOT!"

It echoed through the open truck windows five times before dissipating.

"I can't; it's too narrow."

"Get me off of here right now!" I said in a voice that rivaled the possessed Linda Blair in *The Exorcist*.

"What do you want me to do, back-up all the way down this mountain?"

"Yes, back-up, if that's what it takes!"

Now, it was about this time that I saw a little cloud of dust off in the

Driving Mrs. Flatlander

distance. I shut my eyes and opened them again. Another truck was approaching. I looked out of my passenger window and could not see the road under my door. What I *did* see were little stones falling from the unstable goat path and careening down the sheer wall of rock as we clung to it. I lost sight of those stones as they fell, oh, maybe a "mere" eight-hundred feet or so to the bottom of the canyon.

"How are you possibly going to get past that truck?" I asked hysterically as I prayed:

> "Though I drive through the canyon of the shadow of depth, I will fear no height. I know that you are with me Lord and that heaven certainly must be flat."

"Oh, will you quit worrying? I see a small cut-out in the rock wall ahead. The truck can pull over there. Then, we can pass it."

Sure enough, the truck pulled over and waited for us to approach. Of course, the other truck was hugging the rock wall. We were the ones who would fly off that cliff if our tires left the path.

Doug approached at zero miles-per-hour and stopped about five feet short of the other truck to survey the situation. It was like a stand-off at OK Corral. They both pulled in their drivers' side mirrors, and Doug crept along at one foot-per-hour: OK, so maybe it was a *little* faster. As we passed the other man, he grinned, waved, and said, "Hi." I couldn't believe it! The fool was actually *enjoying* this moment of terror! Well, I certainly didn't feel very friendly, and—I must confess—I stuck my left hand under my coat and flipped the man the bird. Then, I directed my upright finger at my husband. Sorry, but it did take away some of the intense anxiety I was feeling.

Somehow, we passed the truck without a scratch. Only once did Doug put on the brakes because he thought he felt our tires slipping off the goat path. A few minutes later the path widened to a one-lane road, and then we descended from the cliff into a wooded, fairly-level area. I began to relax a bit and heard the woods come alive with the songs of birds. I couldn't resist, and I identified numerous birds with my ears. I do have a special talent: I can spot birds with my ears way before anyone picks them out with their binoculars. I guess I bird-hear instead of bird-watch. Since I am bragging, might I add that I am a great asset to

Smiling Places

take along on bird walks? *Flat* bird walks!

Of course, I had had a rough afternoon, and after my latest flatlander thriller, I was hungry. I had digested the last remnants of my breakfast burrito when we saw the lone buffalo.

"Would you like an apple?' I asked the man (I was still furious at.)

"No, thanks. I'll wait until we get to the visitors' center."

"Maybe his will have a worm in it," I thought reaching into the back seat for the cooler.

I was fumbling with the handle when I heard Doug's unmistakably chilling words, "Holy Bleep!"

The color drained from my face. I didn't want to turn around, but, of course, I had to. Then, I came face-to-face with—and I am not kidding here—an M-16 rifle pointed right at our truck.

A man in fatigues yelled, "Stop! Identify yourselves!"

I noticed Doug kept his hands on the steering wheel in plain sight and calmly answered the man.

"I am Doug Tomsu and this is my wife Melodee Tomsu."

"Why are you here?'

"We were visiting Custer State Park and followed this dirt road from the other side."

"Please pull over there," he said while pointing to two other men also wearing fatigues and holding M-16 rifles. He said something into his hand-held radio as we pulled forward.

As you can imagine, I was a basket case.

'Now you've done it," I whispered to Doug.

"Don't worry. It's just a National Guard Reserve Unit," he whispered back.

Worry, why in heaven's name should I be worried? It was very simple, really. Let me lay it out for you: The bivouacked encampment stretched for a quarter mile and stood between us and the main road. Camouflaged vehicles and canvas tents lined both sides of the dirt road. Everybody—and I mean *everybody*—was carrying an M-16 rifle and a radio. Were they loaded? Do you think I was stupid enough to ask one of them? There was no way in Hades that I was going to turn around to go back up that mountain on that cliffhanger path to get my husband out of this mess. No way! So, quite simply, we had two choices: Either these Reservists were going to let us pass through their Checkpoint Charlies to reach the main road, or I was going to push Doug out of the truck

Driving Mrs. Flatlander

and floor it. That Tundra had great pick-up.

At our next checkpoint, one of the two men motioned for us to stop.

"May we see some identification?" he asked.

"It's in my pocket," Doug answered.

"Go ahead and get it."

Doug reached into his pocket and pulled out his wallet. He handed the man his driver's license, my driver's license, and his Department of Defense identification card.

The Reservist stepped away from our truck with our identification and radioed someone. A few minutes later, he handed them back.

"It's OK. We are going to let you pass," he told us.

Well, that about concludes my big adventures in the Black Hills. Pretty exciting, huh? We went through several Checkpoint Charlies that afternoon before we found our freedom on the paved open road.

I felt like I had lived numerous lifetimes in those hills as we pulled away from our campsite the next morning.

Doug told me this *flatlander* hadn't fooled him about her fear of heights. He knew from the very beginning—the first time I saw the Black Hills.

"The expression on your face was priceless," he laughed.

"Oh, and that time the restroom was closed and you came back to the truck, well, you looked like you had seen a ghost."

"Talking Stoneheads," I said correcting him. "So, you drove me to those dizzying heights on purpose?"

"Just to help you conquer your fears. Of course, I did enjoy watching you squirm and attempt to hide your fears from me. I don't think too many women can do that," he quipped.

I was not amused.

"But seriously," he added, "I think it helped you, and I am glad I did it."

I wouldn't admit it, but he was right. I had left some of my flatlander genes in the Black Hills. I should have left my husband there, too, with the next remark he made.

"You just wait until Montana!" he said with a big old grin on his face. "This was just a warm-up exercise."

Smiling Places

Oh, really? Give me those Yellow Pages. Let's see...Towing... Truck Towing...Truck Towing and Husbands Towed Free. Now *that's* the company I want to call. I wonder if I throw in our cat, whether I could get a discount?

21 - Bumbling Through

So, what is worse than two bumbling idiots from Ohio? How about two bumbling idiots from Ohio in Montana? Or worse yet, how about two bumbling idiots from Ohio who think they are in Montana but are actually in Wyoming? That happened to us the next morning when we left the Black Hills, got on Interstate 90, and headed towards our next destination: Billings, Montana.

We had reservations in Billings that night at—get this—the very first KOA Kampground in the world, established in 1962. Can you imagine all the VW camper buses and Airstream trailers that had camped there in the 1960's and 1970's? Personally, I was excited—a world's first with a touch of nostalgia thrown in but that nostalgia was six to seven hours northwest of us, off of Interstate 90.

So for us, it was one of those long-drive days, and I hated long-drive days, especially on interstates. They were so B-O-R-I-N-G! I could only stare at sixty-five mph moving terrain for so long before I felt like my brain had been lobotomized. And I certainly didn't expect to take an unplanned, sixty-mile, out-of-the-way sightseeing excursion on one of our long-drive days, but that is exactly what my adventuresome husband decided to do—much to my chagrin.

We hadn't been traveling on I-90 too long when Doug pointed to a sign that flew past my window.

"Did you see what was on that sign?" he asked.

"I think it was a Meadowlark," I answered.

"No, not the bird, but what was written on the sign."

"Mileages to cities?" I guessed.

"How about Devil's Tower National Monument? It's our next exit."

"You aren't thinking of going there, are you?"

"Well, as a matter of fact..."

I interrupted him. "Do you realize we are now about six hours from Billings?"

"But Mel, you loved *Close Encounters of the Third Kind*."

Smiling Places

He was trying to bribe me, of course, and normally I would have jumped at the chance to see the mysterious rock formation and to relive Steven Spielberg's movie, but it was just one of those days when my high-spirited self had taken a temporary hiatus. I felt drained and saw myself relaxing at a KOA campsite instead.

"How many miles is it from here?" I asked reluctantly.

He shrugged his shoulders. "I don't know. But I'm sure it can't be too far."

"Yeah, yeah. I've heard that one before," I said as I unfolded a Montana map—quickly, I might add. The exit was within sight.

"Hey, it's free," Doug said. "We can use our National Park Pass."

"Let's see, if I crook my pinky finger like the road, the distance is from the tip of my finger to my knuckle, and when I put my pinky finger on the map legend, that's...THIRTY MILES ONE WAY!"

"Where's your sense of adventure?" Doug laughed.

"Where's your sense?" We can't make Billings by nightfall!"

"Sure we can," Doug said veering off at the exit.

And that was that. The man had ignored my concerns. I was headed to Devils Tower with Mr. Pea-Brain—whether I liked it or not. I put away the map. Let the man find the place himself; I certainly wasn't going to help him. But if we ever got to Billings, and at this point I had my doubts, I was planning my very own close encounter—of the wife kind. And believe me, it would be scarier than anything Steven Spielberg could dream up.

So, at our unplanned exit lay Sundance, Wyoming, the friendliest of small towns. My sour mood melted as I returned the many waves and smiles from the residents as we drove through the town. Even the county courthouse displayed a "Howdy" sign, but my favorite was a carved wooden bear on an old tree stump—paw raised in a "welcome" greeting.

Too bad our cat couldn't take a lesson from that friendly bear. When Doug ran inside a local gas station to ask for directions to Devils Tower, I stayed in the truck with Sushi. She jumped to the front seat, stretched her legs, and stood on my lap with her head stuck out of the passenger-side window. Her blue eyes stalked an older lady carrying a grocery bag, like a lioness waiting for the kill.

"Look at the nice kitty," the woman said with a smile.

Just about that time, Mr. Pea-Brain opened the driver's side truck door and scared the nine lives out of our cat. Sushi tried to leap out of my truck window, but I caught her and her tail at the very last second.

Bumbling Through

"Wraauugghh!" Sushi screamed. She twisted her eight-pound, muscular-clad body in mid-air and tried to bite me. I held her fast, but then the blue-eyed demon turned her wrath on that poor older lady who had made the mistake of getting too close to the "nice kitty." Sushi emitted a growl that sounded like a 4,000-pound grizzly bear, if there was such an animal. She slid her sandpaper tongue out between her front teeth, and I swear that cat's blue eyes became translucent.

"Oh my!" the older lady uttered as she ran down the sidewalk, her grocery bag swinging to and fro behind her.

"Oh my!" I said quickly unloading Sushi into the back seat.

Oh, well, so much for the friendly tourists from Ohio.

So, we left the town of Sundance where Harry Longabaugh, also known as the "Sundance Kid", was jailed for eighteen months for horse stealing. We headed out to a lonesome but beautiful area where ponderosa pines filled sweeping valleys, and lush grasses covered steep hillsides. It was here that we were told the best whitetail deer in the world could be found. Now, I don't have a clue as to what constitutes the best whitetail deer in the world, but it sure sounds impressive when you later tell your friends you saw them.

"Really? Where at?"

"Sundance, Wyoming of course."

"In Wyoming? The best whitetail deer in the world?"

"Sure enough—the absolute best. Everyone should see those whitetail deer at least once in their lifetime! They are AWESOME!"

And, of course, watching all those four-legged prime cuts of deer steaks running from our truck and trailer didn't help my hunger pangs much. My gastric juices had struck up a chorus of *"The Stars And Stripes Forever"* that rivaled the Boston Pops on the 4th of July.

"Feed me," my stomach demanded.

"OKAY," I answered.

"What did you say?' Doug asked.

"Nothing," I answered.

"Feed me," my stomach repeated.

"Shut up," I answered.

"I heard that," Doug said.

"Oh, brother," I thought rolling my eyeballs once again.

My stomach hounded me for miles because, in our haste to get an early start that morning, I had not packed any food for the truck. It was all stashed behind us, riding merrily along in our bouncing trailer. So,

Smiling Places

it's no wonder that my first glimpse of Devils Tower, from fifteen miles away no less, reminded me of a hot fudge sundae. This rock abomination rose 867 feet in the horizon. Its perpendicular sides had been formed into fluted columns, just as if hot fudge had dribbled down a mound of soft-serve ice cream, but the Tower's top was flat; so, my sundae had no whipped cream or cherry. Strangely enough, this conspicuous rock protrusion stood alone on the horizon with no other hot fudge sundaes around. I know. I am so pathetic! I really should eat breakfast.

"Wow, isn't that rock something?" Doug said. "Remember the dead cows on the side of the road and Richard Dreyfuss speeding past them?"

"Oh brother," I thought rolling my eyeballs.

Yet, the man kept babbling, obviously excited about his decision to visit this "Close Encounters" place.

"Do-Do-Do-Do. Remember that tune? The government played it to communicate with the Aliens. Do-Do-Do-Do"

"It didn't sound like that," I answered him. There were five notes, and the last note was held...Do-Do-Do-Do-Dooo."

"Nope, there were four notes...four, like this...Do-Do-Do-Do."

"Five."

"Four."

"Five notes."

"You are so wrong...four notes."

"Oh brother," I thought rolling my eyeballs for the third time.

I am not kidding. Our famous argument about that little ditty continued until we pulled into the Devils Tower parking area thirty minutes later. Doug hopped out of the truck determined to find someone, to hum those notes, and to prove me wrong. I, on the other hand, had more important things to do—like eat, for instance. I took Sushi to our trailer and we ate breakfast together—hairball care formula and chunky applesauce. Then, we cleaned our whiskers, and my stomach quit complaining. Just about that time, my husband stepped into the trailer—gloating, of course.

"It's unanimous," he said. "I asked three people, and they all agreed. It is four; notice my emphasis on *four* notes."

"If you say so," I said as I walked out of the trailer.

I have mustered up two flimsy excuses for not knowing we were in Wyoming and thinking we were in Montana when I walked out of that trailer. Excuse number one has to do with my folding up our map and refusing to take it out again when Mr. Pea-Brain veered off course at Sundance. I knew somewhere near Devils Tower, the state borders of

Bumbling Through

South Dakota, Montana, and Wyoming all met. I just didn't know exactly where, and by the time we had reached the Tower, I felt like we had traveled far enough north of Sundance to be in Canada—let alone what I thought was "Montana."

My second excuse: the man sang four notes, and our ensuing argument distracted us from noticing the Wyoming signs posted around the park, until we left, of course. With that in mind, I descended upon Devils Tower, thrilled to be in "Montana," one of my life's dreams. So much so, that I told everyone I met how beautiful Montana was—huge skies, wide-open spaces. No wonder I got the strange looks! Then, a very astute young man spoke up and said, "Hey Lady! This is Wyoming, not Montana...Get Real." Well, he sure told me—that little wisecracking smarty-pants! So, in a defensive 'I'm-gonna-get-you-back posture,' I asked Mr. Smarty-Pants if he knew how Devils Tower, our very first National Monument, had been formed. Ten minutes later he was still talking about sixty million-year-old molten magma that had cooled underground and fractured into columns. I faded into the large crowd that had gathered around the boy genius.

"How come it's so tall if it was formed underground?" someone in the crowd asked.

"Millions of years of erosion," Mr. Smarty-Pants answered.

The kid was definitely *Jeopardy* material.

Doug and I left the crowd and began hiking a paved, wooded walking path around the perimeter of Devils Tower. The close-up views of the Tower were phenomenal, but eerie. About halfway up the trail, we heard voices that sounded as if they were right next to us. We stopped and looked around. No one was there.

"See that crevice over to your left?" one voice asked.

"Yes, OK, I see it," another voice answered.

Doug and I looked to our left. All we saw were scattered boulders and trees. We picked up our pace and rounded a bend.

A girl was sitting on a boulder looking straight up. We followed her eyes above the tree line. There, approximately 300 feet above us, were two rock climbers, dangling from a network of ropes fastened to the sheer face of Devils Tower. We heard them speaking and realized it was their conversation we had just heard as plain as day—from 300 feet in the air. How strange!

"Hi," the girl on the boulder said to us. "Those are my friends up there."

Smiling Places

"That takes a lot of guts," I muttered as I watched the two juggle the network of ropes.

"Well, the one guy up there in blue, it's his first time climbing up something this big. My boyfriend is teaching him."

"Really? How long has your boyfriend been climbing?"

"About fifteen years," she answered.

I figured her boyfriend started climbing minutes after he was born.

"Do you climb?" I asked her.

"Yes, but I recently had toe surgery, so I couldn't climb today," she answered.

Well, as soon as she said toe surgery, my eyes darted to her open-toed sandals. Thank goodness her foot was bandaged. I was already spooked by the voices from above, and I certainly didn't want to see her grossly-disfigured, purple, swollen appendage. So, I told the young lady we had to go. We left her as she whistled to her climbing buddies, attempting to catch their attention.

We resumed our little hike and scared up two cottontail rabbits. They made an awful racket when fleeing us and scampered in zigzag patterns through the brushy woods until they were out of sight. Apparently, an avant-garde of chickadees heard all the commotion and came to investigate the bothersome humans. The tiny birds fluttered amongst the trees and scolded us as we sauntered through their homesteads. Each step along the path we encountered more critters—bluebirds, chipmunks, nuthatches, woodpeckers, deer—and a soaring prairie falcon, whose back shimmered in the rays of the morning sun. Surprisingly, in the shadow of this sullen but grand rock, we had discovered a delicate metropolis teeming with life.

Then we stumbled upon a stand of trees and a park ranger kneeling beside them. It was obvious the base of the trees had been attacked—by whom or by what—was the park ranger's call. We had never seen tree damage like that before. The outer bark had been stripped, almost peeled like a banana, leaving the white inner bark exposed. Unfortunately, the perpetrator did not stop there and ate or tore out chunks of the tree's fleshy innards. Sadly, gaping wounds penetrated several of the trees, possibly dooming their fragile lives.

The ranger stood up and brushed off his pants. We asked him what had happened.

"That's porcupine damage," the ranger explained.

"Really? We have never seen a porcupine in the wild," Doug said.

Bumbling Through

"They are nocturnal," the ranger said. "And I bet there's one sleeping around here somewhere." Then he looked up in the trees.

"What are you doing?" I asked.

"Looking for a porcupine. Sometimes they sleep in the tall crooks of trees," he answered.

Doug and I looked up and scanned the numerous trees. When my epiglottis became stuck to the roof of my mouth, I returned my head to an upright position.

"Aren't they dangerous?' I asked.

"They aren't dangerous unless they touch you with their quills. They don't throw their quills like some people think."

My preconceived notion of a porcupine bristling its back and firing off an arsenal of quills abruptly came to an end. I relaxed—until my husband asked the next question.

"How many quills does a porcupine have?" Doug asked.

"A lot, about thirty thousand, and the quills grow back if the porcupine uses them," he added.

Thirty Thousand? Grow back? Tree-ripping teeth? Was the ranger *kidding*? My first thought was to use those rodent critters as weapons of mass destruction. Just hurl a few of them at those naughty insurgents; that would teach them! My second thought was to get the heck out of there! I certainly did not want to see a fully-loaded porcupine coming *my* way. So, we thanked the ranger for his time and proceeded up the trail, watching our behinds for the rest of our hike.

Just past the porcupine danger zone, we saw several tree branches that had small pieces of cloth tied to them. I joked that they were probably bits of tourists' clothing stuck to the trees by porcupine quills. Unfortunately, my ignorance prevailed. We found out later that they were prayer bundles placed by Native Americans who considered the area sacred, and during June, the month we visited, a voluntary ban on rock climbing was in effect to honor those beliefs. I thought about the rock climbers we had encountered; they must have known since they were required to pre-register with the park office. Should they have been up there—personally, I didn't think so—I was saddened by their behavior.

When we came to the end of the trail, we noticed a tour bus unloading its passengers a short distance away. Maybe we were at the beginning of the trail and had hiked in backwards. It really didn't matter, I suppose. I mean, one way or the other, we saw the huge object the tourists were staring at. Their binoculars were glued to their eyeballs and

Smiling Places

fixated upon the tower wall. I took out my binoculars and stared.

"I still don't see it," a lady next to me said.

"I don't, either," I said.

"OK, start at the crack right in front of you and count over four cracks. It's wedged in between a crevice," a man said.

"OK. One, two, three, four," the lady counted. "Oh, now I see it. That's huge!"

"What is it?" I asked the lady.

"A 350-foot wooden ladder. It was built by two men in 1895 to help them scale Devils Tower."

I looked again, this time with my naked eye, and sure enough, there was a huge ladder wedged against the face of Devils Tower. Had it been up there since 1895? I didn't know, but thank goodness they didn't leave the man up there who, in 1929, had parachuted to the top of Devils Tower. They rescued him six days later.

Soon, we left behind the ladder, the purple toe, and the porcupines, to continue on our quest for Montana. We wound our way back to I-90 on a different route; it took us further west of Sundance and closer to Billings.

Was I still upset with Doug? Nah, I had a good time.

OK, a great time. Yes, I was glad we had detoured.

Oh, all right! I'm sorry I was cranky. I won't call him Mr. Pea-Brain anymore—at least not while we are in Wyoming.

Hey, don't push it.

That's all you are going to get out of me.

Well, there is one more thing, since I have the last say on the matter: That little "song-ditty" Doug and I argued about? It is *five* notes. Really.

We continued west on I-90 for a Wyoming-eternity, and then the interstate turned north. Before long we had found Montana. We know this because the Federal Highway Administration told us so. We pulled over to the sign on I-90.

"Yep, the sign says Montana," Doug said.

"Yep, it sure does," I answered as goose bumps tickled my arms.

Finally, we had arrived.

Montana. They call it "The Last Best Place." I was both excited and nervous. Montana was wild country where grizzly bears roam and avalanches pound the earth. Only God's hand could have built the mountains so high, painted the streams so blue, and created a sky so big! Urbanized Ohio seemed eons away to me—the traffic, the stores, the

Bumbling Through

crowds. I didn't miss the frenetic pace or the creature comforts. What worried me was our inexperience in a truly wild America, where Mother Nature could change her mind at the drop of a hat and living things could become deadly if you crossed their paths. We would just have to be careful out here—real careful. Then, we would be OK, right? Unfortunately, that "other me," the doubting-Tomsu, wasn't so sure. I thought back to my Girl Scout days. "Always be prepared," they taught you, but be prepared for *what*? How do you prepare yourself for a rockslide, wildfire, or even a defensive wild animal? I didn't have a clue, but I did know one thing: I wasn't about to turn around and run back to Ohio, at least not today. I had more exciting things to do.

"Hey, do you know what?" Doug asked me as we resumed our trek toward Billings.

"Now what? We aren't getting off at another exit, are we?" I asked.

"No, no, nothing like that. But if you scramble the letters in Montana, it spells Ant Mona."

In my head I spelled Montana from the letters in Ant Mona.

"It sure does," I answered.

Now my brain was sizzling like frying bacon over a campfire. The man had challenged me.

"Let's see...Ant Mona, huh," I thought. "What about Atom Ann, now that's a good one.

Wait a minute. Montana has the word Man in it.

That leaves o-t-n-a. Mantano? Nah.

O Man Ant? Nah.

Oh, yeah, this is it: Not A Man! Ha, Ha! Scramble the letters in Montana, and you get Not A Man!"

So I told Doug.

"That's not funny," he said stifling a smile.

"It is, too. I saw the corners of your mouth twitch."

Well, that game was obviously over. No man would ever acknowledge my brilliant letter-scramble of Montana. I put my seat back and stuck a pillow behind my head. I closed my eyes to catch a nap, but the constant chuck-coom, chuck-coom, chuck-coom, chuck-coom of our tires rolling along the section breaks of the interstate pavement kept me awake.

"This isn't going to work," I thought to myself. "Now what can I do?" I looked around the front seat and saw a book. I put my seat in an upright position again and removed my pillow. I opened the book and

Smiling Places

laid it on my lap. The words jitterbugged across the page as we hit our one-millionth bump.

"Ok, enough of this—dizzy displeasure setting in," I thought. "What about some music instead?"

So I turned on the radio. Static filled our ears.

"How about a Willie Nelson tape?" Doug asked.

Now don't get me wrong. I love Willie Nelson, but I hated Doug's rendition of On The Road Again. His head bobbed like a spastic colon. His off-beat foot jerked the gas pedal, lurching our vehicles back and forth. And that voice…let's just say it wasn't a pretty picture.

"No thanks, not again," I answered trying to erase his image from my mind.

Ho Hum…Ho Hum. What to do now? I know. I can play the cloud game. Hey, look at that cloud. It looks like Richard Nixon. Oh, no! His nose is breaking off! Now it looks like a boot. Oh, this is silly. No more clouds. Wait a minute. Here is something very interesting. There is a fly on my window. Probably from Devils Tower. Does it have an alien head? Nope, just a green head. I bet Sushi could catch him.

"Hey, Sushi! Sushi! Wake up! Time to catch a treat," I said.

Buzz…Buzz…Smack.

"Eeewww…what did you do that for?" I asked Doug.

"Because it was bothering me."

"At least you could have rolled down your window and shooed him out. Here's a tissue."

"Thanks."

"Hey, was the Marlboro Man from Montana?" I asked.

"How do I know?"

"Well, I was in love with the Marlboro Man."

"You never told me that."

"Yep. When I was a little girl, I watched TV just to see him. He sure was one cool dude."

"I'm one cool dude," Doug said.

"Not in Montana you're not."

"What do you mean by that?"

"Because you look funny in a cowboy hat."

"I've never worn a cowboy hat."

"Exactly my point. You don't wear boots either."

"So what?"

"Well, that would make you a Dud, not a Dude. A Dud wears base-

Bumbling Through

ball caps and sneakers in Montana."

"I guess I'll be a Dud in Montana," Doug concluded. "What about you?"

"Dud. But a *cute* Dud."

We arrived at the Billings KOA under a barrage of dime-sized hail. It was late afternoon; yet, the sky was purple and black with low-rolling clouds. We registered for a few nights and pulled into a perfectly level campsite. Did you hear me? I said *perfectly level*! I could have kissed the ground we parked on.

So, Doug plugged in the utilities at our campsite, but he didn't bother unhitching the truck and trailer. That could wait until morning. I opened up our refrigerator and was thankful we had prepared fruits and vegetables the day before. I didn't feel like cooking, but you know me—I was always ready to eat. So, I threw the prepared food containers on the kitchen table and sliced some low-fat cheese and served it with pita bread. Surprisingly, we only ate a few bites, put the food away, and went to bed. It was six p.m. We fell asleep listening to the churning waters of the Yellowstone River, and that was our very first night in Montana.

When I awoke the next morning, I crawled out of bed and got dressed. I hated dressing before my showers but I just couldn't bring myself to wear a bathrobe and slippers in the campgrounds like some women did. I slowly made my way to the private family restrooms. I would rather have been on a scenic byway in the Black Hills than face yet another shower.

"Another day, another shower disaster," I thought to myself.

My stressful travel experiences with women's bathhouses were vivid in my memory. I mention this now because our campground had advertised private family restrooms in our travel guide. This certainly peaked my curiosity, but I must admit that I was skeptical. Is it any wonder? Remember the shower stories I shared with you? Well, there are more, and as long as we traveled with our current trailer, one thing was certain: I would never have my own private shower.

I am sure you know by now that our trailer's shower was nothing to write home about. It was large enough for a wee little person and produced sixty drips of water per minute. We only converted it from a closet with a cat litter pan to a shower in the utmost emergencies: Either the campground showers were filthy, or their water smelled like dead skunks. So, each day I begrudgingly collected my shower essentials— shower shoes and disinfectant—and trudged off to a public restroom.

Smiling Places

Every campground we stayed in seemed to have a new and exciting shower surprise waiting for me.

For instance, I endured one most memorable shower surprise when a woman pulled back my shower curtain and exposed "naked me" to the world. My shampoo-filled eyes popped open, and we both screamed. She apologized and ran out of the bathhouse. My eyes *and* pride burned for the rest of the evening.

Another surprise hit me during my flush-and-run shower experience. Someone in the bathhouse flushed a toilet, and my water temperature changed from warm to scalding hot in a matter of seconds. I felt like a lobster that had met its fate.

Then, there was the dope-with-a-rope fiasco. I pulled a short rope far above my head and got water. I let go of the rope and got no water. I played the game of Twister while scrubbing and rinsing. That was not my idea of a fun time.

My favorite, though, was the attack of the slimy shower curtain. I turned on the shower. The bathroom's air pressure blew the shower curtain into my stall. I wrestled with the slimy thing and tried to beat it back, but it wrapped around my legs and bodice—rendering me helpless. I was no match for *The Blob*.

And speaking of *The Blob*, I picked myself up off one slimy shower floor after I slipped on the tiles – and I was wearing my shower shoes, no less! Another time a snake decided to take a shower with me. Yet another time, 500 flies on a window screen tried to join me, but the most blatant creatures were the mosquitoes that drank my blood as I showered. And how about that *alien water*? It smelled like water; it looked like water, but it didn't feel like water. How could I forget the pre-set water temperature that rivaled the temperature in my freezer compartment or the broken showerhead that just missed my skull after paying an extra three dollars for the privilege! Unfortunately, I could recall several more shower incidents, which did not speak volumes for our full-timing lifestyle.

But every once in awhile, a shining light appeared among the burnt out bulbs. Such was the case at the Billings KOA. Their bathrooms were about the greatest thing I had seen since we left home—pure luxury to an old shower warrior like myself. I lavished in my own private, tiled bathroom complete with my very own toilet, sink, and large shower. I soaked in gallons of hot water and treated my muscle aches to a steady stream of water pressure. I dressed in the privacy of a locked room, and

Bumbling Through

the bathroom was so sparkling clean that I didn't use my shower shoes or disinfectant. What a wonderful way to start my day!

That wonderful feeling just kept getting better when I smelled those grilled pancakes and sausages on my way back to our trailer. Many campers had already followed their noses to the open-air eating area where our campground was serving up breakfast for a nominal fee. I knew where I was going to be headed in the next sixty seconds. I hoped Doug would join me.

He was outside unhitching our truck and trailer when I approached.

"Weren't those showers something?" I asked Doug.

"The best I've had since we left Dayton. I didn't want to get out."

"Me either. I love that family bathroom concept."

"Me, too. And after messing with this truck and trailer, I need another shower. Poor me, right?"

"Uh-huh. Hey, do you want to go eat over there?" I suggested and nodded toward the pancake area.

"Well, we could. I'll tell you what. I'll hold off on that shower, but I need to wash up first."

"Oh, OK," I answered, as I drooled on myself. Was that one of those senior moments?

"Wait a second. Didn't you promise to do something first?" Doug asked.

"I give up...what did I promise?"

"We are on a level site now."

"Oh, you mean weigh myself. How about tonight?"

"Melodee, Melinda..."

"Oh, OK."

So, I went into the trailer and pulled our scale away from the bathroom wall. I stepped on—ever so gingerly—and shut my eyes. This was going to be a true reading—no leaning to the left, no holding onto the sink, and no more fooling myself. I slowly opened my eyes. Wait a minute! I stepped off the scale, and then I stepped on again. The dial stopped short of where I thought it would land. I had lost another four pounds, for a grand total of ten pounds since we started this journey. I was ecstatic and beat a path to the breakfast area with Doug in tow.

Now, here is some food for thought: Just the other day I read that if you don't eat enough, your metabolism slows down and you don't lose weight. I figured I was covered by the flip side—eat a lot and I would increase my metabolism and thus lose weight. So, I sat down at a long

Smiling Places

wooden table—or trough as I like to remember it—with an overflowing plate of creamy butter and thick, sugary syrup. My mile-high stack of pancakes and sausages were buried under that gooey concoction somewhere. I fished with my fork and dabbed a huge piece of pancake with all the butter and syrup it could possibly hold and threw the dripping glob into my mouth.

"Yummy," I said to Doug, who couldn't take his eyes off my plate.

"You aren't going to eat all of that, are you?" he asked me in total disbelief.

"Sure I am. The more I eat, the more I lose," I said and took another huge bite.

"What? Say that again?" Doug asked incredulously.

"Mow fu," I answered and pointed to my chomping jaws.

I had eaten my way through half the daily calories in Montana when *she* sat down across from me. Of all the people in that breakfast area, she had to sit down across from me. Her plate consisted of one plain pancake and a dollop of fruit. Her tight jeans and halter top clung to her size .005 body which was like a carved Goddess at the Louvre, and believe me when I tell you, all male eyes were upon her—and all female appetites were instantly suppressed.

I watched her meticulously cut a ¼ inch by ¼ inch piece of pancake with a fork and knife. Then, she laid down the knife, and her tiny hand clasped the oversized fork with tines that raised the pancake piece to her pursed lips. Carefully, she chewed that piece of pancake, ten, twenty, maybe thirty times. And then she swallowed it, ever so daintily, like a butterfly drinking nectar.

Sure, I would eat like that—when in another lifetime when I came back to earth as a flea. I tell you: Bodies like that should not be allowed to attend pancake breakfasts. They ruin all the fun. I never saw so many gastronomically-challenged people suck in their flabby tummies all at the same time. The whole breakfast area lost 500 visible pounds in a matter of seconds. I was amazed: Even Dr. Phil couldn't work a room like this tiny woman did, and I couldn't wait to get out of there. So, I fed the rest of my pancake breakfast to an unsuspecting garbage can and returned to my trailer, ever mindful of my daily battle with my bulge.

Late that morning I became immersed in another battle of sorts, an historical event that took place on a scorching June day in 1876. We bade good-bye to Sushi, whose tiny pug nose fogged our kitchen window as we pulled away. We retraced our steps of yesterday about sixty

Bumbling Through

miles or so, and found ourselves standing within the boundaries of the Crow Indian Reservation at the site of the Little Bighorn Battlefield National Monument. This was the very place where George Armstrong Custer took his last stand against hundreds of Lakota and Cheyenne Indian Warriors. And it was here that Custer, his two brothers, his brother-in-law, his nephew, and many soldiers of the U.S. 7th Cavalry perished.

The battlegrounds for the most part could not have changed much since Custer saw it. The stark, windswept hills are just that; they are desolate and remote with a smattering of a few houses and barns. I-90 runs fairly close, but the low traffic volume did not seem to intrude upon our experience. When we arrived, the skies were cloudy, and the winds whipped our t-shirts like a boat unfurling its sail. By afternoon, the unrelenting sun made temperatures feel like three-digits, similar to what Custer must have felt the day of battle. Several times during our visit, I experienced weird sensations, perhaps even ghostly; one time I had Doug slow down along the 4.5-mile road that traverses the battlefield. I thought I saw a man close to Weir's Point—limping, in tattered clothing. I blinked, and he was gone.

After a cursory drive of the battlefield grounds, my Mr. Museum Man hurried back to the visitors' center to do "whatever it is that men's brains do" with the bits and pieces of information he had gleaned from the outdoor exhibit panels that were set up at various sites. I watched him pinpoint map locations and put troop movements to memory, like he was readying for his own battle that afternoon. I, on the other hand, couldn't even figure out the orientation of the battlegrounds, let alone my east-from-west and my north- from-south. I slipped outside, and discovered an outdoor lecture being given by a park ranger about the events leading up to the battle. Now this was something that peaked my interest, and I personally remember the lecture went something like this...

> "Go find your sister."
> "No!"
> "Then be quiet so I can hear."
> "No!"
> "Jimmy, look! There's your mommy and sister eating your chocolate chip cookies."
> "MOMMY...THOSE ARE MY COOKIES!"

Wow! That Jimmy sure carried a hefty set of lungs with him. I

Smiling Places

inched toward the front of the lecture area and found a vacant seat. The park ranger seemed only too happy to share her knowledge with the audience. And my own personal observation was one of fitting the pieces of my travel puzzle together. At Custer, South Dakota, we had seen a stone mountain carving of Crazy Horse—the largest in the world. Crazy Horse was also the famous Lakota leader at The Little Bighorn. While we were in the Black Hills of South Dakota, we had hiked close to the place where Custer had successfully led a gold expedition. The park ranger mentioned how that discovery of gold was a major catalyst of the events leading up to The Little Bighorn.

When Custer discovered gold in 1874, the Black Hills didn't belong to the white man. The Hills had officially been given back to the Indians in 1868 through a treaty agreement at Fort Laramie, another place we had visited. So, government officials decided to purchase the tract of land back from the Indians, who wouldn't sell. They considered the Black Hills sacred and at the core of their culture. But gold-seekers swarmed the area and violated the treaty. Skirmishes broke out, making both sides angry. Many Indians escaped from government reservations at this time, and others vowed not to give up their ways of life without a fight. Government officials prepared for the Great Indian campaign and vowed to round up all defiant Indians.

And so it was, in the spring of 1876, three army columns mobilized to converge upon a huge concentration of Indians, believed to be in the Little Bighorn Valley. Some who saw this Indian village said it was the biggest they had ever seen—5,000 to 9,000—mostly Cheyenne and Sioux, including 2,000 warriors who had joined forces together, under the leadership of Chief Sitting Bull and Crazy Horse. Custer and his 7th Cavalry of 600 men arrived at the Indian village first. Others would arrive later, but not in time to help Custer. Custer further divided his unit of 600 men into three battalions; Custer ordered one of his battalions, led by Major Reno, to attack the village. They were overwhelmed and retreated to a ridge approximately three miles from where Custer met his fate. Custer sent a message to his second battalion led by Captain Benteen.

"Benteen –
 Come on. Big Village. Be quick. Bring Packs –
PS Bring Packs.
              Lt Col Custer"

Bumbling Through

The messenger who carried this note to Benteen is believed to be the last surviving soldier to have seen Custer and his third battalion alive. According to eyewitness accounts, Benteen did attempt to join Custer; however his unit came under attack, and he never arrived. Custer and his battalion of more than 200 men perished at the hands of the Indian warriors. Reno's and Benteen's battalions survived an onslaught when additional Army columns appeared, and the Indians withdrew.

Then, unfortunately, this informative lecture came to an abrupt end.

"If you haven't already," the park ranger said, "I would suggest you go to our visitors' center, right next door. There you can learn about the historical events that took place here, and please pick up a free map and guide of the Little Bighorn to orientate yourself while you drive the battlefield tour route."

That afternoon Doug and I did drive the route again, and we dutifully got out at each site and reread the outdoor displays exhibited. They made more sense the second time around. We wandered down several walking paths that encircled the sites, flanked by "You are in Rattlesnake Country" warning signs. I am afraid that my usual cautious self had been replaced by a mental time-warp, for I had traveled back to 1876.

I looked out over the bluffs from the Reno-Benteen Battlefield site and visualized a cavalryman, lying behind a mule pack, taking aim at his enemy. I peered down into the valley from Custer's lookout site and imagined seeing the monstrous Indian Village for the first time. Would I have attacked the village like Custer ordered, or would I have waited for reinforcements? Then, I stood on Weir's Point and searched for Custer's Battalion, just like Captain Weir had done on that fateful afternoon. Where were Custer and all his men? Why was it so quiet? And I thought of an Indian warrior who stood in his village and looked up into the surrounding hills. He saw many intruders coming. He protected the women and children. He defended his way of life.

We continued our somber journey at Custer Hill and joined a ranger walk already in progress. We shuffled down the hill, toward an area called the Deep Ravine. The ranger explained that sometime during Custer's Last Stand, forty-five soldiers from his battalion had run toward this deep ravine. Someone in our group asked if they were seeking shelter or trying to make a run for it.

"There's no way to tell," the ranger answered. "I imagine at the end of the battle, they got up and tried to escape. The Indians caught up to them and killed them all."

Smiling Places

As Doug and I traversed the area, we saw numerous markers dotting the battlefields: Each one carved to look like a headstone, and each one placed where a soldier was believed to have fallen. At the top of Custer's Battlefield, a cluster of markers stood in the tall grasses. Custer and his family died together, defending that hill: Custer's marker read:

"G. A. CUSTER
BVT. MAJ. GEN.
LT. COL.
7th U.S. CAV.
FELL HERE
JUNE 25, 1876"

Unfortunately, war is a reality of life. I will never forget the images of markers scattered throughout the hills of those battlefields, nor the meticulously placed gravestones at the National Cemetery, also located on site. The honor and valor of many brave hearts are buried there, from the casualties of The Little Bighorn to the Korean War. We stood at the edge of the National Cemetery; its border was defined by majestic pine trees. A tiny bird flitted in and out of the top of one pine. Here, in the midst of death, life seemed so precious. We paid our respects and prayed for those who had given their lives for us and our country.

The Indian nation suffered terribly after their victory at Little Big Horn. Custer, a celebrated Union General in the Civil War—in fact, the youngest General in our military history—lay slaughtered at the age of thirty-six, his men scattered around him. On the eve of our country's Centennial, our nation cried out for revenge and harsh retributions.

The Sioux nation fell apart. Indians were hunted down or forced to live on reservations. Crazy Horse was murdered one year after Little Big Horn at Fort Robinson, Nebraska. Sitting Bull was killed in 1890, a prelude to the massacre of the Sioux at Wounded Knee. The boundary lines of the 1868 Treaty were redrawn, and the Black Hills opened.

"I don't think anyone won this battle," I said to Doug while on our return trip to Billings. "I mean, look at the consequences. To me, Custer's Last Stand was the Indian Nation's Last Stand as well. It seems like everyone lost so much." There was much to think about.

22 - Doubts and Certainty

Tomorrow we would hit the trail again—to Bozeman, Montana. Tonight we would stand under those soothing showers for one last splurge. I settled back in my seat for the long drive home reflecting on that day in history—June 25, 1876.

I can never really know the thoughts of those who one day are here and the next day are gone. Were Custer's men filled with doubt the day before the battle? Were they prepared for the destiny to come? Had they done all they wanted to with their lives? If they had a chance to do one more thing, what would they chose? The day after-battle brought a certainty that those questions would remain unanswered.

My reflections turned inward—toward my life. I had accomplished what I set out to do work wise: Working with my dad in his business in his last years; gathering awards and rising to a first level supervisor in the financial department at WPAFB,; and running my own businesses. The level of successes in large part due to education from Purdue University. When dropping me off at college for the first time, my dad told me that I could achieve in life whatever I set my mind to. He was right, and I did.

And in one of the ironies of my life, shortly after graduating, I married an engineer from Ohio University. I had gone to a highly ranked college with literally thousands of engineers—and turned down several marriage proposals. I wasn't going to be settling down anytime soon. *Yeah right!* My history with Doug: first date June 1st, engaged July 1st, and married August 1st. Twenty-five years later still seems like yesterday. From a woman's perspective, we were compatible from the start: My female strengths and his male weaknesses. My dad also must've known something as Doug was the only guy he seemed to approve of.

I have been blessed with wonderful family, friends, and co-workers. So many "sister" friendships formed along the way. On the road I do miss the daily contact with them all. My mind wandered from the past reflections to the unknown future. With traveling and no longer living the cubicle life, dotting i's and crossing t's, I was beginning to feel a creative

Smiling Places

spirit awaken. Writing seems to take you someplace different—a world unto its own—if you let it. Several people said I put a funny spin on our travels—little did they know—that was easy given Doug, Sushi, and me. There is such a rush when you hit the "write spot"—and people laugh.

My writing could become a fossilized footprint—a legacy for ancestors to read. We had often wondered about some of our family who came before us; we knew little of their thoughts. One of Doug's relatives was Henry Leland, an inventor who built the first Cadillac, then Lincolns. One of my relatives came over by boat through Ellis Island. Wouldn't a diary of theirs have been fascinating to read? A hundred years from now, my book could give a peephole look into our lives and who we were. A book would continue to entertain long afterwards.

But writing a book? Doubts creep in. Would it be good enough? It would require lots of time and effort. And worse yet, what if I got more than halfway done, and then something happened to me? All that work, and it would simply turn to dust in someone's closet, or be made obsolete by the next generation of software. Well, Doug would just have to pick himself up—finish it for me. But, if he just published what I had finished, my readers would feel cheated if they didn't know how the book ends. They would demand their money back for sure—but he can't write creatively or with humor—he is an engineer. My readers would finish my last chapter, then start reading his, and say "What the heck happened?" But he couldn't use a ghostwriter—they would lose the chemistry between Doug, Sushi, and me.

Of course, he could use my emails and personal logs. Well, he is just going to have to come up with some kind of transition between my chapters and what is to follow. Knowing him, he would probably put *his* name on *my* book—just like all those Christmas cards I write every year. Well, I guess that is only fair if he does some of the work, but he better give me top billing if he knows what's good for him. I could guide him in finishing the book if need be. Doug has acquired a healthy fear of electricity over the years due to his bumbling. If he was doing something I didn't like, I'd simply send a warning shot across his bow by flicking a few GFI circuits. If he was doing well, I'd send a few rainbows, owls, or horoscopes his way. Serious doubts again creep in. Will he do it? *For me*, he certainly would. As with most women in love, I sometimes have long conversations with myself. Then, I expect Doug to know what I said. Somehow, he always does. We had barely spoken a word to each other until we unlocked our trailer door back at the KOA in Billings.

23 - It's Better than Nothing, Isn't it?

The next day we put down our jacks in Bozeman, Montana, a very nice city of around 30,000 people about 90 miles north of Yellowstone National Park. The town had Montana State University, a new hospital, new mall, many new homes, apartments, and condos. We signed up for a ten-day stint that included the 4th of July holiday so we could get a good "feel" for Bozeman.

When we hit the road, in the back of our minds, was a desire to seek out potential retirement places. We had no intention of retiring our traveling ways anytime soon, but while seeing the country, it seemed like a natural. Bozeman is one of those "hits" we came upon during an Internet search. Our ideal place would be small in size—countrified, yet a city—good grocery stores, good medical facilities, a college town, and conveniently located to lots of nature-orientated resources. We were excited to see if we could become Romans in Rome.

I asked myself, "Melodee, just what is it that Montanans do that I need to do like they do?" After many minutes of astute observations, it became apparent that Montanans had lots of trucks with dogs in the back, cowboy hats, and boots. Montanans do drive their vehicles a bit faster than the rest of us—probably a throwback from the days of no daytime speed limits on highways—and they have great distances to travel, as Montana is the fourth largest state in area. Or maybe it is just as simple as heavy boots hitting the gas pedal instead of sneakers.

They so seem to enjoy putting their barking dogs in uncovered truck beds and driving around town showing them off. I always wondered why the dogs didn't jump out at red lights. And even when not standing next to their trucks, you could always still spot a Montanan in a crowd. They were the ones wearing those rugged cowboy hats, boots, and huge belt buckles.

Due to that overly optimistic mood traveling retirees always have, it

Smiling Places

seemed as though we might be able to fit in. We already had the pickup truck, and there isn't much difference between a cat and a dog. So, we decided to give the "western apparel thing" another try—after we tied Sushi to the truck bed. So, Doug and I, in our best jean-sauntering western walk went to the clothing store in the downtown area. A very nice young lady named Amy asked if she could help us,

"Why, but of course!" I replied as I swept Amy across the floor toward the cowboy boots.

"Are these the ladies' boots?" I asked her.

"Yes, they are," she answered exuberantly.

Unfortunately, that was the last moment Amy and I shared in any type of exuberance.

"I just love these boots, Amy," I said as I imagined myself as a petite Dale Evans. "Do you carry them in size 8 or 8-1/2 and in a wide version?"

A worry line appeared on her youthful face.

"I'll have to check," she said running for the secret shoe storage area. She disappeared behind the dark curtain hanging in the narrow doorway, and a few minutes later, she returned with a large box.

Both Amy and I worked up quite a sweat getting those dream boots over my oversized calves. When I stood up, my legs looked like two raw Italian sausages with split casings at the top. So now, I had the look and could walk the walk, but the pain from those boots contorted my face like a branding iron taken to a cow. Don't even ask how we got them off. Let's just say the store manager was ready to run down the street to an auto parts store to buy some axle grease.

When a sufficient amount of blood had returned to my legs, I asked Amy if she carried any Stedmens?

"Stedmen's? What are those?" she asked as a bead of sweat dropped from her lip.

"Those would be a brand of cowboy hats," I replied.

"Cowboy hats? Stedman's? Oh, you must mean Stetson's," she smiled. I think Stedman is Oprah's boyfriend.

Amy smiled at me, in a pathetic, hope-this-customer-leaves-soon sort of way.

"Sorry about that, but do you have a hat that might fit my husband's head?" I asked her.

"Well, I'm not sure," she muttered, an apprehensive look in her eyes.

It's Better than Nothing, Isn't It?

I knew why she was hesitant. It was Doug's head of hair: gray, thick, wooly—kind of like a wiry S.O.S. pad pinned to the top of a Mister Potato Head. And when she placed that cowboy hat on top of Mister Potato Head, he destroyed all images of cowboys that Amy had ever known since she was a little girl. The poor thing was in a stupor with her mind desperately clinging to a picture of an adorable cowboy riding a bucking bronco. There were even a few tears trickling down her cheeks. I took one look at that hat floating six inches above Doug's fuzzy hairline and decided we could not become Bozemans in Bozeman. We were born to be sneaker people with baseball caps—and would always remain so.

The Grizzly's are here! We had tent camped for close to twenty-five years in the Great Smoky Mountains and saw lots of bears without incident. The only eastern bears we ever saw were black, but we learned out here that both our eastern bears and these western grizzly bears can be black, brown, blond, etc. The secret to telling the difference is readily apparent if you come across a grizzly in the wild. You simply pull out your bear identification literature and ask the bear to turn sideways to see if it has a hump. Also, check what type of facial profile it has—straight face or dished face? It is very important to determine what type of bear is going to get you because the experts tell you to react differently to each type of bear. For me, if a bear is close enough for me to see its hump and facial profile, I know my mind will go into a "brown" out or maybe even a "black" out regardless of the bear's color!

The word "Grizzly" invokes visions of bear attacks with no survivors, and we had recently heard of a "crazy" bear at Glacier National Park in Montana. It had attacked people in four or five separate incidents that summer and had yet to be caught. We became more and more confused about the various actions humans should take if they were approached by eastern bear as opposed to grizzly bear. So, we decided to take the better-than-nothing approach. Back in Ohio, this meant outfitting our cars with one of those "silent deer alert" things attached to the bumper because it was better than nothing. Out here in the wilds of Montana, we decided it meant getting some bear spray, but not just any bear spray. We came across a story of a spray manufactured in Bozeman by a man who had been attacked in 1992 by a female Grizzly—and lived to tell about it. His hunting partner had a very small can of pepper spray

Smiling Places

with him and sprayed the attacking bear. The bear ran, but only after inflicting extensive bite lacerations on the victim. Doug got to talk to the "survivor" of the attack and bought one of his products for our upcoming hikes in the wild. We decided also to keep it in our trailer at night by our bed because "who knows—bears, people, whatever—it would be better than nothing." It sprays forty feet, but bears can run thirty to forty mph so you have to be quick.

"How quick?" I asked Doug

"Well, sixty mph is eighty-eight feet per second, so thirty mph is forty-four feet per second." He replied in that manly matter-of-fact way that can be so annoying. "If we come across a bear one hundred feet away, I will have two seconds, *more or less*. I'll just carry it on my belt in a holster like they did in the old days. You know, Quick Draw McDoug."

Sometimes a wife just needs to let the husband have the last word. So, I did and decided not to burst his bubble with the concept that a fifty-year-old man reacts slightly slower, *more or less*, than a young and hungry bear. Or how about what he is going to do if the wind is going the wrong way? With my luck, Doug will likely end up spraying me, but I *am* very glad we got the bear spray. My plan is to throw a candy bar at Doug's feet and then sneak away while *Quick Draw McDud* is trying to unholster his bear spray. It's better than nothing, isn't it?

We hiked high up in the Bridger Mountains outside of Bozeman one day. We found an old road and started walking; it opened up into one of the most beautiful mountain meadows we have ever seen. For as far as we could see, wildflowers of all different colors spread before us for miles. The wildflowers were breathtaking and unlike anything we had experienced. Thousands of bees raced all around us and never bothered us. I'm sure it was the sight of Doug with his bear spray that kept them at bay.

For a day trip, we went west of Bozeman to see a couple of sites—the Madison Buffalo Jump, Lewis & Clark Caverns State Park, and Missouri Headwaters State Park.

We visited the Madison Buffalo Jump early one morning when no one was around. Yes, this is where the Indians used to drive buffalo off the edge of a huge hill to their deaths so they could have food and clothing from the buffalo. There were many rattlesnake signs in this area, and hot, desert-like conditions encompassed the bottom area of this hill. The area was full of yuccas, sage brush (which actually does smell just like sage from your Thanksgiving dressing), and prickly pear cactus. I walked

It's Better than Nothing, Isn't It?

"loudly" but didn't see or hear any rattlers; I'm sure it was the sight of Doug with his bear spray that kept them at bay.

We also went to Lewis & Clark Caverns State Park. Yep, you guessed it: They have "Montana" cave tours there. You see, I call them "Montana" cave tours because the people who have lived there all of their lives are used to the heights, oxygen deprivation, and daredevil stunts that we in Ohio would only dream about—but rarely do.

I am sure you know about Mile High Stadium in Denver, where even the greatest athletes must take oxygen. Well, these caverns were at least that high up; in fact, the tour itself went up 300 feet and down 600 stairs. It was a two-mile, two-hour walk that even involved some stooping. I was so glad when Doug told me the tour was sold out for the rest of the day (It was Sunday.) because I was questioning my physical ability to do this tour. The trail leading up to the caves was really scary! It was about an eight-foot wide trail of rock; there was no handrail on one side, and the mountain rose up on the other. Brave souls and would-be hikers had to walk on this mountain trail for about a mile with that sheer, 1,000-foot drop-off on one side. It was extremely windy that day. WOW! This was not like the Ohio Caverns—that was for sure. As we watched one tour, about ten percent of the people turned around about half-way up the side of the mountain and came back down the trail. We spoke with some of them, and they said it was just too physically challenging for them. I am glad we didn't take it—I just don't know if I would have made it.

We did so enjoy our visit to Bozeman, though. Snow-capped mountains surrounded this town on all four sides, and the 4th of July fireworks were spectacular. Since fireworks are legal in Montana, the nightly shows started around July 1st and went well in the night on the 4th. Many thousands of people gathered around the fairgrounds on the 4th to see fireworks that could rival any of the big cities out east. At the beginning, around eight p.m., private individuals were setting off fireworks everywhere.

I could see them exploding into brilliant colors in a 360-degree circle against the mountains and rising up into that clear, Montana sky where "millions" of stars can be seen nightly. There were also many fireworks being set off in the Big K-Mart parking lot, which was our location at the time—dangerous, but close and beautiful!

Then, the public display from the City of Bozeman started around ten and lasted until eleven—some of the most spectacular I ever saw.

Smiling Places

There were constant "oooh's" and "aaah's" from the crowd. A local radio station played "patriotic fireworks" music and every truck with "dog in tow" had the radio tuned to that station. It was a beautiful, moving, experience and one I won't ever forget.

24 - Keeping a Safe Distance, Mind You

We made a deliberate decision to approach Yellowstone National Park from the town of West Yellowstone. Of five ways into Yellowstone National Park, this appeared to be easier and more level than other entrance roads. Being fearful of Thing, we talked with other experienced travelers who guided us. True to form, the pull-down there was pretty easy, and Thing behaved well. Breaking camp from the Bozeman KOA, we headed for a section of the Gallatin National Forest about two to three miles north of West Yellowstone.

We would be moving fairly often as we took in the grandeur of Yellowstone National Park, Grand Teton National Park, and many other wondrous sites out in this neck of the woods. We were now into peak tourist season, so it was beginning to be harder to find "unreserved" parks with spaces available for longer periods. We did not want to make too many reservations in advance, as we did not want to be on a set schedule. Doug was in a daily state of "giddiness," most of the time thinking of what he was doing now compared to a year ago. I was in heaven enjoying all the sights and sounds.

We initially found a beautiful campsite right on the Madison River; it was a huge pull-thru on 1/4 acre. The drawback was that we would have to "dry camp" with no on-site utility hookups for water, sanitary, or electric. Thing came with water storage as well as tanks for the "used water." We have a furnace, refrigerator, and stove that run on gas, but that is all we can use and still have our battery perform for long periods. In the next five weeks, we would dry camp for three and a half weeks. This would actually bring back memories of our camping days, except we would be in a big, hard shell "tent" instead of a nylon tent—a must in grizzly country. Many of the places will not allow tent camping. Somehow, I didn't place a lot of faith in Thing's walls keeping out a determined grizzly, but, of course, we now had our bear spray so that was comforting. Not!

Smiling Places

We quickly found out where we could dump locally for five dollars, take a shower for three dollars, etc. Our battery seemed to last from five to seven days. Doug could have gotten another battery as a back up, a solar battery charger, or even a generator but chose to tough it out.

With Doug being Doug, life is rarely dull. If nothing else, he is consistent. His concept was to take out the trailer battery, go to an auto repair shop, and recharge it. I started to tell him what I thought, but putting up his hand he said, "I know what I'm doing. How hard can it be?" So, as a dutiful wife, I stood back, keeping a safe distance, mind you.

He went to re-hook up the now fully charged battery. I was somewhat disappointed in the *display*, as he has done much better in the past. We once owned a rental property and while getting it fixed up to sell, Doug had to replace the stove. Once the stove was delivered, he had to hook up the electric cord which never comes pre-hooked to the stove. I started to tell him what I thought, but putting up his hand he said "I know what I'm doing. How hard can it be?" So, as a dutiful wife, I stood back, keeping a safe distance, mind you.

He put the one end of the cord into the wall outlet and while turning to face the stove, he moved the other end of the cord ever so slightly. Just enough, so the two contacts made contact. Wow! Now *that* was a display, and the sound effect of the fuse box door flinging open against the wall was spectacular. This time, he just managed to blow most of the fuses in the trailer with nary a scratch on himself.

The recharged battery was now without power once again, so, back to the repair shop after marking the battery cables with masking tape "pos" and "neg". Why is it that husbands get so defensive when wives say "Shoulda, coulda, woulda?"

We only saw cable TV for three days since we had left May 2nd. Regular TV was also very infrequent because the places we tend to camp have no TV signals. I refused to buy a satellite dish since we are trying to keep this as simple as possible. Also, I don't really want Doug poking holes in our trailer for re-wiring. Would you? We really don't miss many of the conveniences at all. Radio, local newspapers, and talking to fellow campers has supplemented for the news. We have also lived without heat so far as the furnace tends to draw on the battery quite a bit. That may sound funny to you in the summer but when you are at these elevations, it may get up to eighty degrees during the day with hardly any humidity—beautiful weather—but then at night it can get to forty degrees or below. Our trailer is not insulated that well, and it gets real cold

Keeping a Safe Distance, Mind You

in here at times.

Yellowstone National Park is huge at 2.5 million acres and is five times as big as the Smoky Mountains National Park. Yellowstone was our nation's first National Park and also has 10,000 thermal features including the famous Old Faithful. Without stops, Yellowstone probably takes about three plus hours to drive from the east end to the west end and another three plus hours to drive from the north end to the south end. Grand Teton National Park is much smaller; it takes around one hour or less to drive each way from north to south and east to west.

While Yellowstone is both mysterious and fascinating, the Grand Tetons have to be one of the most beautiful places on earth I've seen. Yellowstone has many mountains and canyons to explore with valleys, lakes, and thermal activities interspersed throughout the park. In contrast, the Grand Tetons rise out of the valley floor and can be seen from almost every vantage point in their park. The terrain surrounding the Tetons in the park is mostly flat and filled with many glacier lakes and beautiful hiking trails—both easy ones and the more strenuous ones that lead into the mountains and canyons. What I loved each morning was waking up and looking at the Tetons; the mountains never looked the same.

In 1988, thirty-six percent of Yellowstone Park burned. Most of the fires were caused by lightning. Now, the baby pines are sprouting out of the forest floor again, but seeing the sheer magnitude of the fire shocked us. Mountainsides appear barren with many large, burnt pine trees—still standing—waiting only to tumble one day. There are warnings posted to hikers to be careful of falling trees which block many paths. Fortunately, the Grand Tetons are still basically green with large pines; although, there was a smaller lightning fire around the Jenny Lake area in 1999.

Driving in the Tetons is very easy, while driving Yellowstone can range from easy to a hair raising experience. A certain sense of queasiness comes over you when meeting a super wide motor home on a 180 degree turn at 9,000 feet—while hanging over a 1,000 foot canyon on one of Yellowstone's crumbling, narrow road systems. You get the picture. Teton National Park seems much nicer and well-maintained.

We had lived at altitudes above 7,000 feet for five weeks now. A ranger last night said we have about one-third the oxygen we had as "flatlanders." In any event, it has taken some getting used to. When we first got here, we would have trouble sleeping at night and also get short of breath. Even the easiest thirty minute hike would take our breath away. Many times, flatlanders will end up at the hospital—usually due

Smiling Places

to altitude/dehydration problems. I bring up the dehydration issue as there is a twenty to thirty percent humidity level out here. Drinking water helps get oxygen into your body. So, they tell you to drink tons of water out here. A ranger told us it takes about three months to get used to the higher altitudes. We improved greatly since our first hike; over time, we got up to hiking for well over three hours without complications.

WARNING!
MANY VISITORS HAVE BEEN
GORED BY BUFFALO

This notice is given to you the very first time you enter Yellowstone's gates. After spending many weeks here, I can see why the buffalo are chasing down people: *because people think these National Parks are petting zoos*! Why is it that people become stupid when they enter? We have seen people put their fingers into boiling thermal pots to see how hot it was. One lady showed us her finger right after she did it. It was red and blistered and needed medical attention. Unfortunately, she wasn't the only person who did it. Another lady took her five-year-old daughter with her to get a great shot of a bull elk. She walked right up behind it, and the elk turned quickly—almost knocking another tourist down to the ground. I thought it was going after the mother and little girl, but thank goodness, it didn't charge—even though they ran. Unfortunately, that wasn't the only stupid photographer we saw. Another tourist tried to "pet" a black bear and ends up in the hospital. If it had been a grizzly, I don't think he would be alive right now. Another foreign tourist walked out on the thin crust of a thermal boiling pot to retrieve a baseball cap that had blown off his head—despite cries of "no" from us and others. If the ground would have given way, he would have been boiled alive. The list goes on and on.

Unfortunately, some innocent people get injured also. A sixty-seven-year-old Australian man was gored in his thigh by a buffalo at Old Faithful Lodge as he was watching Old Faithful erupt. We arrived at Old Faithful to watch the helicopter evacuate this man to an Idaho Falls hospital. According to eye witnesses, the buffalo just started charging people right and left, and this poor man could not get out of the bull's way. Park officials still do not know who or what caused the charge. The man will recover but needs therapy. "The hole in his thigh was big enough to

Keeping a Safe Distance, Mind You

put your fist in," said his wife.

While looking at waterfalls, canyon, and osprey, we also saw an older lady evacuated from a steep trail at the Tower Falls junction in Yellowstone. She descended the trail in sandals, tripped over some logs and rocks, and may have broken her leg. The park rescue squad came and put her on this wheelbarrow-like contraption with a huge wheel. They then pushed her up that steep trail with her leg secured by an "air" cast. While waiting for the rescue to be over, we helped another lady get back into her car. Our famous coat hanger has now unlocked four vehicle doors. This is one thing Doug does very well, for some reason.

We came upon a "bust" taking place in one of the pull-offs and parked our truck about fifty feet away. We saw the park rangers handcuff a man, search his vehicle, and throw him in the back of their vehicle. We, of course, broke into a verse of *Bad Boys*. Do you know what the funniest thing was, though? Others were actually pulling up between us and the ranger to photograph the bison herd that stood nearby. None of the twelve cars or so that pulled in at various times even noticed the bust, and they were right next to it.

"Boy, if I was Jane Fonda, I would have asked for this gorgeous 113,000 acre ranch for a divorce settlement!" I exclaimed while driving past Ted Turner's Flying D Ranch.

We pulled over to watch bison grazing in the field. Ted Turner has amassed over 1.7 million acres in nine states in his quest to protect wildlife. A truck rambled by us, and I peered inside.

"Was that Ted Turner?" I asked Doug.

"Yeah, sure," he smiled as he continued watching the bison.

We found out later that Ted Turner had been at that ranch with his girlfriend the very same day we had been there. I still say that was him in the pick-up. Is this like sighting Elvis?

We also celebrated our 25th wedding anniversary on August 1st. Among other things we did that day, we had a wonderful anniversary dinner at the Jackson Lodge in the Grand Tetons—seeing moose off in the distance.

There are so many other stories I could tell. We have hiked some beautiful trails and seen the results of a 1959 earthquake that toppled a whole mountainside here and created a new lake. We took a "whitewater" raft ride that was only a river float trip since the rivers are very dry, and the whitewater experience was all of ten seconds. Oh, well, at least it was the Snake River. The canoeing on Jackson Lake in

Smiling Places

the Tetons was awesome. Swimming in the icy cold Glacier Lakes was exhilarating—the waters are so clear and blue! The thermal features of Yellowstone were fascinating, and we hiked the entire boardwalk trail system provided around the beautiful boiling pots and geysers. I have to admit, though, the sulfur smell from these natural wonders was a little overpowering at times.

Before we left the area, the western fires began to appear all around us. From the news reports, it seems like the whole west was on fire at times. From our campsite, we saw spectacular "dry" lightning displays high up on the mountains—without the accompanying rain, and that is when you worry. A local paper is quoted here as saying that dry thunderstorms in the west generated 75,000 lightning strikes that sparked more than four hundred new forest fires in a SINGLE DAY! In our five weeks' stay, we had two good rainstorms—one in Yellowstone and one in the Tetons. It was extremely dry in other parts of the west, but it didn't seem so dry here. Our own campground in the Tetons banned any open campfires.

The video pictures we have taken of the wildlife would rival Marty Stouffer's *Wild America* (Some great close-ups, I am sure.) We never hike or drive without our video camera, and on the way back, near the place where we hiked last week at Paint Pots, we saw a grizzly. He walked around that area, and then walked down the same boardwalk, and crossed the street. Next, chased a bull elk out of the trees, and the elk ran right past our truck at top speed. The bear then disappeared into the woods and apparently followed the road in the same direction we were going. We were in a ninety-minute, slow-moving traffic jam. The neat thing was that we almost got the whole thing on tape. We also captured on video, beavers building damns, pine martens running up logs, elk, moose nursing their calves, bald eagles/osprey splashing into the water and catching fish in the Snake River, many new species of birds (too numerous to mention), coyotes hunting, black bears, buffalos charging, and so many more. We now have ten video volumes. Too much to do now, so we haven't watched them, but they will make for great trips down memory lane later. We experienced one of the greatest summers of our lives, and these experiences will be with us for the rest of our lives. I just hope my memories will all make sense. Remember, I am operating with less oxygen to my brain! I can tell you that I haven't noticed any change in Doug due to the lack of oxygen. For some reason, I didn't have any expectations of change, but I am still *keeping a safe distance, mind you.*

25 - As Luck Would Have It

There are many important rules and principles of life that we are taught along our journeys. In school, we are taught about Archimedes, Galileo, and asking permission to use the restroom. At home we are taught the Golden Rule, Mom's rule (Do your homework before watching TV.), and Appleseed's Rule: "An apple a day keeps the doctor away." Then, some things we just do by instinct. One such principle we instinctively come to know is the Law of Unintended Consequence, or LUC. You may know this rule by the common phrase "As LUC would have it," never knowing that the "k" was an erroneous addition made as the phrase was handed down from generation to generation.

When we enter a world of leisure activities such as Yellowstone National Park, we are given maps, a list of things to see and do, and a list of things not to do. Using the good manners we were taught at school and home, we graciously take what is offered, and then—just as graciously—hand them to our spouse and say instinctively, "Put this in the plastic bag; I may want to read it later." This leads to the unintended consequence of having to say later, "Boy, was that stupid of me! Wish I had read this earlier before I did that." This would be an example of the Law of Unintended Consequence. This is also why more and more products have more and more safety warnings on them. Each revision of the warning labels becomes smaller and smaller to handle more LUC. We could keep the safety warnings simple with one label on every product that reads: *WARNING: Avoid LUC—Read the literature so you won't say, "Boy was that stupid of me! Wish I had read this earlier before I did that!"*

I would later learn—after reading the literature—that there are over 3,000 elk in Yellowstone National Park, . It would seem that a great number of tourists do nothing but go around the park counting up the number of elk they see. It almost appeared as if there was some sort of elk rally going on. You know, Elk Rallies—people speeding around the park to get all 3,000 elk counted before anyone else.

Smiling Places

I couldn't help but ask myself, "Why is it that national park tourists leave their cars in the middle of the roads with doors hanging open every time they see wildlife?"

Having not yet read the literature, I followed up with a thought-provoking comment to Doug, "They need to publish procedures for wildlife viewing etiquette."

Doug answered in the sincere, well-thought-out, but perhaps too condescending manner of a spouse, "That's a good idea, Mel."

So, after watching tourists photograph the elk at Yellowstone, I came up with ten common actions of tourists, and the LUC for not reading the literature provided by the National Park Service. Here they are:

Tourist Action	LUC Result
While driving on a busy park road, constantly scan the landscape for elk.	Vehicle goes 20 MPH too slow. Begin to hear honking horns.
Upon seeing elk, excitedly throw your arm out of the window and point in the direction of the elk.	Check hand for injuries after being hit by car going opposite direction.
SLAM on your brakes to stop your car.	Ten cars behind you pile up.
Grab your camera!	Twenty cars now behind you. Horn noises increase.
Exit your vehicle quickly, leaving driver's door open. Note: Up to three willing passengers can also play this game by leaving doors open.	Now, have thirty cars behind & fifteen cars in opposing lane stopped. Horn noises increase significantly.
Proceed quickly to field where elk are grazing. Don't worry about finding your car afterwards; you can follow the sounds of honking cars.	The famous Two-Hundred-Car-Elk-Jam. Some join your search. Horn noises become non-stop distraction.

As Luck Would Have It

Tourist Action	LUC Result
Since you didn't read the zoom lens literature, get within two feet for a good close-up.	Elk *will* charge—making for better "action" photography.
As elk charges, run quickly toward car—if you can find it—as horns have stopped.	Two-Hundred-Car-Elk-Jam tourists laugh at you hysterically; forgetting to honk their horns.
Jump in car and shut door, thankful you escaped charging elk and got its picture.	Find bear in car eating your picnic, since you unintentionally left doors open.
Get picture of bear. Wow! Two close-ups of an elk and now, a bear. What's this—a lens cover?	Your loving spouse paraphrases LUC and says, "Boy, was that stupid of you; why don't you ever read the literature first!"

26 The Great Escape

The best of plans can be waylaid by outside influences. During the Fire Season of 2000, the Governor of Montana closed 6.5 million acres of forest lands to the public due to the extreme fire danger. Sports games were either being canceled or moved to other cities further east. County fairs were being canceled. "Follow Me" construction cars were leading people through the smoke-filled interstate I-15 which had been closed off and on. People were being evacuated from places in western Montana. Others were walking around towns in surgical masks trying to breathe. The only road between southern Grand Teton National Park and northern Yellowstone National Park would be temporarily shut down due to a 2,000-acre wildfire. This wildfire, set by "dry" lightning, was blazing about one mile from Flagg Ranch, the resort where we had camped earlier.

Our plan had been to go from the Grand Teton area north to Glacier National Park. The smoke seemed to be getting worse at the Grand Tetons, so we decided to go back to Yellowstone National Park to decide where we were going next. We felt we had tracked the fires pretty well and thought we were at least 50-150 miles east of the major fires. Then, we heard that Butte, MT, which was between us and Glacier National Park, was having darker skies filled with ash and smoke. After one night in West Yellowstone, we decided to head east—and fast! It was seven a.m. in the morning. The sun was in the sky but appeared like a round ball through all the smoke and haze. The sky was an eerie shade of red, orange, and pink. As we drove deeper into the Gallatin Forest heading north to I-90 at Bozeman, the smoke got denser and denser. When we left our truck to take some breaks, our throats and eyes were burning from the smoke.

As we reached Bozeman, we just hoped that in the last few days, no new fires had started from the dry lightning storms that seemed to be everywhere. To refresh your memories, Bozeman, was where we saw the beautiful fireworks display against the mountain ranges surrounding

The Great Escape

the whole city. This time, when we pulled into Bozeman, you could not even *see* the mountain ranges. The town appeared totally flat, and the second and third stories of buildings were hidden from view. The daylight was obscured by smoke and tiny particles in the air. The odor of smoke was everywhere. We never stopped there because I knew I couldn't stay in that environment long.

We pulled out onto I-90 east and passed Livingston, MT, about twenty miles east of Bozeman. "Poor air quality," the Billings paper predicted for Livingston. We couldn't even see the town from the highway. This was to be the longest travel day we would have in our experiences. We drove for about nine hours that day to find fresh air. Most travel days would be three to five hours, which would take us between 100 and 200 miles. Our great escape took us all the way to within seventy miles of Montana's eastern border. Tired, we pulled into the town of Glendive—happy to be away from the fires—but not knowing what to expect, or where we had arrived.

27 - The Out of Towners Revisited

As we walked through the center of town in Glendive, Montana, the banks' sign read 103 degrees. One of the locals was complaining about the high humidity; it was in the upper 20's. We had no complaints; the air was fresh and clear with no smoke from the fires further west. The whole town was shutting down early today. Many store signs read: "See you at the fair." Tonight, the out-of-towners would be attending the annual Dawson County Fair Rodeo.

Will I never learn? Why do I keep trying to buck the laws of nature?

"No, I am not buying this cowboy hat." Doug said firmly after I begged him to try again.

I took one look at him, and I knew why he was saying that. He looked like that little Chihuahua on those Taco Bell commercials.

"OK," I said, "but will you try on the boots?"

"Do they have any boots with a soft, running shoe sole?"

"You know they don't!"

Again, the lesson I can't seem to grasp is that I can't take the city slicker out of my husband.

My biggest concern today was not fashion, however—but the top of my head. If I had never seen the sign proclaiming Glendive as the "Paddlefish Capital of the World," my scalp would not have become poached. We are not "fisher people," but even *I* know that a fifty-five-pound prehistoric fish that must be caught with heavy-duty rods and reels would be a sight to see.

"Look at the river," Doug said, "It is dry this time of the year. Those fish aren't running now."

"If you know so much: Why do fish run? And how can you tell if a fish is running or simply walking fast?" I asked, knowing a woman again using her higher intellect had bested and befuddled her man. Leaving him speechless, I grabbed my sun visor and took off. I walked along the Yellowstone River; it flows through the middle of Glendive—searching for these giants. I stood on bridges peering down into the very shallow

The Out of Towners Revisited

waters of the river. I did not see any fish, let alone the paddlefish. When I returned, my husband was smiling.

"I read the literature after you left. *As luck would have it*, paddlefishing season is May 15 to June 30. Since it is August, you may have quite a wait. Why don't you ever read the literature first?"

"You are such the comedian," I said as I removed my sun visor and discovered my sunburned scalp.

"Ouch!" I said while peering into the mirror.

"Why didn't you take your hiking hat?" my husband asked.

"Because you can only look for paddlefish when wearing a sun visor; it is part of fishing etiquette!" I snapped back, trying to bluff my way through the conversation.

He just gave me that all too familiar (Are you nuts?) look and dropped the conversation.

We got out of our truck at the county fairgrounds that evening wearing jeans, t-shirts, and running shoes; Doug wore a baseball cap. I didn't want to enclose the top of my head since the temperature up there was hitting 130 degrees. As we walked towards the gate, I noticed row upon row of Montana license plates.

"Looks like we are the only out-of-towners here," I said.

Believe me, we didn't need to tell anyone we were from out of town. We stuck out like zebras in a horse barn.

As soon as we took our seats in the grandstand, a sea of cowboy hats surrounded us. Cowboy boots clanged loudly on the new metal bleachers, which had just been renovated by volunteers from the area. A lady with a baby stroller was trying to negotiate the stairs. A man jumped out of his seat and carried her stroller up to her seat. Chivalry is alive and well in Montana.

"So where y'all from?" asked the man I was sitting next to. All of a sudden the immediate crowd around us got quiet so they could hear our answer.

"We are just passing through on our way back home to Ohio," I said in my "funny-talking pilgrim" voice that would have made John Wayne proud.

"You *are* a long ways from home. Have you ever been to a rodeo before?"

"Nope, this is our first one."

"Well, you are in for a real treat, Lil' Darlin'."

I just loved being called "Lil' Darlin'."

Smiling Places

Doug and I learned many things before the start of this rodeo. One man from the row below us said that the origins of the rodeo probably began in the 1800's when cowhands would round up cattle and drive the herds to market. To celebrate these roundups, informal competitions would be held so cowhands could display the skills of their trade.

We also spoke with a man whose brother used to compete in rodeos. "My brother said to respect the animals. Every time you get on one to ride, it is different. You constantly try to improve yourself through form, speed, and consistency.

A lady from our row told me to look at my rodeo program.

"Do you see the events listed here?" she asked.

I scanned the page and saw bareback riding, calf roping, saddle bronc, steer wrestling, bull riding, team roping, and barrel racing.

"Generally, the first five events listed here are at most rodeos. Team and steer roping are also popular. Barrel racing is usually an event for female riders."

"What is a bronc?" I asked her.

"A bronc is a horse that bucks or tries to throw a rider off," she told me.

Just then the rodeo began. We all stood up and sang *"The Star Spangled Banner."* Bucking horses were released from chutes and they bolted into the arena with riders trying to remain mounted for eight seconds. Lassoes were thrown around calves' necks by riders on horses, who then dismounted and tied three of the calves' feet together—vying for the fastest time. Riders slid from their horses and grasped the horns of steer many times their weight and tried to throw the steer to the ground in the fastest time. Did these people have rubber spines? These animals were not always cooperative in heading back to their pens after the events. They chased the cowboys, who in turn, would fling themselves up on fences to avoid these angry beasts. I wondered aloud why these cowboys would do something so dangerous.

"They want a chance to compete at the National Finals Rodeo," said the man next to me.

"How do they get to the Nationals?" I asked.

"These cowboys work all year to build up points to qualify for the Nationals. There is lots of money to be made."

"How much?" I asked.

"They can share in millions of dollars in prize money."

"Wow!" I said.

The Out of Towners Revisited

Wow, indeed! Those cowboys had already built up points with me. I really didn't care how the judges scored them. I had my own scoring system: Five points for the largest belt buckle, ten points for the cutest smile, twenty points for the tightest jeans, and a whopping fifty points for the best physique. I was giving out points all over the place. I decided right there, on that bleacher, Montana men were the best-looking guys in the USA.

During intermission, I noticed everyone got out raffle tickets, and the announcer rattled off some numbers.

"Yahoo," yelled the nice man next to me. "I won!"

We all cheered as he left to collect his prize.

"Would you like a soft drink?" a lady offered. "You ought to try their taco salad," she said. "It is wonderful."

It smelled wonderful, too, so we split one and weren't disappointed.

An announcement was made on the loudspeaker. People from England were visiting the rodeo and won a small gift.

"We told them about you being from Ohio," another lady said, "but they told us they already had someone who had traveled the farthest. Imagine that, England."

"Oh, well, thanks for mentioning us," I said.

"We aren't the only out-of-towners here," I thought. "I wonder if they are wearing cowboy hats."

During the second part of the rodeo, the skies began to darken with thickening clouds. A spectacular lightning show was flashing in the distance. My favorite event, the bull riding, was last. I hoped the storm would hold off until the rodeo was over. It didn't. Halfway through the bull riding, lightning struck a tall light pole in the field adjacent to the metal grandstand. My hair stood up. Doug and I scrambled off the metal bleachers in a hurry—with half the spectators on our heels.

The skies opened up as we raced toward our truck. A gust of wind blew Doug's baseball cap off his head. As he did a little jig trying to catch his dancing hat, I felt the rain and wind soothing my sunburned head. Doug did manage to stomp on his cap with his wet, muddy shoe. I now understood why cowboys wore big hats and boots.

The fun part of attending this rodeo was obviously talking with the locals, but also the fact the rodeo was a real event—not something just set up to attract tourists. The out-of-towners were very pleased and would put Glendive on their list of places to revisit. When we got "home" from the rodeo, I noticed the front cover of our program. A huge

Smiling Places

bull with mean-looking eyes was looking at me. The caption read "Grasshopper: Former Professional Rodeo Cowboys Association (PRCA) Bucking Bull of the Year."

"Wow," I thought. "Even the animals become famous."

28 - Laughing with Buffalo

Our disappointment with not being able to see more of Montana due to the fires was quickly replaced with a sense of wonderment at all that North Dakota had to offer us. Frankly, we entered North Dakota with no preconceived notions of what we would find because neither of us had really ever heard very much about the state. It started as more of an "It's on the way to Minnesota," but we wound our way around much of North Dakota for the next three weeks and were very pleasantly surprised! We left Glendive, Montana and crossed into the southwest corner of the state to go see Theodore (TR) Roosevelt National Park. Somewhat uniquely, the park is broken into north and south units, about 60 to 70 miles apart.

Back in the late 1800's, before TR was president, he owned two ranches out here. He said that living in North Dakota prepared him for the presidency. He saw the buffalo and Audubon Bighorn sheep wiped out. He saw grasslands reduced to stubble because of poor grazing policies. TR was one of the first "environmental" presidents and used his "Bully Pulpit" to set aside many acres of land that you and I enjoy today.

When we first arrived, we camped at an RV park in Medora, a neat little historical town situated right next to the south unit of the park. Again, it was quite hot at 100-plus degrees. We quickly made the decision to stay at the RV park rather than the national park's non-electric campground since we wanted air conditioning for our trailer.

For whatever reason, TR National Park was not crowded and proved to be a wildlife extravaganza for us. We would walk by prairie dog towns at sunset to watch the coyotes and badgers, sometimes in tandem, trying to find a doggie dinner. Bison were everywhere. We would hike to the middle of the park and not hear anything. Perfect peace and quiet. We also were very lucky to see Big Horn Sheep, both rams and ewes. A porcupine had a two-minute standoff with our truck one evening. There it was in the middle of the road, and it wouldn't move one way or another. It just kept standing there looking at us. I thought before it was all over that we were going to have "quilled" tires. Finally it sauntered off

Smiling Places

into the grasses at the side of the road. No prairie rattlers or black widows were spotted even though we foolishly looked for them.

We saw a flock of about fifty mountain bluebirds, the most bluebirds we have ever seen at once. We also saw a bunch of Sharp Tailed Grouse. They didn't strut their stuff for us, though.

One time, we were watching wild horses standing in a field of trees; a man with Maryland license plates drove up, and we pointed out the wild horses to him. Well, I guess he didn't like the horses just standing there and wanted to see them run. So, do you know what he did? He starts blaring his horn to see if he could scare them. He didn't scare them, but he scared the stuffing out of me! Here it is seven a.m. in the peaceful morning, and we hadn't heard a car horn for days. His horn echoed off of every hill in that park for miles around. I thought he was goofy—the way he kept sitting there, beeping his horn. He finally sped away. He didn't get his running horse picture, so maybe he will not use his honking-horn trick in the future. At least, coming across individuals like this man was a rarity.

We also had what I consider one of the best wildlife experiences since I left Dayton: Yes, here while camping in this park. It was eleven p.m., Doug and I had just crawled into bed. We had heard coyotes calling earlier in the evening. The moon was full, and it was very quiet. Suddenly, a wolf started howling. He was very close to our trailer, as his call was almost deafening. He called for about a minute, and then there was silence again. I can still hear his call when I think about it. What a beautiful sound of the Wild West!

We watched four prairie falcons perform one night over a canyon. Their wings are the most aerodynamic of any bird. They are shaped like boomerangs, allowing the falcons to hover in mid-air and then, all of a sudden, dive at over one hundred miles per hour. They are among the fastest flying birds in the world. The birds we were watching would be riding the air currents. Then, two of them would bang together in mid-air, free-fall for about twenty to fifty feet, and then pull up again into the winds. We think they were practicing their hunting skills since they do bang into their bird prey in mid air to catch/kill them.

When the heat wave relented, we decided to dry-camp again at the north unit. We were now camping in the middle of the park because the temperatures had cooled down into the 70's and 80's during the day. Our clothes were crusted with dirt and burrs from hiking in the Badlands of southwest North Dakota. Trying to conserve our water, we had not

Laughing with Buffalo

showered in three days—except for the plastic water jugs that we warmed in the sun during the day and poured over ourselves in the evening. That was satisfying, but my gourmet dish of peanut butter and Ramen noodles no longer tasted good to either of us.

It was here that we came up with our own catch phrase of the day, Laughing with Buffalo. It became our saying for those situations when we saw Mother Nature have the upper hand with mere humans. The situation also dictates that *we were spectators* and not mere humans being toyed with. I had just gotten up about seven a.m. and heard grunting. You can sometimes hear this grunting ten minutes before you see anything. I sat up in bed and pulled the curtain back a tiny bit to see where the noise was coming from. As I peered outside, two black, beady eyes looked right back at me. I realized those beady eyes were on a massive, wooly head with pointed, curved horns.

"Yikes!" I said as I jerked the curtain closed. "Am I dreaming, or is a buffalo standing outside my bedroom window?"

"Doug," I whispered, "Doug, wake up!"

Of course Mr. Braveheart didn't stir and was oblivious to this 2,000 pound creature, whose horns could turn our tin can travel trailer into shredded mulch. He was oblivious—that is, until the back of our trailer started shaking.

"What's going on?" Doug asked and sat up in bed.

"Either we are experiencing a 10.5 earthquake, or a buffalo is trying to get in bed with us," I said while holding onto my closet.

The buffalo had decided that the back corner of our trailer made a good scratching post for its wooly head. Not having the presence of mind to conjure up Buffalo Bill Cody, I became worried that our leveling jacks could break, and that buffalo would roll us a few hundred feet into the Missouri River—while continuing to scratch its head, of course. My man was worried about whether or not he had charged his video camera batteries. Didn't matter—the camera was in the truck.

"I think that is a male buffalo because the bulls have those black beards," Doug said matter of factly.

I couldn't believe this! *Now* my man was identifying which *gender* this buffalo was, the same buffalo that was eating our taillights for breakfast.

In the meantime, our cat Sushi was howling, and she was bouncing off our trailer's walls like Gene Kelly.

I made my way to the front of our trailer and realized what she was

Smiling Places

howling about. Out of the woods, about twenty-five feet from our trailer, came a herd of forty to fifty buffalo!

Now, up to this point, this is not a "Laughing With Buffalo" moment as we were the ones being toyed with by Mother Nature. But then, the buffalo moved away from our trailer, stood around the restrooms, and grazed for about thirty minutes. This did not pose a problem for us since we had a self-contained restroom; however, the few tenters in our campground didn't think this predicament was humorous at all. I don't think it was the fear factor of having the buffalo so close to their tents. Rather, these buffalo were unexpectedly upsetting the campers' morning rituals. Now, that is a "Laughing ith Buffalo" moment!"

29 - Off Track Out Back

Well, the fires followed and caught up to us in North Dakota. Our favorite park, Theodore Roosevelt National Park, was closed for a few days after we left because of fires caused by lightning strikes. This was the southern section around Medora. There were also other lightning related fires in the western section of North Dakota. One spokesman said he estimated there could have been thirty-five burning at once. We were beginning to get a complex. Mother Nature was Laughing with Buffalos as tornados chased us out west; and now the fires were chasing us back east. On the positive side, we were moving more quickly from place to place—and we hoped, ahead of the fires.

We started our journey in the southwest corner of the state at Theodore Roosevelt National Park. Then, we proceeded north and discovered Ft. Union & Ft. Buford. We begin to appreciate the fact of why Lewis & Clark spent more time exploring the North Dakota area than any other. The Missouri River acted as their guide. At Ft. Buford, we stood at the confluence of the Missouri and Yellowstone Rivers. With a little imagination, it was just like it was described in the journals of Lewis and Clark. Ft. Union was built by John Jacob Astor and became the American Fur Company in 1828. This company dominated the upper Missouri region for years and became the headquarters for trading buffalo and beaver furs with the Indians.

We then ended up at the Canadian border (Manitoba) at the International Peace Garden. To help you picture in your mind where this is, go thirty-one miles north of the geographic center of North America (close—in Rugby, North Dakota). Didn't that help? The USA shares this garden with Canada to honor the friendship between the two countries. In addition to the formal gardens, there are 2,300 acres of lakes and forests. These gardens and lands are a free-zone where you can walk unrestricted between the US and Canada. The formal garden's features reminded us of the Washington D.C. Mall overlooking the Monument. At one end are the formal gardens containing more than 150,000 planted

Smiling Places

flowers. At the other end is the tall monument of peace with the Chapel of Peace. Everything is centered with two sidewalks (one on the USA side and one on the Canada side) going along the edges of the garden with symmetrical flower and shrub displays. It is about a 1/4 to 1/2 mile walk to Peace Chapel. The main features of the chapel are the three circular walls engraved with quotations from people of peace throughout history. As the indoor waterfall trickled down into a pool of stones, we read some of the quotes:

> *"The measure of life, after all, is not its duration, but its donation."*
> Peter Marshall

> *"Consider that this day will never dawn again."*
> Dante

The Dante quote would come back to us when we later saw a modern-day version on a campground sign that read: "Life is not a dress rehearsal." We stayed inside the chapel awhile meditating and praying. The only question Doug and I kept asking ourselves: "Why hadn't we ever heard of this place before we came to North Dakota?" It was very inspirational!

To best explore North Dakota's back roads and towns, we armed ourselves with binoculars, our video camera, bird books, and a good map. As we were driving around some really remote roads (the state only has ten people per square mile), we saw a sign that said it all:

WELCOME TO AMERICA'S OUTBACK!

We found much humor throughout the state. For example, one town had twin water towers. On one tower, the word HOT was painted, and the other—COLD! North Dakota is also home to the biggest buffalo, turtle, golfer, and fish (all statues). We will let you find them if you ever visit. As we left the western badlands area, the rolling farmland reminded us of home in a way, *but* the farms are a lot bigger. We passed many fields cultivated in wheat, rye, and gorgeous yellow fields of cultivated sunflowers; they meandered for miles. Oil and gas rigs also dot the countryside.

One of the most amazing features, though, was the sheer number of

Off Track Out Back

wetland areas that dotted the plains. North Dakota has more wildlife refuges than any other state, and being the crazy birders we are, we had a blast. We lost track of how many refuges we visited, but it didn't matter. Everywhere you drove, flocks of birds would be present. We literally saw thousands, maybe hundreds of thousands of birds, throughout the state. Close your eyes for a moment and imagine 500-1000 swallows flying around within one acre. How about 500 pelicans closely huddled together in a small pond, and on seeing you approach, they all take off? Not to mention the thousands of ducks and numerous hawks we saw perched on the rolls of baled hay along the sides of the roads. If there is a birder's heaven, this just may be it. We are so confused now on our water birds that we can only identify the stuffed, labeled ones. At least they pose for you.

We also saw a mink and a bobcat in the wild for the first time. North Dakota also has moose in the north central portion and a national refuge of buffalo and elk around Devil's Lake. Of course, there is all that wildlife at Theodore Roosevelt State Park. Our only birding advice is *wear a hat when birding in North Dakota!*

We stayed at many nice state parks throughout the state. The larger towns we visited centered around Minot (population around 35,000), which has Minot Air Force Base, and Bismarck, (population around 50,000), the capitol. Fargo is the largest city with around 75,000 people. Bismarck was a very nice city with a beautiful state capitol building and a wonderful historic center located right next to the Capitol. If you ever visit Bismarck, do not miss them.

The best BBQ restaurant honors go to Space Aliens restaurant. Located in both Bismarck and Fargo, their fire roasted BBQ pizza is awesome! It is one of the few restaurants where we returned a second time for another sampling.

As we were eating dinner at the Homesteaders Restaurant in Minot, a bolt of lightning came down out of the sky and struck the field below us. Our paranoia about fires went to next level. A huge roll of baled hay and the grasses surrounding it caught fire. The fire department arrived quickly and stopped it from spreading.

We also visited many small towns, some thriving and others just surviving, but all were friendly. Nebraska still has our vote for the friendliest state we visited, but North Dakota is a close second. We just loved those steering–wheel-waves, and the friendly conversations struck up while stopping at different places.

Smiling Places

A few weeks ago, we saw a PBS special on TV about old abandoned farmhouses in Minnesota. It could have been written here. We saw many, and as we drove past, we wondered about the people who had lived there and the farms they had managed.

My vote for favorite town goes to Jamestown, population of about 16,000. Jamestown is located in a valley where the James and Pipestem Rivers meet; it provides a setting for many water and birding activities. Jamestown College is located here as well. It was chartered in 1884 and has a beautiful campus. Jamestown was also the boyhood home of Louie L'Amour, the famous western writer who wrote around 117 books. We walked the trail of L'Amour in town and went into the library where Louie spent many hours reading before he became famous. Guess what I bought yesterday? Louie L'Amour's first novel!

30 - You Bet

If there is anything we learned from our travels, it is that each state is different. Each has its own characteristics and exciting treasures to share with its visitors who have time to look. Minnesota was no different. We quickly picked up that the expression "You Bet" was commonplace and thrown into most conversations by the locals. Minnesota is packed full of surprises, ranging from beautiful biking to "get serious" shopping extravaganzas! We would find a one-of-a-kind gas station, see a blow down area, and learn about a brotherhood of doctors. We discovered, to our surprise, that Minnesota was the second largest producing state of wild rice; much of it is cultivated by hand—I felt this enhanced its taste. At Chippewa National Forest, you can find the largest community of nesting bald eagles in the USA (except for Alaska) with over 150 active nests at last estimate. We drove through parts of the forest and did some hiking. We even managed to see one bald eagle soaring close to the shoreline of a beautiful lake.

Unfortunately, we didn't have time to visit International Falls, MN. Since I was a little girl, I have watched TV 7 in Dayton; I remember them always talking about the temperatures in International Falls. Supposedly, International Falls has a giant thermometer in town for that special Kodak moment. We don't want to burst any bubbles, but according to some locals, International Falls is NOT the coldest place in the US. Reportedly, Tower, Minnesota is the coldest. It is located south of International Falls in the northeast Boundary Waters near Ely, Minnesota. I was told if you blink your eyes when going through it, you could miss it. Go figure! Voyageurs National Park is also near International Falls and has its boundary on the Canadian border. The other place we missed around Ely, Minnesota is known as the gateway to the Boundary Waters Canoe area. National Geographic has named the Boundary Waters area as one of the fifty places everyone should visit in their lifetime. Our list of "places to return" just keeps growing; however, the threat of snow was building in the fall air.

Smiling Places

We started our Minnesota adventures in the St. Paul-Minneapolis area. The four stories of the famous Mall of America towered over the Bloomington, MN skyline as we sped down I-494, right by St. Paul/Minneapolis. OK, towering may be stretching it, but to shopaholics, this place is on the same scale as the Sears Tower. I mean, how often do you get to visit 520 stores under one roof in the largest shopping and entertainment mall in the USA?

The day I chose for our visit to the mall was a rather stupid choice on my part, but was an integral piece of my husband's devious plan. I had given him notice that we were going to the Mall on Monday, and he could chose what to do the day before. He chose the Minnesota State Fair. The fair was packed since we went on a Sunday, but the people were laughing, and everybody was so nice and courteous. It was like going back to the Ozzie and Harriet era. Anyway, my legs were worn out from the fair after seven to eight hours. Never admitting he secretly planned it this way. My husband probably thought, "You bet! If I wear her out at the fair, how long can she shop?

Well, I showed him! After walking the mall for eight to nine hours, we finally limped back to our truck. That was about a sixteen hour hike in two days! I don't know how Doug kept his foot on the accelerator driving back to our campground. My shoes were off, and I was giving myself foot rubs all the way home. Can you believe we didn't buy hardly anything? Birthdays and other gifts had already been given, and I never have been able to plan far in advance for Christmas. You bet! I am the great procrastinator.

So, we walked and walked seeing the layout of the mall and visiting only five to ten percent of the five hundred or more stores. The mall is probably around four times as big as the size of the local Fairfield Mall in Dayton, OH (just my guess). The Mall of America has four stories, is basically square-shaped, and anchor stores occupy each of the four corners. On the east and west sides of the mall, there are free parking garages, and to the north is an outside parking area at ground-level. There are more than 13,000 parking spaces, and believe it when we say that you had better memorize *exactly* where you park at the mall. In fact, you just may want to carry a "which-way-is-north-whistle." We saw many people scratching their heads inside the parking garages.

The mall features a huge LEGO Imagination Center, an Underwater Adventure (1.2 million gallon walk-through aquarium), and over forty restaurants and nightclubs—including Planet Hollywood, Rainforest

You Bet

Cafe, and Knuckleheads Comedy Club. Camp Snoopy is located in the middle of the mall and is the largest indoor theme park in the USA. Watch out below as the four-stories-high roller coaster swoops over your head! The whole fourth story is filled with restaurants, bars, and a movie complex. Some of them open by eleven a.m. and stay open late into the night. You can get some great videos of the center of the mall while standing on the third and fourth floors. We also managed to find the largest sports store at the mall and played a fun game of racket ball in one of their demo setups. So, is this the place to go if you want to experience the wisdom of Minerva's "Shop-until-you-drop" motto? You bet! Should you leave your husband at home? You bet!

After our mall excursion, we proceeded south to Rochester. Our curiosity about this city had always been piqued because it ranked as one of the ten best places to live in the US. No wonder: the Mayo Clinic is located here, right in the heart of downtown Rochester. We took the Mayo Clinic Tour and I had visions of surgeons performing operations, research labs, and trauma rooms. Reality set in quickly when the tour guide pointed out the beautiful architecture of the buildings and the Mayo Brothers offices. They also told us not to take any pictures due to the privacy of the patients. The architecture of the buildings was magnificent. The buildings were accented by built-in marble and rook wood (yes, the rook wood from Cincinnati) and trimmed by large, delicate, wood carvings.

In 1883 and 1888, Dr. Mayo's two sons—Will and Charlie—joined him in practice in Rochester after they finished medical school. They had helped their father in his practice during their boyhoods. Their father once mortgaged their home to buy a $600 microscope needed for his practice and research. It took many years to pay off that obligation. A tornado devastated Rochester in 1883, and six years later, the Sisters of St. Francis and the Mayos built the twenty-seven bed St. Mary's Hospital. The concept of group practice evolved in the 1890's with the Mayo's inviting many famous physicians to join them in Rochester. By 1914, the first building constructed for an integrated, group medical practice was completed, and the Mayo Clinic has been growing ever since.

Mayo Clinic's transportation system is particularly interesting: They still have many miles of pneumatic tubes to transport medical files and other information. These are the same type of tubes we use every time we pull up to a drive-thru window at a bank. Those tubes send our banking paperwork from our car to the tellers sitting behind the glass win-

Smiling Places

dows. Mayo Clinic has a central transfer station that moves the records and information from one tube to another—and they arrive at the right destination. Many thousands of tube mailings are sent through this system daily. Can you imagine the magnitude of this operation? We were told that the Clinic was trying to computerize all their operations, but that is still probably years away. They do have their own subway system of underground walking hallways for pedestrians; they connect most of the Mayo Clinic buildings.

In 1919, all the assets of the Mayo Clinic were transferred by the Mayo brothers into an endowment—the Mayo Foundation. This foundation includes two other hospitals in Rochester, and Mayo Clinics in Jacksonville, Florida and Scottsdale, Arizona. Other Mayo health system facilities are located throughout Minnesota, Iowa, and Wisconsin.

The Mayo brothers died in 1939 within a few months of one another. If you ever visit Rochester, don't miss the famous "Pill Hill" residential section located close to the hospitals. Many old, beautiful, two- and three-story Victorian mansions line the hilly, curving streets bordered with many large, majestic trees.

The Mayo Mansions are also open for tours. A tower high atop one of the Mayo medical buildings, houses a carillon of fifty-six bells—the largest bell weighs 7,840 pounds. The "singing tower" rang out as we were ready to leave the clinic. Such a beautiful, sweet, melody poured forth—so soothing to one's spirit.

Remember *Little House on the Prairie*? Some of the places that Laura Ingals Wilder lived in her early years are located in the southern part of Minnesota; we visited a few of them. What I found fascinating about her life was that Laura did not begin writing her *Little House* book series until age sixty-five. Laura and Almanzo did marry and they eventually settled a short distance from Branson, Missouri. Laura died there at age ninety in 1957. Melissa Gilbert, who played Laura in the TV series, looks so much like the real Laura Ingals Wilder; it is uncanny to see their pictures right next to each other.

Minnesota really brags about its bike paths, and we can definitely understand why. It seems like every abandoned rail line has been converted to a biking path. We read that they have more biking trails than any other state. St. Cloud, Minnesota is about eighty miles northwest of St. Paul/Minneapolis. This is where we bought our dream bikes: Trek Navigator 200's that were even *on sale*! They are comfort bikes for old people like us—suspension coils and well-padded seats.

You Bet

Our problem: how would we transport these bikes around the country with us? We needed to get a bike rack to fit our truck hitch, so we could take the bikes from our campground to nearby bike trails without taking "Thing" along. We also needed the same rack to fit on Thing's bumper for transport around the country. Our bumper says one hundred pounds maximum weight, and I didn't like that since the bikes and rack added up to around eighty pounds. We have hitched them back there a few times, but now we are putting one of them into the trailer when we pack up to go. I wanted Doug to secure the bumper better—especially after we heard a story of someone who was going down the road dragging their bent trailer bumper with bikes behind them. We heard the bikes were totaled after they stopped and discovered their misfortune. I do want to emphasize *this was not us*. We have only purchased one set of bikes, thank goodness.

Just up from Saint Cloud is the quaint, friendly town of Sauk Centre. We camped at the Sinclair Lewis City Campground on Sauk Lake. This has our vote for the most beautiful city campground we have visited thus far in our travels. Complete with band shell and boat ramp for some fantastic fishing, it is another town with a famous author. I'm beginning to think something is trying to send me a message. If you are familiar with Garrison Keillor's novels, the towns surrounding and including Sauk Centre make up the Lake Wobegon area. Even though not born in Sauk Centre, Keillor wrote "...where all the women are strong, all the men good looking, and all the children are above average." Now, don't get me started again about good-looking men. Remember the Montana rodeos? Best of all, a new twenty-eight mile asphalt bike trail called the Lake Wobegon Trail has its western trail-head right near the campground, and it was a beautiful bike trail!

This town was also the birthplace of Sinclair Lewis. Did anyone ever read *Main Street* written in 1920 by Sinclair Lewis? This was not only one of his most famous novels, but also one of his most controversial. In the 1920's, this novel outraged some people in this town because they could recognize themselves in this book, and of course, did not appreciate his mocking portrayals of their characters. He was the first American to win the Pulitzer Prize for Literature in 1930.

I had just finished reading *Main Street* as we walked down the center of town. Many of the same buildings mentioned in this novel are still here. Main Street Drug, known as Dyers Drug Store in the book, was actually built in 1903; Sinclair's father had his medical offices upstairs.

Smiling Places

Those offices are now apartments. We walked inside and noted the old soda fountain area had been removed. The Palmer House Hotel is across the street from the drug store. Sinclair worked—and was fired from there—as a young man.

We were fortunate enough to tour Sinclair Lewis' boyhood home which has been restored to just how it was when he was growing up. Since we were visiting after Labor Day, the tour was open only by appointment and on weekends. However, the tour guide for the home came to our rescue and graciously agreed to let us see it before a large tour group was coming through. She gave an outstanding tour which certainly paralleled much of what I had read in the book. I could "see and feel" Sinclair throughout the house—upon completion of this tour—it provoked an even deeper understanding to me of *Main Street*. Sinclair Lewis died in 1951 and is buried next to his father in the Greenwood Cemetery in Sauk Centre.

Since I haven't mentioned "Thing," our travel trailer for a while, I don't want you to think that I am getting used to living in this spacious two-hundred square-foot travel trailer. Doug is always worried about the trailer's weight, so he keeps a tight reign on my shopping. However, I do manage to smuggle in books by the various authors we have run across. Wives always hate to admit when their husbands are right. You bet! When walking the Mall of America, Doug kept muttering about the small trailer that was our home. Whenever I would pick something up, he would say, "If you can't consume it, you can't buy it." So, I'll admit this was one of the *few* times he *might* have been right, but I won't swear on a stack of Bibles that he was. *You* can take that *bet* to the bank!

31 - The Pillsbury Dough Girl

Grab your cameras! You don't want to miss a must-have moment with the greatest north woodsman of all times: Paul Bunyan, and of course, his blue ox Babe. Their giant statues were built in 1937 and have remained in Bemidji, Minnesota ever since—to the delight of all who visit. Bemidji is also home to Bemidji State University, a beautiful college campus set on the banks of Bemidji Lake. We camped in Bemidji State Park about six miles north of the city; running alongside this park are two Bunyan-sized trails. One is one hundred miles long and paved; and the other is twenty miles longer, but only parts of it are paved.

This is where we first started having trouble with the cold weather. One night while camping there, I got up and turned on the water, but nothing came out of the faucet. My man was sleeping when I notified him of my dilemma.

In a trance-like state, he muttered, "flashlight," which I promptly handed him.

He then ventured out into the cold, dark night. *Thump, bang*, and an *expletive* the whole campground probably heard—then the door opened.

"It's frozen," my man declared triumphantly. "I disconnected it."

"Well, how do I get water now?" I asked.

"The water pump and water tank should kick in," he said.

Sure enough, I got water by turning on the faucet. What a man! I thought as he went back to his warm bed. For that instant, I saw John Wayne rescuing his damsel in distress! However, this John Wayne was a bit grumpier than the one I remembered in the movies.

The cold weather issue also affected Sushi. Did I mention that in her early years she had the run of a home with gas heat when winter came? Sticking her in a trailer with limited heat and minimal insulation tends to make her surly and somewhat revenge-minded. So, when the temperature drops at night, she heads for the nearest sleeping humans and their warm blankets. She places her eight-pound body in strategic locations under the blankets; this in turn gives human beings back aches and sore muscles. Somehow, the law of weights and measures does not add up.

Smiling Places

Everyone can move an eight-pound object—yet, our eight-pound cat becomes immovable.

"That will teach you for not keeping me warm today." she purred while curling up against my back.

The last day at the park for us was quite chilly. It was late afternoon, and the wind had grown quite strong. The skies were threatening, but nonetheless, we needed our "bike fix." Have you ever craved exercise? I can't believe I have reached a point in my life when I need an exercise fix. The ride would also stretch out those kinks in my back from Sushi. Anyway, I insisted we go out for one last ride. Donning gloves, sweatshirt, and a large, blue windbreaker with a drawstring hood, I set out.

The first part of the trail was through woods, and the trees provided some shelter from the sun and wind, but it was on the next part of the trail where the trouble began. This old rail line sat on top of an embankment with a thirty-foot drop off on each side. There were no guardrails, nor trees nor any other object of protection between me and the thirty feet below. We were biking that part of the trail when all of a sudden, a huge wind gust kicked up. The wind caught my blue windbreaker which suddenly blew up as if I had just pulled the ripcord on an inflatable boat. I looked like the blue Pillsbury Dough Girl! My hood was also all puffed out while those drawstrings pulled at my neck and choked me. The wind was pulling me toward the edge of that bike trail! I heard my man burst out laughing and yelling the famous words, "Zig Zag!" You see, many years ago, Doug's brother told us that the only thing about sailing we would need to know, before we set out in a small sailboat on Lake Michigan, was "Zig Zag." That is how you move the boat in relation to the waves, the wind, and where you are trying to go. I guess my man thought I had set full sail, but I didn't think it was so humorous. I slammed on my brakes and decided I could pedal no further. I walked my bike back toward the wooded part of the trail. Doug, of course, rode back, but he had not set sail with his jacket...and then the sky opened up! Unfortunately, we still had a few miles of the wooded trails to ride before we would be back to Thing, and this was fall in the north woods! That rain was freezing cold, and we were both soaking wet when we arrived at Thing. I suddenly remembered those previously-forgotten lessons warning about the year-round dangers of hypothermia. I dried off, grabbed Sushi for warmth—despite her protests—and snuggled under the blanket with her. In retrospect, I wouldn't have done anything different. It was another exciting adventure—just another day with the bumbling idiots.

32- Parting the Headwaters

From Sauk Centre, we ventured north and eventually ended up in Itasca State Park which encompasses about 32,000 acres. This is the must-see of the Minnesota State Parks as it contains the Headwaters of the Mississippi River. It also features paved biking trails, canoeing, birding, fishing and swimming. There are also wonderful, well-marked hiking trails along a sixteen mile wilderness loop drive loop abounding with wildlife.

One chilly morning, we decided to drive the loop road and do some hiking. We walked along a "blow down" area where, in 1995, strong winds (over one hundred mph) knocked down a huge stand of trees. Some trees were left upright with their tops gone—it was eerie to see as Ohio didn't have anything like it. On another trail, while surrounded by majestic pine trees in a deep, dark forest, we heard the haunting call of the Common Loon, the Minnesota State bird. Did you know the loon is the earth's oldest living bird species?

Our feet were tired and hot from our hikes that early morning, so we decided that this was the day! As we pulled into the Mississippi Headwaters parking lot, I peeled off my hiking boots and threw on my loafers. It was about forty degrees outside as we approached the mighty Mississippi. I noticed the sign:

> "Here 1475 feet above the ocean
> the mighty Mississippi begins to flow
> on its winding way 2,552 miles
> to the Gulf of Mexico."

"Don't be wimpy," a native Minnesotan had warned us a week ago. "Walk across the river like we do—BAREFOOT!"

I discarded my loafers at water's edge and rolled up my pant's legs. I stuck my foot in—and quickly pulled it out. "Boy, is that cold!" I shivered.

Smiling Places

"OK, let's go," I said as I gritted my teeth and began my journey across the frigid waters. We passed the log bridge (It was set up for the wimps.) and reached the other side. Then, we went back across the same way we had come since we left our shoes on the opposite bank. DUH!

A crowd was gathering on the banks watching us. "Cold? You Bet!" one man said.

"Why did you do that?" another asked.

"Because it was there," we both said in unison, then looked at each other and smiled.

I slipped back into my loafers and went straight to the gift shop where I bought my badge which read "I walked across the Mississippi Headwaters at Itasca State Park, Minnesota." I pinned it on my Jenny Lake hiking hat from the Grand Tetons and wore it proudly.

By the way, the mighty Mississippi is a mere trickle at this point, but it doesn't matter to me. I walked across twenty-five feet of the largest river in the USA. I really had you fooled there for a minute, didn't I? I know you were thinking about those Mark Twain stories and imagining those huge steamboat paddlewheels floating down the river. Not here—not in twelve inches of cold, cold water.

While in Minnesota, we read an article from a national newspaper discussing the recent shark attacks in Florida. Pretty typical information except for the statement that bull sharks can survive in both freshwater and saltwater. Actually, they have even been spotted in the Mississippi River, north of St. Louis! The article failed to mention how far north. Maybe next time we part the headwaters of the mighty Mississippi, I will use the wimpy log bridge, and Doug can cross in his bare feet.

33 - Shore was Great

In my humble opinion, Lake Superior is the most beautiful of all the Great Lakes. It is the cleanest and has fascinating rock structures—much like they were many, many years ago—on its shoreline. Our short excursion centered around Duluth, Minnesota--on Lake Superior.

I expected—and got—the obligatory groan when I told Doug we were going to Cloquet, about twenty miles southwest of Duluth to see a Frank Lloyd Wright design. In Doug's previous life (before retirement), he had the distinction of supervising a talented group of engineers and architects. The engineering part was right up Doug's alley as he was one. But architects? This man is colorblind, and it was a constant source of amusement in his organization as he tried—in vain—to compensate for this deficiency. Doug knew that Frank Lloyd Wright was the architect of architects, but he didn't know we were so close to the one gas station he designed. We don't know why he designed it, but that Phillips 66 station is still operating. As we drove toward the gas station, you could hardly miss it. The copper roof sprayed the sun's golden rays across our windshield. The glass expanse on the front of the station was characteristic of Wright's vision of building with harmony with the surrounding land. I expected--and got—the obligatory groan from Doug as I explained Wright's vision, and then I asked him to tell me what colors the gas station was painted. It helps every so often to compassionately point out your man's limitations to him. Keeps him humble. You bet!

We were unsuccessful in our search for the colorful Northern Lights. We had been watching the skies since North Dakota, but no luck. We did manage to drive along Skyline Drive, a scenic route sitting high above the city of Duluth providing beautiful views of Lake Superior. Along this route was a place called Hawk Ridge, which we were told was a definite "must-see."

It was a beautiful Saturday afternoon when we arrived at Hawk Ridge. Parked vehicles crowded the roadway, and people were sitting on rocks and talking in groups high above the city of Duluth; everyone had

Smiling Places

a pair of binoculars. We knew we loved this place immediately. It was full of our fellow birders—not just the casual birders—but the professionals. We were in the presence of greatness! These people knew their birds through years of study. A large chalkboard was sitting by the road with the day's date on it:

September 23rd, 2000

Species	Today's Count
Sharp Shinned Hawks	440
Broad Winged Hawks	400 + or -
Turkey Vultures	148
Bald Eagles	24
Red Tailed Hawks	60
Kestrels	71
Northern Goshawks	15
Coopers Hawks	10
Northern Harriers	7
Merlins	4
Swainson Hawks	1
Sandhill Cranes	2

WOW! This was just part of one day's count! We found out why this is such a great area for watching birds. In fall, the birds are migrating south and eventually hit the shoreline of Lake Superior. Since they can't see any land on the other side of the great lake, they do a ninety degree turn to the west and follow down the coastline of Lake Superior on their migration route. The hawks follow the warblers and other small birds for breakfast, lunch, and dinner.

"Why is that crowd gathering in the field over there?" I asked.

"It looks like they are holding a bird," Doug said as we hurried over.

Sure enough, an Audubon member had caught and banded a sharp shinned hawk and was ready to release it. "Does anyone want to adopt this bird for twenty dollars?" she asked the crowd.

Upon hearing those words, Doug quickly glanced my way and saw a twinkle in my eye. He warned "Don't go there; you are not going to put me up for adoption."

"Oh, well," I smiled. I already had one lady interested: She took one look at Doug, then looked at the sharp shinned hawk, and decided to adopt the bird. She went to the front of the crowd, said a few words to

Shore was Great

the bird, and then let him go. He quickly flew into some large brush near the crowd and then took off for the wide-open skies.

The day continued, and we drove part of the North Shore Scenic Drive which extends from Duluth, MN all the way to Thunder Bay, Ontario. It is two hundred miles long, and we drove around sixty miles of it. Many beautiful state parks with interesting rock formations dot the coastline. Pretty coastal towns with food specialties and crafts shops are found all along this drive. Our favorite town was Two Harbors which included a view of the massive operations of the giant ore carriers entering and leaving the town's busy port. Two Harbors also hosts the beginning of the North Shore State Trail which is approximately 150 miles long. This beautiful town with population of 3,600 is a definite stop on this scenic drive.

"Ten dollars! To see a lighthouse?" I said. "There must be another way."

We were at Gooseberry State Park on the shores of Lake Superior, north of Two Harbors. The lighthouse was surrounded by prison-like walls.

It was as if the historical society was saying, "If you don't pay the five dollar for each admission, you can't see us!"

When I saw that wall, it then became a challenge to see the lighthouse free of charge. "Let's go to the picnic area," my man suggested. He was right. We hiked about a quarter of a mile and walked out to the shoreline. There it was, plain as day, in all it's shining glory, extending out on a point into Lake Superior. We got some good free videos.

"Sixteen dollars! For a a pie?" I gasped.

I saw the World Famous Betty's Pie sign on the side of the building. We were on the North Shore Drive about thirty-five miles north of Duluth. Betty's parking lot was packed, and obviously, Betty had built herself a new restaurant from the sale of all those pies. Not deterred, we went inside and sat down to have lunch.

"I hope the food prices aren't indicative of the pie prices," I muttered as I opened up the menu.

The food prices were very reasonable for lunch, so we ordered, and we did get one piece of cherry crunch pie to go. It was delicious, and we would highly recommend a stop at Betty's. As we left, Doug left the tip along with one of his less-than-memorable, bad puns written on the napkin: "Shore was Great!" He expected—*and got*—the obligatory groan from me.

34 - Running from the Cold

One day we drove in some light snow flurries, and that is when we decided enough is enough. Nature was again dictating our travel pattern. Even though this part of the country in the North Woods of Minnesota is absolutely gorgeous, we must leave for a warmer climate. We decided to head to the Upper Peninsula of Michigan and go south through the Lower Peninsula. As we raced through Wisconsin that day, I dreamed of the time when we would return to ride on more miles of bikeways and to visit Door County, the Wisconsin Dells, and—since he was born in Wisconsin—many more Frank Lloyd Wright structures.

Unfortunately, with the weather turning for the worse, we could not stay long enough to visit the many important sites and cities in Michigan's Upper Peninsula—including Houghton, Calumet, and Copper Harbor. Copper Hopper is one of those places that just might explain my man's behavior. It seems when he was vacationing there as a little boy with his family, the locals were exploding dynamite to construct a new road through the rock bed. When the dynamite exploded one early morning, he fell from a "second story" bunk bed in their cabin. You would expect a little boy to be excited about the cool explosion, but in this case, Doug didn't even wake up after falling. I think this explains a lot—I would have liked to see Copper Harbor for more than one reason.

We arrived at beautiful Lake Gogebic State Park on a sunny crisp fall day. Lake Gogebic is the Upper Peninsula's largest inland lake. The fall colors were almost peaking as many of the brilliant reds and oranges were already on display. We nestled Thing into its campsite along the shore of this clear blue lake. We noticed the State Park personnel working on some water lines. Doug went over to talk to them.

"Having water problems?" he asked.

"Nope, just not taking any chances. The weather is turning colder, and these water pipes could freeze up—so we are shutting them down."

Running from the Cold

Doug found out the only place to get water was a long walk from our trailer at the only restrooms left open in the park. Many of the parks in the Upper Peninsula close between October first through October fifteenth each year. We had to be careful where we planned to stay because we were now in this "window of closure."

We chose to stop at Lake Gogebic because it looked like a great place to set up camp to explore Michigan's Porcupine Mountains, affectionately called the "Porkies" by the locals.

"Oh, my knees!" I gasped as I had climbed a steady ascent of stairs up a huge hill. We were hiking to the lookout tower of Summit Peak to view the highest point in these mountains. "I now dub thee The Stair State," my man dictated. Upon reaching the top, we were treated to some spectacular views—Lake Superior's blue waters in the distance.

It seemed like every trail we hiked that day in the Porkies had "bunches" of steps. More steps to the Lake of the Clouds, more steps to the Presque Isle River Scenic area, and so on. Do you know what? Once you started hiking these trails with boardwalks and steps, you were locked in—you couldn't jump over the boardwalks to escape the steps. If you went down, you had to climb back up. I mention this because we found out that some people have forgotten that "what goes down, must come up."

A lady we met on one such stair trail was complaining to her husband. "I just can't climb one more step." She turned toward us as we were passing them and asked, "How was the trail the way you came?"

"Lots of steps," I said too quickly.

"Oh, no!" she said quietly with a sense of despair. We found out they also were from Ohio, had just recently retired, and had not been hiking in quite a long time. I told her to be positive; she could do it. She just needed to take it slow and easy, and she would do fine. They passed us and started walking toward the dreaded stairs.

Signs and literature proclaimed,

> "Black bear are frequently encountered in the park. When camping, hang all food and valuable items on a rope between two trees at least twenty-five to thirty feet above the ground and at least one hundred feet away from your camp. DO NOT FEED THE BEARS ANYWHERE IN THE PARK. Do not cook food inside your tent."

Smiling Places

There are an estimated 12,000 black bear living in the Upper Peninsula of Michigan. We didn't see any.

We did "encounter" black bears on TV that evening. We watched a local hunting show that showed how black bear are hunted in the Porkies. Now, please note the above warning posted for tourists. Hunters, on the other hand, bring bags of old doughnuts, rolls, cookies, and then dig a pit, drop these food morsels in the pit, and cover it with leaves. The hunters then wait by this food pit to see who wanders by. If it is a larger black bear, he may be shot. My point is: what is this teaching the bears? To eat human food! Yet, campers are continually scolded about food storage techniques, and if a bear starts harassing humans for food, it is sometimes shot and killed. Then, the blame is cast upon bad campers—*they* should have stored their food better. Well—what about the bear *hunters*? Some mysteries of human beings just escape me.

The Pictured Rocks National Lakeshores is located by Munising, Michigan on the south shore of Lake Superior in the center of the Upper Peninsula. We hiked to many beautiful rock formations and beaches. There is also an underwater preserve which offers diving to explore the many shipwrecks and sea caves that are so numerous to this area. We chose to take the afternoon Pictured Rocks Boat Cruise. This is the cruise you always see on TV shows. The afternoon was cloudy and windy with temperatures in the fifties. "The only time we won't leave is if there is a strong northwest wind," said the guides. We figured the boat could be bashed against the rocks fighting that wind.

The cruise lasted about three hours, and we were treated to many colorful, carved rock formations. We sat on the outside top deck of the boat while the wind picked up water and sprayed us wetter than a sponge in dishwater. We were told during the cruise that the lake was so clean in these parts that you could drink the water right out of the lake. I don't think so. All kinds of things have happened on previous tours, but not during ours. They have witnessed weddings up on the rocks, cave-ins, terrible weather, people have jumped off the boat. Once, in a thick fog, a swarm of bees invaded the boat!

Unfortunately, we did not make it to the Grand Sable Dunes on the eastern side of the park because weather reports predicted the possibility of an early snow—up to ten inches in parts of the Upper Peninsula. We decide—*Run, Don't Walk*—to the nearest exit—The Mackinaw Bridge.

35 - My Bridge of Revenge

Doug saw the monster bridge miles before we reached it. The steel superstructure sparkled in the bright sunlight, pulling Thing towards it in a magnetic way. We stopped at a pull-off on SR 2 in the Upper Peninsula of Michigan. As soon as I stepped out of the truck, the wind blew my hair into a totally upright position. It looked like I had just gotten zapped by 5,000 volts of electricity. I stared at the Mackinac Bridge, linking the upper and lower peninsulas of Michigan. Doug came over and stood beside me.

"It's quite windy today," I said to my nervous husband.

Men are *so slow* to realize that women remember the slightest things, even years later. I, for example, clearly remember the first time I saw Doug get real nervous. It was twenty-five years ago on our way to a vacation in Canada. You guessed it: Via the Mackinaw Bridge. His nerves went into high gear driving in that small, lightweight car when a gust of wind unexpectedly hit us at the center of the bridge—moving us into the next lane.

I, of course, had remembered this fact weeks ago when we were discussing our travel route south from Minnesota. Doug had suggested simply driving south through Wisconsin. I feigned disappointment at not being able to see the Upper Peninsula since we were so close. He, of course, relented too easily, and the trap was set. *Poor man*!

"I wonder if the bridge is open," he said (hoping it would be closed due to high winds).

"Oh, of course it is open," I said. Just look at all those little specks traveling across it. Do you want to take a look?" I asked as I offered him my binoculars.

"No, I'll take your word for it," he sighed.

Ah, *revenge is sweet*, isn't it? After all those scary experiences my husband had planned at my flatlander's expense for the last five months, I was finally getting revenge! After all, I didn't have to drive Thing over that bridge—he did! I just had to sit back and enjoy the moment. The

Smiling Places

moment of my husband's fear, not mine!

"Hey, you know that brochure we picked up about the Mackinac Bridge?" I said innocently. "Do you know that bridge is five miles long, and 550 feet tall to the main tower? Wow! The waters below it can reach depths of 295 feet!"

"I really don't need to hear this now," Doug said.

I continued as if I didn't hear him. "The height of the roadway above the water is 200 feet! I wonder if anyone has ever blown off that bridge. I don't see any accident reports in here."

"Of course there wouldn't be any accident reports—they can't recover the bodies in that depth of water," Doug said.

As we approached the monster bridge, I kept reading the portable signs to Doug:

> High Wind Warning
> Maximum speed 20 mph
> Utilize the outside lane
> Turn on 4-way flashers
> *Do you feel lucky today?*

Doug's knuckles were getting whiter and whiter, along with his complexion. We made one last turn, and suddenly the bridge's entrance gates were looming before us. We were trapped! We couldn't turn around. We had two choices: either go over the bridge, or go *over* the bridge. Before November 1, 1957 when the bridge first opened to traffic, ferryboats would transport vehicles across the water where the bridge now stands. That option did not sound too bad to Doug.

We paid our fare and started slowly up the bridge.

"Wow, listen to this!" I said as I started reading the brochure again. "This is the third longest suspension bridge in the world. Do you know what suspension bridges do?"

"Oh, I know what they do; I'm a civil engineer. You can stop reading now," he grumbled with clenched teeth.

I continued as if I didn't hear him. "They move to accommodate wind. It is possible that the deck at this center span can slowly move as much as thirty-five feet if the winds are strong enough. I would guess that with all the wind up here today—they are probably moving *forty feet*!" I snickered. It was I all could do not to break into a chorus of Gordon Lightfoot's *The Wreck of the Edmund Fitzgerald*.

There was a noise that sounded like screaming baboons as a car

My Bridge of Revenge

passed us on the inside lane. "What's that?" Doug asked without taking his eyes off the road.

"The road is making that noise because the inside lane is built of steel mesh. You can see through it to the waters. Want to switch lanes to try it?" I giggled.

"No!" he growled.

I noticed porta-johns were placed precariously along the edges of the bridge for use by maintenance workers. The term "extreme sport" entered my mind. Can you imagine the bathroom rush you might get from using one of those?

I found I was taking more video pictures of the driver than the bridge and the waters. The driver's actions and words (bleep) were more entertaining. This video would be great fun to show everyone at a party. Great fun to everyone but the driver that is. I was definitely enjoying my bridge of revenge moment.

A Mackinac Bridge Authority vehicle passed us. Now, that is the job I would not like to have—transporting people, bicyclists, bikes, snowmobiles, vehicles. (Na na na na na na…you won't drive across this bridge!), I wondered if their employees got some type of drivers' training. Why should I trust these drivers over my own abilities? What if it was their first day on the job?

The Mackinac Bridge Authority is very busy on Labor Day each year because they drive buses back and forth across the bridge transporting walkers to and from the annual Mackinac Bridge Walk. It begins at seven a.m., after the governor's party begins to walk. The route starts at the north end of the bridge and ends five miles later at the south end; the average walker takes two hours to walk the complete route. Some traffic lanes are closed to vehicles to accommodate the walkers, and there are no restroom facilities available to the public on the bridge. Can you imagine walking on one of those steel mesh lanes, looking down through the mesh 200 feet below into 295-foot-deep waters—and *not* having to go to the bathroom?

As we approached the end of the bridge, I asked Doug about his new towing experience on the bridge.

"Were you scared?"

"Well, I wasn't comfortable. The lanes seemed narrow."

"I read the outside lanes were twelve feet wide and the inside steel mesh lanes were eleven feet wide. Is that narrow?"

"Let's just say there was no margin for error."

Smiling Places

"What about the wind? Did it *take* our trailer?"

"My hands hurt from clenching the wheel, but the wind wasn't bad. I did worry when we crossed some large metal strips in our lane. They seemed to affect the trailer's tires and my control of the trailer. I don't know. It just felt funny when we crossed them."

I asked Doug one final question.

"So, will we be crossing the Mackinac Straits next year?"

"Yeah, if this trailer can float," he said.

"Very funny," I said. "I took lots of video pictures up on the bridge."

"Good, I'd like to see what I missed."

"Oh, *you will*!" I smiled.

36 - Pictures in the Eye of the Beholder

Doug drove the truck. I took the video pictures. Doug and I hiked the trails. I took the video pictures on this trip. It was not always that way. After years of watching Doug's video pictures showing heads cut in half, legs cut off at thighs, or 1-1/2 people sitting on a park bench, we decided to retire Doug to the Husband's Amateur Photographer Hall of Fame. I would take the video pictures of our adventure of a lifetime—so they would be perfect.

I knew how to do four things with our video camera: turn it on, record, zoom, and turn it off. Any dummy can use a video camera, right?

"Quick, get the video camera!" Doug said while easing the truck to the side of the road. He had spotted a bull moose by willow bushes, now ten feet from our truck. I grabbed the camera and turned it on. I looked into the eyes of the moose and pressed the record button.

"Wait a minute! What happened to the camera?" I asked as the screen in the viewfinder turned bright pink.

"Let me take a look," Doug said.

I handed him the camera while the moose disappeared into the willows.

"You accidentally pushed the special effects pastel button," he said.

"How do you know that?" I asked.

"Because I read the instructions," he said.

Another time we were hiking in the mountains. A mature bald eagle swooped over our heads and landed in a tree so close to us that we could see its yellow talons clutching the branch. I turned on the video camera and took footage of the eagle that would rival a *National Geographic Explorer* TV special.

"I got some beautiful pictures of that eagle," I said proudly. "By the way, what does that little flashing circle with the diagonal line through it mean in the viewfinder?" I asked my husband.

"It means you are out of film."

"How do you know that?" I asked.

Smiling Places

"Because I read the instructions," he said.

So what if I had lost the perfect moose and eagle pictures. Other photo opportunities were right around the corner—like the time I took the video of the covered wagon monument while flying past at fifty-five miles per hour because we didn't want to pull over. Or the time a black bear was eating by the road, and I used my zoom lens to capture every feature on every square inch of the bear's body, zooming in and out, in and out, in and out. Or the time I quickly took a 360-degree dioramic video of a lake's shoreline with forest behind me. Round and round, round and round, round and round, went the water and trees.

Sitting in Michigan and feeling melancholy about our travel adventures coming to a close, we thought looking through our homemade videos would refresh us. I was in the trailer alone, and the video camera case was sitting by the TV. I opened the case and saw it—the instruction booklet, *Video Cameras for Dummies.*

I picked up the booklet. Did I dare read the instructions? I pulled down all the shades and locked the door. I didn't want Doug to see me. In our marriage, my husband always read the instructions, and then briefed me on how to turn the item on and off. He knew what the 246 other little buttons on the item were used for. I only knew how to use four buttons. All men read instructions. All women quiz their husbands on what they read. "How do you turn this on? That's all I need to know." Have you ever noticed when men receive a new man-toy that they carefully open the box, take out the item, lay open the parts sheet and make sure all the parts are in the box? Then, they read the instructions. After they are finished, they carefully put the box away with the parts list and instructions.

I sat down on the couch and began on page one. By page two, I was already skimming through the rest of the book to find the good stuff. On page thirty-two, I found the paragraph that would change my picture taking life forever. "Taking pictures with a video camera is no different than taking pictures with a camera. You must focus first. Don't zoom in and out unless you are in the standby mode."

Fast Forward: Five months, twelve states, and ten recorded video cassettes later, as luc(k) would have it, I realized that I may have been a little too hasty in taking over the video camera.

Later that evening, Doug hooked up the video camera to the TV so we could watch our "home movies." We began at cassette one. My shaking, waving, zooming video pictures would make the *Blair Witch*

Pictures in the Eye of the Beholder

Project show like the *Sound Of Music*. We watched parts of all ten recorded cassettes, and all ten made me sick—literally. I felt like my brain had been dislodged from my head, spun around in the spin cycle of a washing machine, and bounced a few times on a basketball court. I also felt nauseous. Dinner was about to make another appearance. I crawled into bed.

"Maybe I could sell my videos to the Navy and Air Force as training films," I thought.

"Must view before going out to sea or flying aircraft."

"If these videos don't cure motion-sickness, nothing will."

It would take me months to forget those videos. If I closed my eyes, I could see the waving pictures. If I rode in our truck, I could see the roads and sidewalks rush by. If I went to a movie, I could see special camera effects zooming in and out, in and out....

The next day we pulled Doug out of retirement from the Husband's Amateur Photographer Hall Of Fame. I decided watching a headless moose on video was better than having motion sickness.

37 - Life Comes Full Circle

Wanting to put some distance between us and snow, we drove all day. We arrived at Ludington, Michigan and passed its beautiful city park. Many an evening we had sat in this park with friendly townspeople and watched spectacular sunsets. Many a summer day had been filled with swimming, biking, and blueberries—sweet, succulent, the size of quarters. Just as a year earlier, the blueberries had already been harvested, and the waters had turned much colder. Even the salmon had taken their last run in early fall. We hoped for one more day in Ludington State Park before the snows blew. Life had come full circle.

Little funnels of colored leaves danced around us as we pulled Thing into our campground space. The crowds had long since departed for the year. A few hearty souls remained in recreational vehicles, and a few more hearty souls braved the elements in nylon dome tents as we had done a year earlier.

I watched a red-bellied woodpecker pecking a hardwood tree trunk nearby. A distinctive gust of wind rushed through the campground, and I, caught up in the moment, yelled "Thar she blows, Matey!" as I had done a year earlier. Doug smiled, very glad to be in Thing, and not a tent.

A younger couple in their late twenties or early thirties, whose tent was being tested by the crisp daggers of wind, was invited in. And, as was done a year earlier, stories were told over steaming mugs of coffee—stories of retiring, selling everything, and traveling to smiling places. There was not enough time in one evening to cover it all. "It would take a book," I said. Laughter filled the trailer when recounts told of things not always going as planned for the bumbling idiots from Ohio. We spoke of an insatiable appetite that only traveling together would cure— a yearning not only to see our magnificent country, but taste its cultures and feel its history.

This splendid evening ended all too soon for both couples. As we all stepped out into the dark, the cold was shocking, and the wind still un-

Life Comes Full Circle

tamed. Tiny specks of snow stung cheeks as shoes shuffled through a glistening blanket of white covering the red and yellow leaves that had fallen—as one year earlier.

Starting out early to head south for warmer weather, a postcard wrapped in plastic was left on the young couple's windshield—showing a buffalo standing on the Great Plains, it read simply

>Home Is Where The Buffalo Roam
>Happy Trails,
>Doug and Melodee

Post Script

We drove south from Ludington, Michigan, and stayed for a short time in both Dayton, Ohio and the Smoky Mountains in Tennessee. The Smoky Mountains were a special place to us, and the fall colors were always enjoyable. Rarely did we fail to spot one or more black bears in the Cades Cove area. The eleven-mile loop road with restored cabins was perfect for biking, hiking, nature watching, and history lessons—all that we loved to do. November 2nd was our sixth month anniversary of being on the road.

Arriving in Florida too soon for our winter reservations, we decided to make a side trip to Tallahassee. Our objective was to experience a historic moment. We quickly met up with Murphy who was having a very good time with the 2000 Presidential election. We arrived Sunday to find a handful of Bush supporters and only three of the sixteen major stations broadcasting. We had our five seconds of "fame" on CNN International, which is not broadcast in the USA. The news lady called us a "small group of protestors" even though we were in the background behind the Bush supporters with their signs. Murphy said he was too busy to spend time with us, but he would catch up to us later. Can't wait.

Over the next three years, we would enjoy the milder winters of Florida, travel the Blue Ridge Parkway, connect with many of the states east of the Mississippi River, and visit with family and friends along the way. A home complete with its own RV porte for Thing and Toy would be built at a great little place outside of Titusville, Florida—appropriately called The Great Outdoors RV/Golf Resort.

Melodee passed away on October 4, 2004, having almost completed her first nonfiction book, *Smiling Places*. It was to be her way of putting a smile on people's faces, and it was to be her legacy for future generations who might want a glimpse into who Melodee and Doug were. She had dreamed of this being the first in a series of humorous adventure books about the two bumbling idiots from Ohio who hit the road. I mentioned to her that as we became more experienced, it would be harder for her to come up with misadventures. She simply said, "You are still bumbling after fifty years of age; I don't think I have anything to worry about for *quite a while!*"

She thought it might be fun to do a book called *Driving the Appalachian Trail* as walking the trail had been very well written by others. An-

Smiling Places

other book was already in her thoughts as well—about the RV resort we now lived in during part of the year. Its broad spectrum consists of mostly retired, friendly folks with a similar interest in traveling. They had that nice "kind of crazy, kind of kooky" outlook that always brought a smile. They definitely had too much time on their hands; the combination generated perfect fodder for Melodee's writing skills, creative ideas, and whimsical mind. Here are folks who go to elaborate lengths by custom painting their driveways, installing custom curbing for landscaped bedding, buying the latest techno gadgets, outfitting their custom golf carts for a Christmas parade, and creating a doggie world for pampered pooches. One character even has temperature gauges—one in the front, and, of course, one in the back of his house! The resort is so unique that others without RV's have come here to live—even though they have no intention of ever purchasing an RV or using the oversized portes for a RV. We were welcomed into this unique community and came to love many of the people here.

I have tried *bumbling through* with my best effort to complete her book with her vision and her "help." Whether you believe in afterlife contacts or not, some things happen that do not fit into the *neat explanations* engineers like me come to expect. Early on, when I was probably not doing as Melodee would have expected, she tripped a GFI circuit twice that had never been tripped before or since. I heeded the warning shot across my bow. When moving along on the right track, I saw rainbows at just the right time, and a screech owl came to visit me in our RV Porte early one morning. The significance of rainbows and owls is part of our personal history that I'll keep to myself for now. While struggling for days to organize the chapter on Yellowstone, I saw a horoscope (I generally don't read them) which read:

> *The super volcano that is now Yellowstone devastated the Western Hemisphere. There's hope for that area of your life you currently think is a catastrophe.*

That chapter flowed out that afternoon. I had often told Melodee that if she was going to do something afterwards, and if she wanted to get my attention, she had to do more than simply moving a picture. She did—and I am more attentive.

I will never be the writer Melodee became. While my bumbling may have been her inspiration, she was the creative perspiration and very

Smiling Places

much enjoyed writing. While working on *Smiling Places,* she wrote *The Perfect Dance*—a short story about her mom written shortly before her mom passed away. While ultimately not accepted for *Chicken Soup for the Caregiver's Soul*, her story was rated in the top four percent—one of forty-one finalists out of the thousands submitted. Her talent never fully developed nor realized.

As for me, I intend to travel again carrying Melodee with me to more *Smiling Places*. As promised, I have completed her book as she wanted me to. Should we meet, don't be saddened by the end of our tales, but tell me a story of Melodee that made you smile. She was always willing to listen, provide a word of encouragement, and help others if she could. Her passion was nature and making people smile. She will be missed by those she touched. A legacy anyone would be proud of. As she became fond of saying "Happy Trails."

SMILING PLACES
BY
MELODEE
&
DOUG
TOMSU